Hacking Google® Maps
and Google® Earth

Hacking Google® Maps and Google® Earth

Martin C. Brown

Wiley Publishing, Inc.

Hacking Google® Maps and Google® Earth

Published by
Wiley Publishing, Inc.
10475 Crosspoint Boulevard
Indianapolis, IN 46256
www.wiley.com

Copyright © 2006 by Wiley Publishing, Inc., Indianapolis, Indiana

Published simultaneously in Canada

ISBN-13: 978-0-471-79009-9
ISBN-10: 0-471-79009-5

Manufactured in the United States of America

10 9 8 7 6 5 4 3 2 1

1B/QV/QX/QW/IN

For general information on our other products and services or to obtain technical support, please contact our Customer Care Department within the U.S. at (800) 762-2974, outside the U.S. at (317) 572-3993 or fax (317) 572-4002.

Library of Congress Cataloging-in-Publication Data
Brown, Martin C.
 Hacking Google Maps and Google Earth / Martin C. Brown.
   p. cm.
 Includes index.
 ISBN-13: 978-0-471-79009-9 (paper/website)
 ISBN-10: 0-471-79009-5 (paper/website)
 1. Geographic information systems. 2. Google Maps. 3. Google Earth. I. Title.
 G70.212.B765 2006
 910.285--dc22
                        2006013971

To Darcy and Leon, the cats that understand everything and nothing, respectively.

About the Author

A professional writer for more than six years, **Martin C. Brown (MC)** is the author of both the Perl and Python *Annotated Archives* and *Complete Reference* books (all four Osborne/McGraw-Hill), *Microsoft IIS 6 Delta Guide* (Sams Publishing), and 14 other published computing titles. His expertise spans myriad development languages and platforms—Perl, Python, Java, JavaScript, Basic, Pascal, Modula-2, C, C++, Rebol, Gawk, Shellscript, Windows, Solaris, Linux, BeOS, Microsoft WP, Mac OS, and more—as well as web programming, systems management, and integration. MC is a regular contributor to ServerWatch.com and IBM developerWorks.

He is also a regular writer of white papers and how-to guides for Microsoft on subjects such as migrating Solaris/Unix/Linux development and systems administration to Windows 2000 and 2003 Server product lines. He draws on a rich and varied background as a founding member of a leading U.K. ISP, systems manager and IT consultant for an advertising agency and Internet solutions group, technical specialist for an intercontinental ISP network, and database designer and programmer—and as a self-confessed compulsive consumer of computing hardware and software. In his formative pre-writing life, he spent 10 years designing and managing mixed platform environments. As a result he has developed a rare talent of being able to convey the benefits and intricacies of his subject with equal measures of enthusiasm, professionalism, in-depth knowledge, and insight. MC is currently a member of the MySQL Documentation Team.

Credits

Executive Editor
Chris Webb

Development Editors
Kelly Talbot
Suzanna R. Thompson

Technical Editor
Ben Hammersley

Production Editor
Pamela Hanley

Copy Editor
Kim Cofer

Editorial Manager
Mary Beth Wakefield

Production Manager
Tim Tate

**Vice President and Executive Group
   Publisher**
Richard Swadley

Vice President and Executive Publisher
Joseph B. Wikert

Project Coordinator
Ryan Steffen

Graphics and Production Specialists
Jennifer Click
Denny Hager
Stephanie Jumper

Quality Control Technician
John Greenough

Proofreading and Indexing
Techbooks

Cover Design
Anthony Bunyan

Contents at a Glance

Contents

Acknowledgments

I'd like to thank Chris Webb for giving me the opportunity to write this book, and Suzy Thompson and Kelly Talbot, who kept me on the straight and narrow while writing the chapters. The unseen members of Wiley's development team for the book also had a serious role to play in the process. I shouldn't forget the vital roles played by my agent, Lynn Haller, and the rest of the team at StudioB.

Helping me ensure the correct content and testing some of the applications were Chris Herborth and the technical editor, Ben Hammersley. It should go without saying that the users and developers of Google Maps applications and the rest of the Google Maps community have served as an inspiration for some of the examples in this book.

Most importantly, I must thank my wife who survives not only my good days, but also my bad.

Introduction

Do you know where you are?

Do you know where you are going?

Could you find the nearest restaurant to your current location?

When you looked at your latest holiday photos, could you remember where you were?

It is just these sorts of questions that drove me to write this book. I'm interested in the answers to all of these questions, and particularly in ways in which I can represent information about my world, and the world we live in, in a way that relates that data to its location.

During the course of writing this book I visited New York (U.S.), Edinburgh (Scotland), and Sorrento (Italy), in addition to many different places within a few miles of my home. In each case, Google Maps and Google Earth could be used to record information about where I had been, to look up information about where I was going, or simply to help me understand the area I was visiting. All of these situations, and more, are documented and described within this book.

Who This Book Is For

This book is aimed at both amateur and professional programmers who want to make use of either Google Maps or Google Earth in their own applications. To get the best out of this book, you should have some basic programming experience and ideally be familiar with HTML and JavaScript. It would also be beneficial to have experience with scripting languages (particularly Perl) and SQL databases, such as MySQL.

Managers and other interested parties might also find sections of the book useful, because it can help them understand how the applications work and also provide background knowledge on what Google Maps and Google Earth are capable of.

How This Book Is Organized

The book is divided into four basic parts:

Part I covers the basics of the Google Maps interface, the fundamentals of the Google Maps API, and how to organize and translate existing information into a format that can successfully be used within Google Maps and Google Earth applications. The section should get you up to speed on the core techniques and abilities you need to work with the rest of the book.

Part II shows you what the Google Maps system is capable of doing. In this section you'll find information on some excellent sample applications and how to create your own Google Maps applications by extending the functionality of the core Google examples.

Part III is crammed full of examples of Google Maps applications, starting with basic markers and overlays, moving through dynamically driven examples and on to methods of highlighting key points and elements for archaeologists and Realtors. The section finishes up with an example of a route description application. All of the examples demonstrated can be viewed online.

Part IV covers the Google Earth application. Google Earth is a standalone application, rather than a web site solution like Google Maps, and offers a completely new set of methods for describing information.

Conventions Used in This Book

In this book, you'll find several notification icons—Note, Caution, and Tip—that point out important information. Here's what the three types of icons look like:

Notes provide you with additional information or resources.

A caution indicates that you should use extreme care to avoid a potential disaster.

A tip is advice that can save you time and energy.

Code lines are often longer than what will fit across a page. The symbol ⊃ indicates that the following code line is actually a continuation of the current line. For example,

```
var newlat = latpoints[0] + ((latpoints[latpoints.length-1] - ⊃
latpoints[0])/2);
```

is really one line of code when you type it into your editor.

Code, functions, URLs, and so forth within the text of this book appear in a monospace font, while content you will type appears either **bold** or monospaced.

What You Need to Use This Book

For the Google Maps examples in this book, you need access to a publicly available web site where you can add and update pages, because the Google Maps API must be able to verify your pages during use. Hosting these pages on your own machine is unlikely to work. Full details of requirements, including those for accessing the Google Maps API are provided in Chapter 3.

Google Maps applications are written using JavaScript and HTML, so you should be familiar with these to be able to understand and adapt the examples. Many of the examples use a Perl script for providing data, and although these operations could also be written in PHP or Python, examples of these are not provided. Finally, some examples use a MySQL database to store information. A similar database solution, such as MySQL, Derby, PostgreSQL, or others will be required to duplicate some of the samples. All of the examples should work within the major platforms (Windows, Linux/Unix, and Mac OS X).

All of the examples in this book make use of the version 1 sequence of the Google Maps API. The API is under constant development and new versions might be released after the publication of this book that supersede the version used in the examples. The availability of the new version will not affect the operation of the examples, which are designed to work with the v1 sequence.

The Google Earth application is available for computers running Windows and Mac OS X. However, new versions and editions for existing and new platforms could be released at any time.

What's on the Companion Web Site

A companion site for the book is available at `http://maps.mcslp.com`.

The site includes the following:

- Full source code for all the examples in the book.

- Working examples of all the applications featured in the book.

- Errata and corrections.

- Regular follow-up articles and information on Google Maps, Google Earth, and the book contents.

The web site also includes a Weblog. Details of how to subscribe to the articles and comments posted to the blog are available on the site.

As usual, all of the code and errata for the book are also available at `http://www.wiley.com/go/extremetech`.

Basics

part

Using Geographical Information

Are you going somewhere in the next few days?

Have you thought about how you are going to get there?

Have you thought about what might be there when you arrive?

Geographical information systems like Google Maps and Google Earth can answer these questions and, with a little work on your part, many more. They enable your computer to think about information in terms of a physical, real-world location and then associate data with that location.

Understanding Your Location

When you think about your current location — whether you're at home, at work, or even at the beach — do you realize how often you think about what is around you? If you were able to monitor your every thought, you'd probably be surprised at how often you consciously and subconsciously think about your environment.

Mapping a Location

Humans, on the whole, are very spatial creatures. We frequently think about and mentally map the information, places, and items around us — from the smaller things, such as curbs and sidewalks, to the larger components, such as the locations of mountains, buildings, and even entire towns and cities. But many humans take for granted the ability to locate and produce a mental map of where we are and where we want to go. (Some of us are better at this than others, mind you!)

Typically, the human brain collects information while simply walking or driving about. Subconsciously, and sometimes consciously, it's fairly common to think about the following:

in this chapter

☑ Find out the ways location can be defined

☑ Learn how to think in terms of location

- Locations of restrooms, police stations, information booths, and other useful places.

- Locations and names of restaurants or coffee bars.

- Interesting-looking buildings or places (such as castles, ruins, or statues).

- Routes to and from locations, including identifying whether a pathway meets up with a past location (somewhere you have been before).

You don't always, however, want to investigate an area and make a mental map of all this information. Suppose, for example, that you want to find a restaurant within a few blocks of your current location. Determining this information by walking about and collecting the data could take hours, by which time you would be much hungrier than when you started — and you still may not have found what you were looking for.

This is why Google Maps and Google Earth are so useful. At their core, they provide mapping (Google Maps) and aerial photography (Google Earth) of many areas of the planet. In addition, Google Maps connects the location information with data about businesses and other sites in the local area, allowing you to find all the restaurants or copy shops or any other type of business within a given area.

As a further expansion of the technology, Google Maps enables you to create applications that combine the mapping or earth information with your own set of data so that you can build customized views of information, all mapped to the geographical location of the items.

This technology can be used for a number of purposes, including (but not limited to) obtaining the following information:

- **Localized data:** You can find all of the restaurants (or any other type of business you choose) within a few miles of exactly where you are now.

- **Maps and routes:** You can find out where you are now and then how to get to other places.

- **Topographical views:** You can get an idea of exactly where you are in relation to other components, such as hills or ruins.

- **Relation of locations to photographs:** You can work out where you were standing and in which direction you were pointing the camera when you took a particular photograph.

- **Statistical data:** You can describe statistical data (such as population levels) by showing it graphically on a map, rather than by providing a basic list.

To make the best of this functionality, however, you need to change the way you think about your environment.

Defining a Location

You can describe your current location in several ways, usually depending on the level of civilization in your vicinity.

With an Address

Suppose you are interested in the National Maritime Museum in Greenwich, London. To write to the museum, you would use this simple address, along with the postal code SE10 9NF. (Postal codes are known by the post office and indicate a more specific location than just the town or city.)

But if you are on the ground and need to actually locate the building for a visit, you need something more specific; Greenwich is too large a district to have to search on foot. You need a street name (in this case, Park Row) in order to locate the museum's precise position. Having this information will help you find the correct street sign (if you already happen to be in the vicinity) or look up the street on a map.

Both of these address options — using just the postal code and using the full street address — have meaning only because the city of Greenwich has well-defined locations, identified in a format that humans can easily understand. They are useful only if you know where a location is in terms of other places (for example, the street name "Park Row" is useful only if you know it is the Park Row in Greenwich, London) and if you have a well-indexed map that shows you that location.

Without an Address

But what about areas that are neither subject to human habitation nor blanketed by roads, such as the Lake District in England or Yellowstone National Park in the United States?

In these situations, assigning an address is basically impossible. A much better solution is to use a map grid reference. Grid references give you a two-dimensional reference (horizontal and vertical) for a given location and are unique to the map you are using. Within the confines of a single local map, a reference like A6 or TQ 387 776 GB Grid (the Ordinance Survey grid reference for the museum) works quite well.

In a global environment, the grid reference is the combination of longitude and latitude. Longitude is the number of degrees, minutes, and seconds east or west of the prime meridian line. Latitude is the number of degrees, minutes, and seconds north or south of the equator. The combination of the two gives you a precise east/west and north/south location on the earth. Each half of the earth has 180 degrees.

The National Maritime Museum is on the prime meridian point, which is the home of Greenwich Mean Time and the reference point for longitude references and time differences between countries. Its longitude is, therefore, 0° 0' 0". Because the museum isn't on the equator, its latitude is 51° 28' 38".

Normally, however, you quote only degrees and minutes (not seconds) in the longitude and latitude references. Thus, the location of Greenwich is 51.28N 0E. For Washington, D.C., use 47.30N 120.30W; for Beijing, 39.55N 116.20E; and for Jakarta, 06.09S 106.49E.

Note Each of the references discussed in this section is useful in its own way, and you'll use all of them as a method for identifying information. Remember to consider them when you look at different data types and think about how you can map them to geographical locations. Also make sure to take into account the direction in which you are facing when you orient yourself on a map. Because your orientation affects what you can see, it becomes important when you build applications that can use this information.

Moving to Another Location

Once you know current location and the location of your destination, you need to work out the best route between them. Movement between locations is generally either direct (commonly referred to as "as the crow flies") or via roads. Once again, the environment will likely determine the route you choose.

If you are on foot or in the car and within a city, you will probably follow the road to your destination. The likelihood of being able to walk directly through a building (let alone drive through it!) is not great.

Within the countryside, especially if you are on foot, a more direct route (as opposed to traveling by road) will save you a lot of time. When traveling by plane, you'll probably use the direct route, as well.

Knowing how you are going to move between different locations is important when using geographical systems. You need this information not only to move between the areas, but also to gain information about your environment (for example, the distance between two points or the total area).

Thinking in Terms of Geographical Location

The first step in making use of geographical information is to change the way you think about the word "information" in general. You need to think about information in terms of how it relates to its geographical location, rather than as the simple data it may describe. To do this you must change the key you use to identify the information.

To Find Places

Imagine that you are stranded on the main street of a typical town, such as my hometown of Grantham. Although you know where you are, you are clueless about your surroundings. You do, however, have access to a computer.

The first rule of survival is to find something to eat, so you do a search on one of the various business directories on the Internet and find a list of restaurants easily enough. Table 1-1 shows a list of some of Grantham's restaurants and their addresses.

The list treats the information you've gained as simply a list of restaurants and their addresses. To make use of information in this format, you either need to know Grantham and its streets really well or you need a map in order to make heads or tails of the addresses. You would then need to use both the list and the map to work out in which direction you need to begin walking and when and where you need to turn left or right.

If you aren't familiar with Grantham, reordering the list by location — the most important piece of information — and combining that list with your map of Grantham would be much more useful, especially if you can show the location of the restaurants relative to your own.

Table 1-1: Restaurants in Grantham

Restaurant	Location
Manthorpe Road Fish & Chip Shop	25 Manthorpe Road
The Market Cross Fish Bar	9 Market Place
Sorrento's	11 Market Place
Catlins	11 High Street
Nicklebys Restaurant	41 The George Shopping Centre
China Inn	4 Avenue Road
Knightingales	Guildhall Court Guildhall Street
Hop Sing	Tudor House, 21 Westgate
Relax Fish Bar	71 Westgate
One on Wharf	1 Wharf Road

To Identify Photo Subjects

During a recent trip to New York City, my wife and I were amazed by how Manhattan doesn't feel like an island when you are on the ground. That perception has a number of effects, one of which is that you can walk for miles around the island, visiting different places, without ever getting a really good perspective on where you are in relation to other places you've visited.

The same can be true of photos: People tend to define the photographs they take in terms of the subject of the photo or the name of the site, and not by the relationship between that location and another one.

To illustrate the difference, I photographed the Brooklyn Bridge from two different locations. Figure 1-1 shows a photo I took of the bridge while standing on Manhattan Island.

If you aren't familiar with Grantham, reordering the list by location — the most important piece of information — and combining that list with your map of Grantham would be much more useful, especially if you can show the location of the restaurants relative to your own.

Figure 1-2 shows another photo I took of the bridge, this time from the Staten Island Ferry.

Both photos show the same object, and I could describe them as merely that: pictures of the Brooklyn Bridge. The problem is that, although both photos show something interesting, neither the generic description nor the photos themselves give you an idea of the relationship between the photos.

FIGURE **1-1:** The Brooklyn Bridge from its base.

FIGURE 1-2: The Brooklyn Bridge from the Staten Island Ferry.

The same can be said of any set of photos that show the same subject. For example, photos of a property don't always give you an accurate impression of a house or building because you don't necessarily know from where the photo was taken, which direction the photographer was facing, or what the content of the photo is in relation to other photos that might be in the same file.

If you treat the photos as merely a record of your visit and describe them with meaningless terms (that is, a description of *what* the photo is, rather than *where* it is), you lose some of the most valuable information about the photo.

By thinking about photos in geographical terms (where they were taken, the direction you were facing) and combining this information with a map of the location (in this example, Manhattan), a vacation photo can become more than just a shot of a famous landmark.

To Understand Statistical Data

My wife and I arrived in New York City the weekend that Hurricane Katrina hit the Gulf Coast of the United States. The results of the hurricane were devastating. But hearing the results, or even seeing the interviews and reports "on the ground" about the effects of the hurricane on New Orleans and the surrounding areas, wasn't anywhere near as informative as the satellite images of New Orleans, taken before and after the hurricane hit. Through the Google Maps and Earth service, Google provided the images that showed these differences (see Figure 1-3).

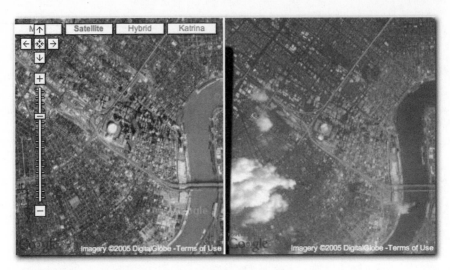

FIGURE 1-3: New Orleans before and after Hurricane Katrina.

Equally instructive were the maps showing the predicted route and, later, the actual route that the hurricane took. As successive hurricanes hit the Gulf Coast of the United States that fall, these maps became a vital method for individuals, companies, and government, emergency, and weather organizations to work out the probable location of landfall.

With a visual representation of the actual or predicted location of the storm, individuals could easily identify, at a glance, where the storm would be at a later time. This made the other information (number of miles off the coast, the towns and cities being affected, and so on) easier to understand.

A picture is worth a thousand words, which is why graphs and geographical data are combined in a variety of situations. Votes in elections, population data, plant and animal areas, even the migration routes and quantities of birds can all be described by marrying map data with the statistical information.

To Generate Data from Maps

While my wife and I were in New York City, we did a lot of walking — using the subway would have robbed us of the ability to view our surroundings and enjoy the city's architecture. On one particular day, we walked to Soho, from there to the Brooklyn Bridge, then around the bottom of Manhattan, across to the Staten Island Ferry, back again, and then back up to our hotel.

In the past, determining how far we'd walked would have been difficult without using a map, retracing our route, and then possibly using a piece of string and some quick math based on the map's scale to determine the distance. Using a Google Maps application, though, I was able to quickly determine exactly how far we had walked. I generated that data using information I'd gained from the map.

In this case, the translation of information into geographical representations is not what proved to be the most useful — the map data itself, in combination with some data points (the streets and places we visited), provided me with the information I needed.

Wrapping Up

Now you know several ways in which a location can be defined, as well as how important it is to think about information in relation to its geographical worth. To learn how to produce applications that convert information and portray it in geographical terms, read on!

The Google Local Interface

Before looking at specific examples of how to customize the Google Maps system, it's a good idea to become familiar with what information and facilities are available to you when viewing a Google Maps page.

Google Local is the name of the web site provided by Google that uses the Google Maps Application Programmer Interface (API) to describe information, locations, and routes within a map. By examining how to use Google Local, you can obtain a good idea of what the Google Maps API is capable of achieving. This chapter examines the Google Local interface and its components and what you can do within the confines of the Google Maps system when developing applications.

System Requirements

Google Maps uses a combination of HTML, JavaScript, maps, and interactive elements. As with any new product, keep in mind that bugs and minor problems may affect your interaction with the application.

At the time of this writing, Google Maps was known to work with the following web browsers (minimum supported version numbers are shown):

➤ Internet Explorer 6.0+

➤ Firefox 0.8+

➤ Safari 1.2.4+

➤ Netscape 7.1+

➤ Mozilla 1.4+

➤ Opera 8.02+

You should be aware, however, that the list of supported browsers, version numbers, and, sometimes, platforms may change.

Tip

If you are having problems, ensure that you have enabled JavaScript in your browser (some users disable it for security reasons). If that doesn't work, check the help section of the Google Maps web site (`http://local.google.com/support`).

Examining the Main Interface

The main, basic interface of Google Local (and the Google Maps API) is incredibly intuitive and straightforward. You can select a map, move it around, and zoom in and out to find the area you want to see. Figure 2-1 shows a typical Google Maps screen.

Note

When developing your own mapping application, you have the ability to alter the look and feel of the page, including any surrounding text and graphics.

At the top of the page is a search field that you can use to search the Google Local database for locations, businesses, and points of interest that you want to be shown on a map.

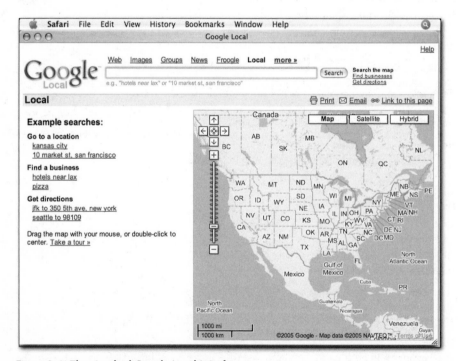

FIGURE 2-1: The standard Google Local interface.

The main content of the window is the map panel that shows the current map view. In the top-left corner of the map are the navigation and zoom controls; in the top-right corner are the view controls (which allow you to switch between map, satellite, and hybrid views). The bottom-left corner shows scale information, and the bottom-right corner shows the copyright data (which Google requires to be shown).

You can obtain a link to a specific page using the "Link to this page" link at the top right (above the map), and you can e-mail a copy of the map or print out the map using the corresponding links in the same area.

Interacting with the Map

The current view location can be adjusted through a series of controls and methods. The first is simply the ability to move around the map, changing the current view in terms of location. The zoom level — effectively the amount of information shown on the map — can also be changed. The closer you zoom, the less ground you see, but more detail is discernible.

Moving the Map

You can easily move the map in four ways:

- Use the search field to find (and, if necessary, select) a location.

- Use the arrow buttons in the top-left corner of the map to move the map in the corresponding direction. The button in the center will move the map to the last known reference point (for example, to an item you selected or a location you searched for).

- Click the map and drag your mouse north, south, east, or west. The map will "drag" beneath the pointer, as though you were holding your head still and moving the map.

- Double-click a spot on the map to center the map on that location.

Zooming In and Out

The zoom slider (on the left side of the map) allows you to adjust your view of the map. The plus sign button at the top of the slider zooms in (for more detail), and the minus sign button at the bottom zooms out (for a more generalized view). You can also select or drag the slider to a specific zoom level within the current map.

The level of the zoom is best described by the scale, or the number of miles to a given marker distance. (This is generally, but not always, constant between zoom levels.) The actual area of map shown at each level depends entirely on the size of the window you are using.

The current scale is shown in the bottom-left corner of the map. It shows measurements and a marker length in both metric and imperial (U.S.) measurements. Because the two lengths are not equal, the map marker may show differently sized markers for the 200-meter and 1,000-foot distances.

The zoom levels, starting from the bottom of the slider (and through increasing levels of zoom), are as follows:

5,000 miles/10,000 kilometers

2,000 miles/5,000 kilometers

2,000 miles/2,000 kilometers

1,000 miles/1,000 kilometers

500 miles/500 kilometers

200 miles/200 kilometers

100 miles/200 kilometers

50 miles/100 kilometers

20 miles/50 kilometers

10 miles/20 kilometers

5 miles/10 kilometers

2 miles/5 kilometers

2 miles/2 kilometers

1 mile/1 kilometer

2,000 feet/500 meters

1,000 feet/200 meters

500 feet/200 meters

200 feet/100 meters

To compare the differences between different zoom levels, check out some maps with progressively closer views of the National Maritime Museum in London:

■ At 5,000 miles, the lowest zoom level (Figure 2-2), you see the entire world map many times over. The red icon marks the site of the museum.

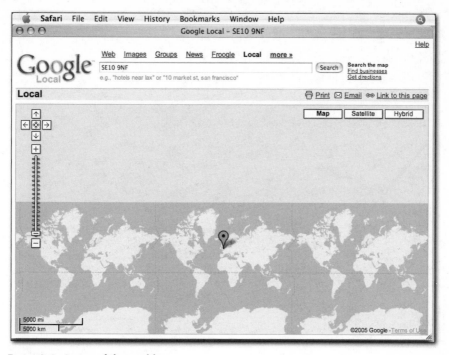

FIGURE 2-2: A map of the world.

- At 50 miles (Figure 2-3), you start to see the detail of the City of London and much of the rest of the country.

- At 1 mile (Figure 2-4), you can see most of the major roads within London and get a rough idea of how to reach your destination.

FIGURE 2-3: A map of the south of the U.K.

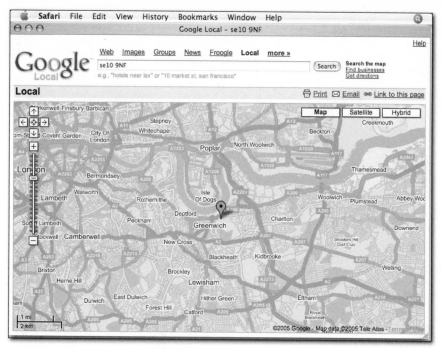

FIGURE 2-4: Greenwich and greater London.

- At 200 feet (Figure 2-5), you can almost imagine yourself walking along the street the museum is on. You can see individual roads and even the railway line running to the north.

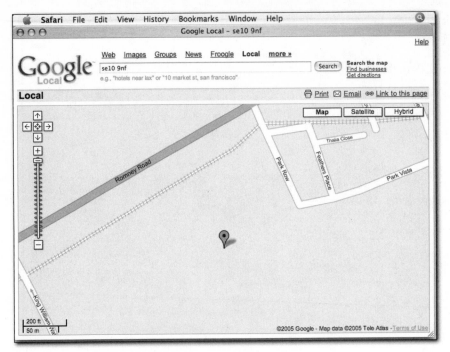

FIGURE 2-5: Greenwich map at the highest resolution.

In comparison, look at the satellite images (taken at the same resolutions) of the same location:

- Again, at the lowest zoom level (Figure 2-6), you see the entire world as a satellite image.

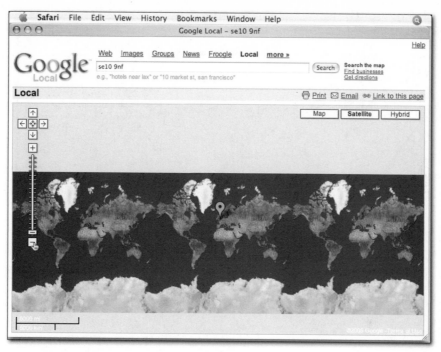

FIGURE 2-6: The whole world as a satellite image.

■ At 50 miles (Figure 2-7), you can see virtually the whole of the south of the U.K. and parts of France and the Netherlands. The patches with a slightly different coloring show areas on the map that are available in a higher resolution.

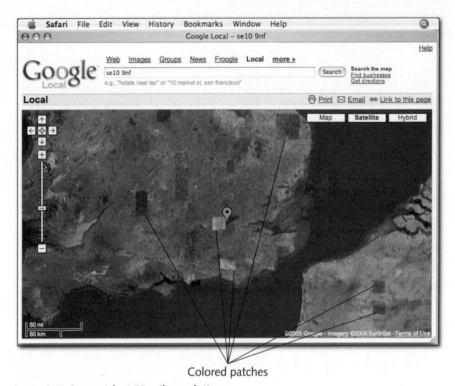

Colored patches

FIGURE 2-7: Greenwich at 50-mile resolution.

- At 1 mile (Figure 2-8), you can see the shape of the river (and you may recognize the shape and image used for the BBC television program *Eastenders*). You can no longer see detail, but you do get a good idea of the main areas of parkland, roads, and buildings. When you are viewing the screen in color, you can note the difference in color; it shows the different ambient weather conditions.

FIGURE 2-8: Greenwich and Greater London at 1-mile resolution.

- At the closest zoom level (Figure 2-9), you can see the layout of the museum buildings.

FIGURE 2-9: Closest zoom on the National Maritime Museum.

Just as Google Maps and Google Earth images are not always available at all zoom levels (within maps, sparsely populated areas are rarely shown below 500 feet, and sometimes 1,000 feet), satellite information is not always available, either. Much of the United States has been photographed at a resolution of 1 meter, making 200-foot images readily available but, as with map information, some sparsely populated areas or extremities are not available at such a high resolution. But a lot of the United Kingdom is unavailable for satellite imagery below the 2,000-foot zoom level, although heavily populated areas such as London, Birmingham, and Manchester *are* available at the highest zoom level. Other parts of the world are similarly split into different levels of higher and lower resolution according to their population density or the amount of interest in the location. Satellite imagery is constantly being updated and improved, and this process is likely to increase as more people begin to use the information.

Resolution quality has no defined boundaries, and it is possible to find a location on the map that shows satellite for only a portion of the area viewed. At certain zoom levels, you can determine where the higher-resolution images are available; for example, these areas of unavailability showed up in Figure 2-9 as differently shaded patches on a map of the United Kingdom.

You, therefore, need to take care to ensure that when you display a map or satellite image, you choose a zoom level appropriate to the area you are viewing.

Note Occasionally, satellite information is obscured by cloud cover (see Figure 2-10). This (and the shadows the clouds cast on the ground) is an unfortunate side effect of taking images from space or from a high-altitude vehicle, and is obviously not Google's fault. You may also see other images, such as boats on the water, planes at airports, and any other structure large enough to be picked up by the camera. These images, despite what you may have heard, are not live. You cannot watch yourself—or anybody else, for that matter—using Google.

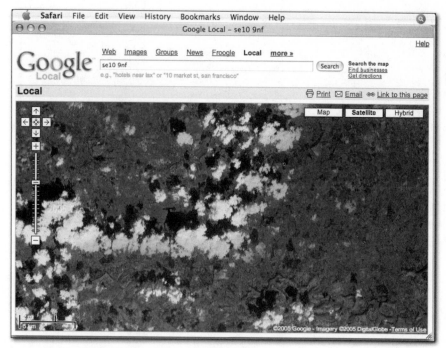

FIGURE 2-10: Clouds and shadows on a satellite image.

Changing the View Types

By now, you know that the Google Local service provides maps and satellite images. What you may not know is that it, in fact, provides *three* different views, between which you can switch at any time by using the links at the top-right corner of the map view:

- **Maps:** These are street-level maps — correct in location, length, and shape — that include the names of roads, open spaces (when named), lakes, rivers, seas, oceans, and other identifiable items. These maps can be used to provide location information and routes for points of interest, such as the Brooklyn Bridge (see Figure 2-11). For roads, the color defines the relative capacity of the road (in addition to the size representation), and as you can see in Figure 2-11, information on the direction of traffic (for one-way streets) is shown where known.

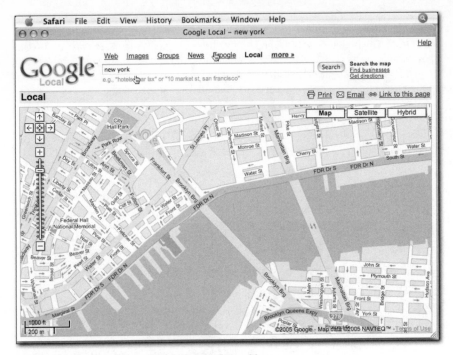

FIGURE 2-11: A map of lower Manhattan and Brooklyn.

- Google Maps also shows country, state, and county boundaries when available; regions and locations; country names (if you're zoomed out far enough); known ferry routes, train lines; and a whole host of other information.

- **Satellite imagery:** This consists of photographs of the surface of the earth as taken from satellite (see Figure 2-12). The information is presented at different resolutions (see the earlier discussion on zoom levels) and is regularly updated with new pictures of the earth. Satellite imagery is most useful when combined with photo, historical, or other information; because you cannot see street names or points of interest, it is less useful for routes or location information.

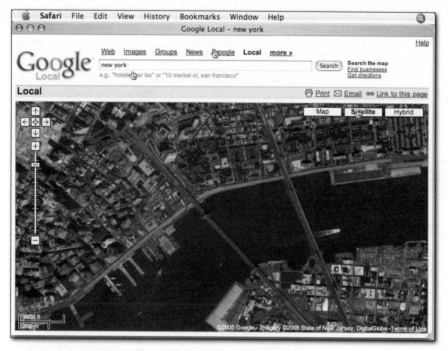

FIGURE 2-12: A satellite image of lower Manhattan and Brooklyn.

- **Hybrid maps:** This type of map overlays the road information, including the road name, size, color, and travel direction, onto the satellite imagery. The hybrid view is most useful when you want to provide location and route information with the context of the location. In particular, the hybrid view can be useful when you want to include a large natural structure (such as a lake, the coast, or mountains), while still showing the street location. Figure 2-13 shows the Brooklyn Bridge street map overlaid with a satellite image of the same area.

FIGURE 2-13: A hybrid map of lower Manhattan.

Conducting Searches

Searches within Google Local return two types of results. If the information you enter into the search box is an address, postal code, or other fully identifiable address, Google Maps or Google Earth will center the map on the address or location you entered. For example, if I enter SE10 9NF into the search field, Google takes me to the location of the National Maritime Museum, and an information window pops up (see Figure 2-14). Google Maps will use whatever the active format is at the time you perform the search; this particular screenshot shows the results in the hybrid format.

FIGURE 2-14: Address information for the National Maritime Museum.

If the information you enter is not an exact location, Google will do a search on the information to find localized objects or business. For example, if you type "Plumbers, New York" in the search field, Google will find a list of plumbers in New York and mark their physical locations on the map with an icon (see Figure 2-15), which is discussed in the next section.

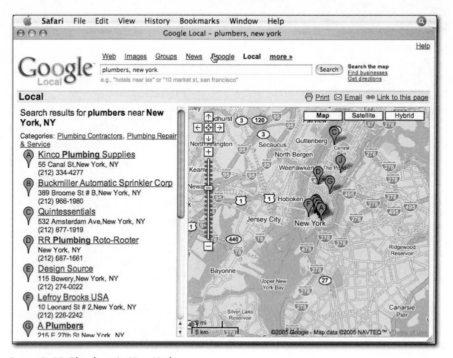

FIGURE **2-15**: Plumbers in New York.

If Google cannot discern from the string you have entered whether it should be displaying a specific location or businesses and objects within a locality, it will return an error and ask for a more explicit description of what you want.

You must be careful when supplying information because Google cannot always determine what you mean — even if the information you provide seems quite explicit. For example, I cannot find the street I live on by entering the full address, although I *can* find it by using the postal code or by ignoring the village in which I live. And without a postal code, I cannot find my parents' street at all, despite the fact that the road has been there for some 30 years and is clearly shown on the map.

Understanding Markers

Markers highlight specific points of interest. In the previous section, for example, the location of different plumbers within New York was highlighted through a number of icons called *markers*. Markers can also provide information windows (pop-ups), and there are other ways of highlighting data using lines and overlays. All of these solutions (and more) are available when developing a Google Maps application, so understanding what is available in Google Local will help you determine the functionality you can use in your own applications.

Markers

Markers are simple little icons that show the precise position of a business or address on your map. If you have performed a search and obtained a list of items, a number of icons (each with its own letter) will appear on the map, along with the corresponding locations highlighted in the list of available addresses or businesses on the left side of the screen (as you already saw in Figure 2-15).

If you are custom-creating a map, you can similarly highlight and mark points on the map and provide information about specific points. Google provides a number of standard icons, including map pins and tags of varying sizes, but you can customize the icons to be used on your map.

Pop-ups

Clicking an icon or its associated description will present you with an icon pop-up (or content bubble). The exact content of the bubble depends on the information that is available. Within a standard Google Maps search, the pop-up will often contain the full address and phone information for the business in question, as you can see in Figure 2-16.

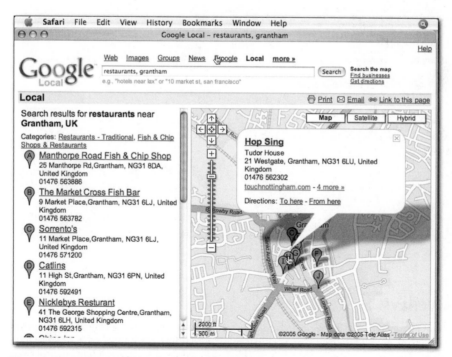

FIGURE 2-16: Business information in Google Maps.

The information content of a pop-up is completely customizable. Because the base of the content is HTML, you can include styles, images, and other content. When developing a Google Maps application, what you use this pop-up for is entirely up to you.

Links

In the case of the standard Google Maps interface you also obtain two "Directions" links ("To here" and "From here") that provide an interface to the Google route-finding service, which calculates, highlights, and describes a route between two points. Figure 2-17 shows a route from a railway station to a restaurant.

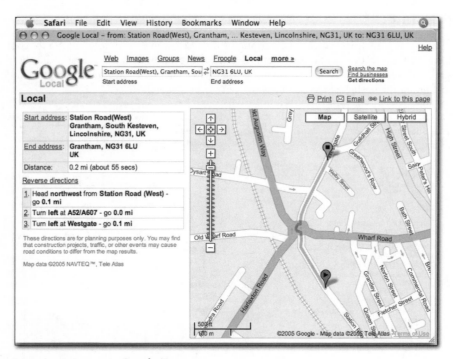

FIGURE 2-17: A route in Google Maps.

Overlays

The Google Maps API enables you to overlay lines and polygonal objects onto a map. You can use this information to provide additional detail about the location you are looking at. The overlay lines are specified in terms of their location within the Google Maps environment, so the lines will scroll and move when you move the map around. A good example of overlays in action is the route highlighted by Google when determining how to get from one location to another.

With some further programming tricks within the browser, you can build in additional overlays using JavaScript and images that can be overlaid on top of the Google Maps display.

Note These custom overlay images will not move like the built-in overlay lines do when you scroll or move the map, or when you change the zoom level.

Wrapping Up

The basics of the Google Maps API interface — the ability to zoom; move about the map; and overlay information such as map points, information windows, and routes on top of a Google Map — are all functions that you can add to your own map when you develop applications using the Google Maps API.

In short, Google Local is a superb example of the capabilities of the Google Maps API when you start to combine information from multiple sources into your application. Creating these elements is not as complicated as it seems; you can start by understanding the classes and functions supported by the Google Maps API.

The Google Maps API

The Google Maps API is based on a very simple suite of classes that you use, within a JavaScript container, directly within an HTML page. All of the functionality of a Google Map is based on this simple premise of an embedded JavaScript object built into a web page.

The interface to the API is surprisingly straightforward, but the simplicity hides some powerful classes, objects, and interfaces that enable you to manipulate the Google Map. By combining this interface with the data that you want to display, you can support interactive elements on the web page without having to reload the page or redisplay portions of the map: The entire process is handled within the JavaScript and Google Maps application.

Using the API Key

Before you start using the API, you must register with Google and obtain a Web API key. You cannot use the Google Maps API without a key; Google will return an error and display nothing if you do not use a key or if you use the wrong key when you try to use the Google Maps API. For this reason, the Google Maps API key needs to be referenced in every Google Maps application you create.

To obtain a Google Maps API key, you must already have an account on the Google system. If you do not already have an account with Google, you will need to register with Google first. You will be asked to supply an e-mail address (which will be used to supply you with your API key).

Once you have you have registered with Google, go to the Google Maps API web site (http://www.google.com/apis/maps/) and request a key. The key only works when Google can verify the web site on which your applications will work. This means that the web site on which you build your applications must be publicly available on the Internet. Unfortunately, this also means that you cannot develop applications locally within a network that is not shared directly with the Internet. This includes most servers in organizations behind firewalls and servers at small businesses and homes connected to the Internet through a standard xDSL connection such as ADSL.

Note If you don't already have a publicly accessible web site service, you will need to sign up to a server provided by a hosting company, where many different solutions are available. All the examples shown in this book, for example, are hosted on a service provided by Dreamhost (www.dreamhost.com).

The Google Maps API is, in fact, more specific than simply the web site hostname. The API key will only work within a specific directory. So, if you register with a URL of http://maps.mcslp.com/examples, Google Maps applications will only work when loaded from this precise URL. Other directories above or below this URL will not work.

Thus, http://maps.mcslp.com/examples/simple.html would be valid for the key registered with the preceding URL. But http://maps.mcslp.com/simple.html would be invalid. So would the same example placed into a subdirectory: http://maps.mcslp.com/examples/simple/simple.html.

These limits mean that you cannot register an entire domain for hosting Google Maps applications unless all the applications are placed into the same directory. The restrictions are designed to protect both Google and your own applications from being stolen and abused because the correct key must be used.

Once you have a web site URL for your Google Maps applications, you can register for a key by going to the "Sign up for an API key" page, entering the URL for your web site, and clicking Submit. Your Google Maps API key will be e-mailed to you. Make sure you keep the e-mail message as well as a separate note of the key in a secure location. Although you can request keys again, and even request multiple keys for multiple web sites, keeping the key safe is a good idea.

Limits and Usage

As mentioned, your Google Maps API key is unique to your web site. You cannot copy the code that you have developed (or that anybody else has developed, for that matter) and use it on a different web site without separately registering for an additional key and modifying the key information.

Once you have an API key, you can create, use, and support as many Google Maps applications as you like. But you need to be sensible about the information and services that you provide. For example, you cannot claim that the Google Map and the information that it contains is solely your copyright. Nor can you claim that there is any official affiliation between yourself and Google just because you are using its mapping service.

The Google Maps API web site contains a full guide to the terms of usage that you agree to when you request an API key. I strongly recommend that you read these notes before signing up for a key and developing applications to ensure that you are aware of the issues and limitations of using the service.

Browser Compatibility

Google Maps is compatible with the same browsers and environments as Google Local (see Chapter 2). This covers the vast majority of the web browsing environments available. Other browsers might or might not support the Google Maps API. The Google Maps API is constantly changing as it is improved and updated. It is inevitable that some occasional problems will manifest themselves. Any significant difficulties should be reported to Google.

Note In your HTML page you can check whether the current browser is compatible with the Google Maps system through the GBrowserIsCompatible function in the Google Maps API. Ideally you should check the return value of this and report any known incompatibility to the user.

Basic Components of a Google Maps Application

The key to the Google Maps API is the JavaScript component that is loaded from Google each time you open a Google Maps web page. This JavaScript component provides the interface to the Google Maps service and generates the map onscreen by loading the necessary image components and tiling them onto the display.

Further customization and extension of these components is what makes a custom Google Maps application.

XHTML (Extensible HTML)

Google Maps will work in any standard HTML page, but Google recommends that you create pages that are compliant with the XHTML standard. This will ensure not only that the HTML is compatible with the standard to which most browsers are now also made compatible, but also the reliable rendering of your web page on as wide a range of web sites as possible.

For this reason, you should make sure that your XHTML pages are correctly marked up as XHTML. Listing 3-1 shows a simple XHTML-compatible page template.

Listing 3-1: XHTML Page Template

```
<!DOCTYPE html PUBLIC "-//W3C//DTD XHTML 1.0 Strict//EN"
"http://www.w3.org/TR/xhtml1/DTD/xhtml1-strict.dtd">
  <html xmlns="http://www.w3.org/1999/xhtml">
<head>
<title>XHTML Page</title>
</head>
<body>
</body>
</html>
```

You can check the markup content for your web page by using the W3C validator at `http://validator.w3.org`. Here, you can supply the URL of a web page on the Internet or cut and paste the page content into the web form for validation. Errors and warnings will be reported for pages that are faulty.

Figure 3-1 shows the result after running the code in Listing 3-1 through the validation service.

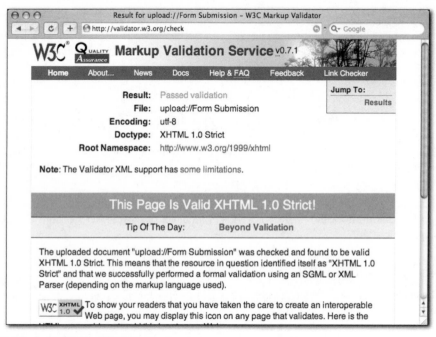

FIGURE 3-1: Validated XHTML report.

VML (Vector Markup Language)

If you are using polylines (that is, any type of line-based markup, such as routes or bounding boxes) on top of your Google Maps applications as an overlay, and you have clients using Internet Explorer, you should include the Microsoft VML namespace within your XHTML definition. Without this option, your polylines will not work.

Note You can ignore this requirement if you are not using polylines of any kind.

Listing 3-2 shows the suggested XHTML header to use for VML and Internet Explorer.

Listing 3-2: XHTML for VML/Polylines in Internet Explorer

```
<!DOCTYPE html PUBLIC "-//W3C//DTD XHTML 1.0 Strict//EN"

"http://www.w3.org/TR/xhtml1/DTD/xhtml1-strict.dtd">
<html xmlns="http://www.w3.org/1999/xhtml" xmlns:v="urn:⤶
schemas-microsoft-com:vml">
  <head>
    <meta http-equiv="content-type" content="text/html; charset=UTF-8"/>

    <title>Your Page Title Here</title>
    <style type="text/css">
    v\:* {
      behavior:url(#default#VML);
    }
    </style>
    <script src="http://maps.google.com/maps?file=api&v=1&key=abcdefg"

           type="text/javascript">
    </script>
  </head>
```

Styles and Elements

You are completely free to develop and design your own styles, stylesheet, and layout according to the needs of your web site. Google Maps does not place any limitation or restriction on how you lay out or style your web site when it includes a Google Map.

However, the map will tend to dominate most pages, and you should take this into account when designing the layout and other content for your pages.

XML (Extensible Markup Language)

The XML standard is a way of representing data in a structured format that is architecture neutral. Although XML is not a required element in Google Maps applications, it is common to provide large volumes of data (map points, information windows, and so on) by specifying the information in XML, loading the XML through the Google Maps API, and then displaying that information using the functionality of the API. The API also supports XSL Transformations, a method of converting an XML document into HTML using a stylesheet.

Cross-Reference

Generating, parsing, and using XML is covered in more detail in Chapter 5.

JavaScript

The Google Maps API is based on the JavaScript language. JavaScript (soon to be referred to as ECMAScript as an official standard) is built into most browsers and provides a rich suite of functionality for developing dynamic elements.

Teaching you how to program in JavaScript is beyond the scope of this book. However, Google Maps does rely on JavaScript, so numerous examples of JavaScript applications are included throughout this book. JavaScript is easy to use and learn, and any programmer that is already familiar with the basic mechanics of programming should be able to adapt her skills to JavaScript.

Note The majority of JavaScript programming is designed to interface directly into the Google Maps API, which itself is based on an object-oriented interface to a suite of Google Maps–specific classes.

Understanding API Terminology

The Google Maps API is essentially a suite of JavaScript classes that you use to build applications within the confines of a web page. Understanding the API relies on knowing the terminology used to define sections of the Google Maps API and interface. Once you understand the terminology, a closer look at the Google Maps API classes will provide the detail required to build Google Maps applications.

All Google Maps applications start off with a simple map. To this map, you can add a number of different elements designed to provide the application functionality. All maps support four main elements:

- **Overlays:** Points of interest on the map or lines denoting areas, routes, or other information about the location being displayed.

- **Events:** Occurrences of an operation, such as the user clicking on a point of interest.

- **Information:** Extended data about the map, a map marker, or map region that is displayed as part of the map application.

- **Controls:** Basic interface controls that enable the user to zoom in and out of the map and move about the map effectively.

A fifth element doesn't have a unique role in the API, but it does support the operations: The ability to load data dynamically is key to providing the interactive elements of a typical Google Maps application. Generally, the information is extracted from an XML file that is loaded from the web server, either as a static file or — for true dynamism — through a dynamic component on the web server, such as CGI script, PHP script, or Java application.

By combining all of these elements, you can create quite complex applications, even though the core of the application code is still based on the comparatively simple JavaScript language.

Overlays

Overlays consist of information that is displayed on top of a map of a particular location. There are two basic types:

- **Markers or points:** These are generated within the application through the `GMarker` class. They are based on an icon and a shadow (at a 45-degree angle) and can be used to denote any information you want. In general, an icon is used to highlight a specific item and is, therefore, usually a pointer, arrow, or other construct that gives a specific reference point. For example, you would use a marker to indicate the location of a business on a map so as to give a precise location. To show more detailed information about a specific location, you use an information window.

- **Polylines:** These are used when you want to provide a route across a map, or when you want to draw a specific shape on the map. For example, you might use a polyline to denote the boundaries of a property on a map.

Events

Events are used to communicate specific occurrences of an operation. For example, an event is raised when the user clicks a marker, moves the map, zooms in on the map, and so on.

To provide interactivity in your application, you can assign functions to be executed when an event occurs. A common example is when the user clicks a marker: Most maps center the map on that marker and provide an information window showing more information or detail about that particular point. In the Google Local system, for example, searching for a business on a map and then clicking one of the available markers provides you with the address, phone number, and, if available, other information for the business denoted by the marker.

Information Windows

Additional information is usually displayed in an info window, which is a sort of speech bubble that is overlayed on the map. The info window usually appears in response to the user selecting a marker, either by clicking the marker in the map or by clicking a separate list of markers that is also displayed on the page.

Information windows can be as simple or complex as you like. They can contain simple text or full-blown HTML, incorporating images and other elements. As already noted, info windows appear in Google Local when the user clicks a business marker.

Tip The Google Maps API includes a suite of functions for triggering, displaying, and formatting the content within an info window.

Controls

The Google Maps API provides a number of standard controls for allowing the user to interact at a basic level with the map. These controls are normally displayed in the top left-hand and top right-hand corners of the map display and include the buttons for moving around the map, zooming in and out, and selecting the map type (map, satellite imagery, or hybrid).

At the time of this writing, the available control types are as follows:

- GLargeMapControl: A large pan/zoom control (with slider).
- GSmallMapControl: A smaller pan/zoom control (without slider).
- GSmallZoomControl: A small zoom control (no slider or panning controls).
- GMapTypeControl: Lets the visitor toggle among map types (map, satellite imagery, and hybrid).

Generally, you choose the type of controls to add to the map according to the needs of the application, but you can also let users select which controls appear.

The Google Maps Classes

All of the functionality of the Google Maps API is provided through a suite of classes designed to build and define the elements of a Google Map. You start with the GMap class and, through the additional classes, define map markers and information windows, and create controls and events that allow the user to interact with the application.

GMap

The main GMap class creates a new Google Map within an HTML container (typically a div element within the HTML). The format for creating a new object using the class is as follows:

```
GMap(container, mapTypes?, width?, height?)
```

 Note   Optional arguments to a function are denoted by a question mark after the argument.

The optional mapTypes argument enables you to specify which map types are available in the application. The default is the three current solutions: G_MAP_TYPE, G_HYBRID_TYPE, and G_SATELLITE_TYPE.

The default size of the map is the same as the container in which the map is created. Alternatively, you can specify the width and/or height (in pixels) when creating the map.

Once the map is created, you can set a number of options, as outlined in Table 3-1. Each of the items in this table is a method to the map object created by GMap.

Table 3-1: Configuration Map Options

Method	Description
enableDragging()	Enables dynamic dragging (enabled by default).
disableDragging()	Disables dynamic dragging.
draggingEnabled()	Returns true if dynamic dragging is enabled.
enableInfoWindow()	Enables the info window on this map (enabled by default).
disableInfoWindow()	Disables the info window on this map.
infoWindowEnabled()	Returns true if the info window is enabled on this map.

To add or remove one of the control types on a map, use the methods in Table 3-2. The con-trol argument uses one of the constants specified in the "Controls" section, earlier in this chapter.

Table 3-2: Adding and Removing Controls on a Map

Method	Description
addControl(control)	Adds a map control to the map.
removeControl(control)	Removes a map control from the map.

You can get status information about the map, such as the current location, zoom level, and area shown using the methods in Table 3-3. This table also shows the methods that allow you to modify these settings.

Table 3-3: Methods for Getting and Setting Status Information

Method	Description
getCenterLatLng()	Returns the center point of the map in latitude/longitude coordinates.
getBoundsLatLng()	Returns the latitude/longitude bounds of the map viewport.
getSpanLatLng()	Returns the width and height of the map viewport in latitude/longitude ticks.
getZoomLevel()	Returns the integer zoom level of the map.
centerAtLatLng(latLng)	Centers the map at the given point.

Continued

Table 3-3 *(continued)*

Method	Description
recenterOrPanTo LatLng(latLng)	Centers the map at the given point, doing a fluid pan to the point if it is within the current map viewport.
zoomTo(zoomLevel)	Zooms to the given integer zoom level, ignoring the request if the given zoom level is outside the bounds of the current map type.
centerAndZoom(latLng, zoomLevel)	Atomically centers and zooms the map. Useful to initialize the map with an initial center and zoom level.
getMapTypes()	Returns an array of map types supported by this map (currently G_MAP_TYPE, G_HYBRID_TYPE, and G_SATELLITE_TYPE).
getCurrentMapType()	Returns the map type currently in use (G_MAP_TYPE, G_HYBRID_TYPE, or G_SATELLITE_TYPE).
setMapType(mapType)	Switches this map to the given map type (G_MAP_TYPE, G_HYBRID_TYPE, or G_SATELLITE_TYPE).

To add an overlay to the map, you must first create the overlay (using GMarker or GPolyline) and then use the addOverlay method from Table 3-4 to draw the overlay onto the map. You can also delete an overlay (providing you have the object definition) or remove all overlays.

Table 3-4: Methods for Adding/Removing Overlays to a Map

Method	Description
addOverlay(overlay)	Adds the given overlay object to the map.
removeOverlay(overlay)	Removes the given overlay object from the map.
clearOverlays()	Removes all of the overlays from the map.

To add an information window to a map, use the methods in Table 3-5. Note that the methods in this table are primarily aimed at adding information windows to areas of the map that do not have a specific marker; there is a separate method for adding information windows to markers that is part of the definition for the GMarker object.

You configure events for a map object, marker, or other element by using one of the event types specified in Table 3-6. These events are common to all places where you can specify an event.

Table 3-5: Methods for Adding Info Windows to Your Map

Method	Description
openInfoWindow(latLng, htmlElem, pixelOffset?, onOpenFn?, onCloseFn?)	Displays the info window with the given HTML content at the given point. htmlElem should be an HTML DOM element. If pixelOffset (GSize) is given, you offset the info window by that number of pixels, which lets users place info windows above markers and other overlays. If onOpenFn is given, you call that function when the window is displayed. If onCloseFn is given, you call that function when the window is closed.
openInfoWindowHtml(marker, htmlStr, pixelOffset?, onOpenFn?, onCloseFn?)	Like openInfoWindow, but takes an HTML string rather than an HTML DOM element.
openInfoWindowXslt(marker, xmlElem, xsltUri, pixelOffset?, onOpenFn?, onCloseFn?)	Like openInfoWindow, but takes an XML element and the URI of an XSLT document to produce the content of the info window. The first time a URI is given, the file at that URI is downloaded with GXmlHttp and subsequently cached.
showMapBlowup(point, zoomLevel?, mapType?, pixelOffset?, onOpenFn?, onCloseFn?))	Shows a blowup of the map at the given GPoint. If the zoomLevel and mapType parameters are not given, you default to a zoom level of 1 and the current map type.
closeInfoWindow()	Closes the info window if it is open.

Table 3-6: Event Types Supported by the Google Maps API

Event	Arguments	Description
Click	overlay, point	Triggered when the user clicks the map or an overlay on the map. If the click was on an overlay, you pass the overlay as an argument to the event handler. Otherwise, you pass the latitude/longitude point that was clicked on the map.
Move	none	Triggered when the map is moving. This event is triggered continuously as the map is dragged.

Continued

Table 3-6 *(continued)*

Event	Arguments	Description
Movestart	none	Triggered at the beginning of a continuous pan/drag movement. This event is not triggered when the map moves discretely.
Moveend	none	Triggered at the end of a discrete or continuous map movement. This event is triggered once at the end of a continuous pan.
Zoom	oldZoomLevel, newZoomLevel	Triggered after the map zoom level changes.
maptypechanged	none	Triggered after the map type (map, hybrid, or satellite) changes.
infowindowopen	none	Triggered after the info window is displayed.
infowindowclose	none	Triggered after the info window is closed.
addoverlay	overlay	Triggered after an overlay is added to the map.
removeoverlay	overlay	Triggered after an overlay is removed from the map. Not triggered if clearOverlays is called — see the clearoverlays event.
clearoverlays	None	Triggered after all overlays are cleared from the map.

Cross-Reference Don't worry if the information presented here seems daunting. Chapter 4 provides more specific examples of how you use the API and the classes, methods, and objects.

GMarker

This class creates a new GMarker object based on the supplied GPoint reference. GMarkers are used to highlight points on a map. All GMarkers are displayed using an icon, either the default icon supplied by Google Maps or a special icon (previously defined through a GIcon object) specified as the optional argument to the function:

```
GMarker(point, icon)
```

The created marker supports a number of methods for adding information windows based on an HTML reference, HTML string, or XSLT transformation of XML data. You can also configure a GMarker object to force a zoomed version of the map for that point. Table 3-7 shows the full list of supported methods.

Table 3-7: Methods for the GMarker Object

Method	Description
openInfoWindow(htmlElem)	Opens an info window with the given HTML content over this marker. htmlElem should be an HTML DOM element.
openInfoWindowHtml(htmlStr)	Like openInfoWindow, but takes an HTML string rather than an HTML DOM element.
openInfoWindowXslt(xmlElem, xsltUri)	Like openInfoWindow, but takes an XML element and the URI of an XSLT document to produce the content of the info window. The first time a URI is given, the file at that URI is downloaded with GXmlHttp and subsequently cached.
showMapBlowup(zoomLevel?, mapType?)	Shows a blowup of the map over this marker. You use a default zoom level of 1 and the current map type if the zoomLevel and mapType parameters are not given.

All GMarkers also support the following triggers when the specified event occurs:

- click: Triggered when the user clicks the marker.
- infowindowopen: Triggered when the info window is opened.
- infowindowclose: Triggered when the info window is closed.

GPolyline

This class creates a line made up of two (or more) GPoints for display on a map. The format of the function is as follows:

```
GPolyline(points,color,weight,opacity)
```

The points argument should be an array of GPoint objects.

Caution

Lines are drawn from one point to the next in the order they are supplied. Ensure that your array of points has the correct order before creating the GPolyline object.

The remainder of the arguments are completely optional:

- color: The color of the line (specified using HTML style colors, such as #ff4787).
- weight: The width of the line in pixels.
- opacity: The opacity specified as a float between 0 (invisible) and 1 (fully opaque).

GIcon

This class creates a new GIcon object, which is the graphic used to highlight points on a Google Map. GIcons can be based on any suitable graphic image. If you create your own GIcon, you must specify at least the following properties before using it in a map:

- image
- shadowImage
- iconSize
- shadowSize

Table 3-8 gives a full list of properties and their descriptions.

Table 3-8: Properties for the GIcon Object

Property	Description
Image	The foreground image URL of the icon.
Shadow	The shadow image URL of the icon.
iconSize	The pixel size of the foreground image of the icon.
shadowSize	The pixel size of the shadow image.
iconAnchor	The pixel coordinate relative to the top left-hand corner of the icon image at which you should anchor this icon to the map.
infoWindowAnchor	The pixel coordinate relative to the top left-hand corner of the icon image at which you should anchor the info window to this icon.
printImage	The URL of the foreground icon image you should use for printed maps. It should be the same size as the main icon image.

Property	Description
mozPrintImage	The URL of the foreground icon image you should use for printed maps in Firefox/Mozilla. It should be the same size as the main icon image.
printShadow	The URL of the shadow image you should use for printed maps. It should be a GIF image because most browsers cannot print PNG images.
Transparent	The URL of a virtually transparent version of the foreground icon image used to capture IE click events. This image should be a 24-bit PNG version of the main icon image with 1% opacity, but the same shape and size as the main icon.
imageMap	An array of integers representing the x/y coordinates of the image map you should use to specify the clickable part of the icon image in non-IE browsers.

To create a new GIcon, use this:

```
GIcon()
```

You can also optionally specify the name of an existing icon from which the properties will be copied. This is useful if you are creating a suite of icons that are the same dimensions (and can use the same shadow), but which have different main images.

GEvent

This class creates a new GEvent object for building event objects for your Google Maps. Table 3-9 provides a list of the available methods for this object.

Table 3-9: Methods for GEvent Objects

Method	Description
addListener(source, eventName, listenerFn)	Calls the listener function (listenerFn) when the event is triggered on the source instance. An opaque listener token that can be used with removeListener is returned.
removeListener (listener)	Removes the given listener, which should be a listener token returned by addListener.
clearListeners(source, eventName)	Removes all listeners for the given event on the given source.

Continued

Table 3-9 *(continued)*

Method	Description
trigger(source, eventName, args...)	Triggers the given event on the given source with the given list of arguments.
bind(source, eventName, object, method)	Binds the given method of the given object to the given source event. When the given event is triggered, the given method is called for the specified object.

GEvent methods are static, so you should always create the object before calling the method (for example, new GEvent(); GEvent.bind()) rather than creating and calling the method in one line (for example, new GEvent().bind()).

GXmlHttp

This class creates a browser-independent instance of XmlHttpRequest that enables you to access remote content (XML, HTML, or XML-RPC). In short, the object provides a method for dynamically loading information that can then be used to build components and items on your map.

The precise operation of this function is covered in more detail in Chapter 5.

GXml

This class creates a new XML object that can be used to parse and access information contained within an XML string. You must create the GXml object first, and then supply a string to be parsed. For example:

```
var xmlparser = new GXml();
```

Once you create the object, you can parse XML by calling the parse method:

```
parser(xmlstring)
```

Or you can access a value from the parsed XML using value:

```
value(xmlnode)
```

Because you parse and then access data after you create the object, you can reuse the object to parse other XML documents without re-creating a new object each time.

Because GXml creates a persistent object that you then use to parse and access XML data, you should take care to ensure that you are using the correct object when accessing a value. Although in some situations it is tempting to reuse the same object to parse an XML document, it may return an odd value if you use the wrong object or forget to reparse the XML you wanted.

GXslt

When providing additional information on a Google Map (for example, within an info window when the user clicks a map point), you can use XSLT to convert a supplied XML document into the HTML to be displayed.

The GXslt function creates a new object that supports a browser-independent method for translating XML data into HTML through the supplied XSLT transformation definition. The conversion tries to use the native XSLT transformation library built into the browser if it is available (it automatically picks a solution based on the browser). If no built-in XSLT engine is available, it defaults to the XSLT transformation engine available within the JavaScript definition.

To create a new object by supplying the URI of an XSLT document, use the following:

```
GXSlt(xsltURI)
```

To perform a transformation, use the transformToHtml method:

```
transformToHtml(xmlDoc, htmlContainer)
```

The preceding transforms the supplied XML document directly into the HTML DOM element in a web page identified by the htmlContainer argument. It does *not* return the HTML.

GPoint

This class creates a new GPoint object representing a two-dimensional coordinate (horizontal/vertical):

```
GPoint(x,y)
```

If you use GPoint to create a point on the map, x represents the longitude and y represents the latitude.

A common mistake with GPoint is that it takes longitude (east-west) and then latitude (north-south) as arguments, in that order, even though you commonly refer to a point on a map the other way around. It is very easy to mistakenly swap the values and end up referring to a point thousands of miles from your intended location.

GSize

This class creates a new GSize object designed to represent a two-dimensional size measurement (such as width and height). The format of the function is as follows:

```
GSize(width, height)
```

Converting Degrees to Decimal

If you know the longitude and latitude of a given point in the degrees, minutes, and seconds format (for example, 52° 54' 40" N 0° 38' 21" W), you can convert each value into its decimal equivalent using the following formula:

decimal = degrees + (minutes/60) + (seconds/3600)

Taking the preceding example map reference:

Longitude = 0 + (38/60) + (21/3600) = 0.6391666

Latitude = 52 + (54/60) + (40/3600) = 52.911111

These values can now be inserted directly into your Google Maps pages, databases, and data stores when you create maps.

Here, `width` and `height` are the appropriate spans. These can be any floating-point value, but are usually used to hold latitude/longitude values.

GBounds

This class creates a new object that represents a two-dimensional bounding box. You would normally use GBounds to determine whether a given GPoint was within a specified range. To create a new GBounds object, use this:

```
GBounds(minX,minY,maxX,maxY)
```

Here, the arguments are usually the latitude and longitude of the box, although they can hold any floating-point values.

Wrapping Up

Probably the hardest part of the process in developing a Google Map is understanding the relationship between the HTML used for the web page and the JavaScript used to integrate with the Google Maps service. Although, in practice, you are embedding the JavaScript for the application into an HTML page, the two should really be considered as separate elements that are merely contained within the same file.

Once you understand that little piece of the puzzle (that is, using the class interface to the Google Maps system and largely ignoring the HTML that acts as a wrapper around it), it becomes easy to start developing Google Maps applications. The Google Maps class interface is simple but effective, and throughout the rest of the book you will see that this simplicity makes it easy to develop complex sites with rich functionality — without getting bogged down in complicated interfaces.

The Google Web API

The Google database contains a massive range of information. Some of it is, of course, based on the web pages that make up the World Wide Web. In addition, Google has worked hard to add other information to the database, such as names, contact details, and classifications for businesses and organizations. As you use the Google Maps API, you will probably want to combine your Google Maps information with data extracted from these other sources.

To do this, you must interface to the Google system through the Google Web API, which provides access to the Google web index of web sites to users working in Java, .NET, Perl, and other environments.

This chapter tells you how to acquire the Google Web API, examines the basics of this API, and shows how you can use it to incorporate additional information to help support the data you will be presenting in your Google Maps applications.

Downloading the Google Web API

To use the API, you first need to download the Google Web developer's kit (from `http://www.google.com/apis/`), which includes the following components:

➤ A Web Services Description Language (WSDL) file that defines the interface to the Google Web Service. The information contained in the WSDL file can be used by any compatible web services client environment using the Simple Object Access Protocol (SOAP).

➤ A Java library that provides a wrapper around the interface to the Google Web system. The Java wrapper makes it very easy to build Java-based applications that access the information in the Google database.

➤ An example .NET project that invokes the Google Web API.

➤ Full documentation for using the Google Web API.

The API kit is supplied as a Zip file, which you will need to extract using one of the following:

- PKZip, the built-in Zip extractor in Windows XP.
- The unzip tool in Unix/Linux.
- The built-in or StuffIt Expander applications in Mac OS X.

The Google Web developer's kit contains the following files and directories:

- `APIs_Reference.html`: Contains the Google Web API documentation and can be read with any web browser.
- `GoogleAPIDemo.java`: A sample Java class that you can adapt.
- `GoogleSearch.wsdl`: Contains the WSDL for the entire Google Web API.
- `LICENSE.txt`: The license for using the kit.
- `README.txt`: A quick guide to the contents.
- `dotnet/`: Contains samples for the Windows .NET environment.
- `googleapi.jar`: The Java class for accessing the Google API.
- `javadoc/`: Contains Java documentation for the Java class in `googleapi.jar`.
- `licenses/`: Contains licenses for using different components.
- `soap-samples/`: Contains SOAP XML samples.

As with the Google Maps interface, accessing the Google Web system requires a unique key. You cannot use the Google Web API without the unique key, and this key must be included in every application that needs to access or use the Google Web API.

Note   To obtain a key, just visit the Google Web API site (`www.google.com/apis`) and choose Create Key. If you already have a Google account, the key will be sent to you automatically. If you do not already have a Google account, you will need to create one.

Tip   If you forget your key, you can ask for another one simply by visiting the Google Web API site and making a request. Google will then e-mail your key to you.

Using the Google Web API

You must agree to numerous terms and conditions before using the Google Web API. The primary points to remember are as follows:

- You cannot use the Google Web API to build a site for commercial purposes without prior agreement with Google.

- You are limited to a maximum of 1,000 queries a day. This averages to one query every 86 seconds, so it pays to be careful with your queries; limit, cache, or count your queries to ensure that you can still get the information when you need it. If you rely on the Google Web API for supporting functionality in your web site, and your web site becomes popular, hitting the 1,000 query limit in a typical day is inevitable.

- Google will return a maximum of 10 results per query, even though your query may actually be made up of many more results than this. Because of this, large searches may require multiple queries, increasing your daily query count on each occasion.

If you have any questions, check the terms and conditions and the FAQ section on the Google Web API site.

Remember to take note of the limits and usage on your key, which is tied to your Google account. In theory, you could create multiple accounts, obtaining multiple keys to increase the number of queries you can make per day. Over the long term, however, you run the risk of Google revoking or restricting your access and your ability to use the service and to obtain additional keys.

Conducting Searches

Once you have your access key, you can start submitting queries to the system. This relies on using web services with a number of parameters to specify the information you are searching for. You also need to understand the format of the results, how the information can be used, and what the limitations of the data that you extract are.

Parameters

Regardless of what language you are using, the Simple Object Access Protocol (SOAP) interface to the Google web service works in the same way: You supply the parameters for the search and Google returns a structure with the search results.

Table 4-1 shows the parameters to the remote function.

Table 4-1: Google Web Search API Arguments

Parameter	Description
Key	The access key provided by Google.
Query string	The query string that defines what you are searching for.
Start index	The index of the first result to be returned within the query.
Max results	The maximum number of results to return. Note that you can never obtain more than 10 results.

Continued

Table 4-1 *(continued)*

Parameter	Description
Filter	Activates filtering to remove similar results or results from the same host.
Restrict	Adds a restriction to the search database. Restrictions can be made on a country-by-country basis or to specific topics. Check the API documentation for a full list.
SafeSearch	Enables SafeSearch, which filters adult content.
Language Restrict	Restricts the search to return only matches within a specified source language.
Input Encoding	Now deprecated. Used to specify the input encoding; all requests should be made in UTF-8.
Output Encoding	Now deprecated. Used to specify the output encoding; all results are now returned in UTF-8.

Some of these parameters have specific settings and formats that will alter the information that is returned during a search. For example, the `query string` parameter supports the query specification available to you when you perform a search on the Google web site. That is, placing a plus sign before a word will require the word to be in the page; placing a minus sign before a word will require that it be ignored; and enclosing a group of words in quotation marks will allow you to specify a certain phrase to search for.

Tip The easiest way to identify the right query string is to perform your search on the Google web site itself. This way, you are not limited by the number of queries and can perfect the string that you want to use before running the query through your application. Once you have the right string, place this into your code or application.

Other parameters filter the results in terms of the information returned, such as removing adult content, restricting to specific topics, and even restricting to specific locations and languages. Check the API documentation for a complete guide of the available options.

Results

The call to the Google Web API returns a large structure of information composed of base data (information about the search, such as the total number of results and indices), as well as an array of results. How you access the information that has been returned depends on your implementation and the language you are using (for example, Perl makes the data available in the form of a nested hash structure). The base data returned is detailed in Table 4-2.

Table 4-2: Base Data from a Search Request

Element	Description
documentFiltering	A boolean value that indicates whether filtering was performed on the results. The value is only true if you have requested filtering and filtering has been performed. If you have not requested filtering, the value will always be false.
searchComments	Any message the API deems suitable to return about the search, such as filtered content or words removed from the query string.
estimatedTotalResultsCount	The approximate total number of matches for the given search criteria. The value given may not equal the exact number of matches; you can determine this by looking at the estimateIsExact value. Results are estimates when results might be removed due to duplications.
estimateIsExact	A Boolean that if true states that the estimate value is the real value.
resultElements	An array of results. See Table 4-3 for the format of each result item.
searchQuery	The original value of the search query text.
startIndex	Indicates the index (of the first result in the list of results) within the total number of results.
endIndex	Indicates the index (of the last result in the list of results) within the total number of results.
searchTips	A text string for search tips, such as alternate searches or misspellings.
directoryCategories	An array of directory categories (from the Google directory) that would match the search.
searchTime	A floating-point value indicating the amount of time taken to perform the search.

The array of results is actually a list of individual structures, and each structure includes the information about the result, including its URL, the snippet of text extracted from the page, and other information. You can see the individual fields in a given item in Table 4-3.

Table 4-3: Data Return for Each Item

Element	Description
Summary	If the search result has a listing in the Google Open Directory Project (ODP), the summary text for the entry appears here.
URL	The URL of the result.
Snippet	A snippet that shows the query text in the context of the page that is being returned. The matching query text is highlighted in bold, with the entire snippet encoded as HTML. In some environments, this will be encoded HTML, where tag elements have been converted to their text equivalents suitable for displaying in a web browser. See the Perl example (later in this chapter) for more information.
Title	The title of the search result, returned as HTML. In some environments this will be encoded HTML, where tag elements have been converted to their text equivalents suitable for displaying in a web browser. See the Perl example (later in this chapter) for more information.
cachedSize	The size of the page in the database. The result is a string, not an integer, including the integer size and quantifier (k for kilobytes).
relatedInformation Present	A boolean value indicating that you can perform a related search on this URL to get pages that reference this URL.
hostName	If results are filtered to remove hostname duplicates, only two results from each host are returned. In that instance, the second result in the result list has this value set to indicate that it is the second of the two de-duped results.
directoryCategory	The category of the URL if the URL also exists within the Google ODP.
directoryTitle	The title of the URL as it is referenced within the Google ODP, if the result URL exists in the ODP.

Again, extracting and using the information contained within the individual results is reliant on the language and environment that you are using. Later in this chapter, you'll see examples in Perl and Java.

Limitations

The search parameters and results have some limitations (see Table 4-4). Some of them I have already described and are imposed as part of the license limitations; others are simply technical limitations. I suggest checking the documentation to confirm the details in Table 4-4, as they are subject to change.

Table 4-4: Search Limitations

Item	Limit
Maximum query string length	2,048 bytes
Maximum number of words in the query	10
Maximum number of "site:" terms	1
Maximum number of results per query	10
Maximum value of start index and result size	1,000

Tip

If your search obtains more than 1,000 results, you can obtain only the first 1,000—and your query string is probably not specific enough to return the information you are looking for anyway. Narrow down your search and try again with a different query string.

As you can see in Table 4-4, you can see only 10 results at a time from Google. The initial search, if you don't specify otherwise, will return the first 10 results. To see subsequent results, you must specify an alternative starting index with multiple requests. This is called paging.

For example, imagine that you search for plumbers in Stamford. Your first query returns the first 10 items. From this first search, you can extract the number of the expected results by looking at the value of the `estimatedTotalResultsCount` element of the base data. If the value of this is 87 and you want to obtain the remainder of the results, you must also perform the following searches:

- Plumbers in Stamford starting at index 11.
- Plumbers in Stamford starting at index 21.
- Plumbers in Stamford starting at index 31.
- Plumbers in Stamford starting at index 41.
- Plumbers in Stamford starting at index 51.
- Plumbers in Stamford starting at index 61.
- Plumbers in Stamford starting at index 71.
- Plumbers in Stamford starting at index 81.

With these eight requests, you've finally got all of the information you need. Well, you've got information, anyway; to determine whether it is what you wanted, you must examine the results in more detail.

Beyond Searches

The primary reason for using the Google Web API is to get a list of web sites that match a particular query and, thus, might be useful to you when building your Google Maps. You can, however, access two other Google systems through the Google Web API: the spelling system and the cache system.

The spelling system provides alternate spellings for words or phrases that you supply. The same system uses the information in the Google database to suggest sensible alternatives when you submit a search (for example, if you searched for "Bratney Spires," it would suggest an alternate — and correct — spelling: "Britney Spears").

The cache system returns the cached document content for a given URL. The text returned is the raw HTML for the URL, assuming that it exists in the Google database, as it was stored from the last Google web crawl.

Both these systems are described further in the Google Web API documentation but are not generally useful for Google Maps applications.

Note   Each individual query counts as 1 toward your 1,000-per-day limit. The limit is by query, not by unique query string. In this case, you had to perform nine queries to get all of the results for just one query string.

Comparing Language Samples

Google Maps examples consist of JavaScript and the HTML that makes up the page. But the backend information that you might store or compose will probably be sourced through an alternative language.

The Google Web API uses the Simple Object Access Protocol (SOAP), which means that it is accessible from just about any language. This section concentrates on Perl and Java for backend solutions, because they are two of the more common languages in use.

Perl

With Perl, you first need to download and install the `SOAP::Lite` package and all the other modules on which the `SOAP::Lite` module relies (including the `XML::Parser` and others).

If you are familiar with CPAN, this should be a simple task. Just use the following command (under Unix/Linux): `perl -MCPAN -e 'CPAN::Shell->install("SOAP::Lite")'`.

Without CPAN, you'll need to manually download the main `SOAP::Lite` package and the modules on which it relies. When using the ActivePerl distribution in Windows, use the Perl Package Manager (PPM) or Visual Package Manager (VPM).

Once you install the `SOAP::Lite` module, submitting the query to the Google search service is relatively simple. Listing 4-1 shows a simple search (without any processing or printing of the results).

Listing 4-1: Simple Perl Example

```perl
#!/usr/bin/perl

use SOAP::Lite;

my $key='*****';

my $googleSearch = SOAP::Lite->service("file:GoogleSearch.wsdl");

my $result = $googleSearch->doGoogleSearch($key,
                                           'MCslp',
                                           0,
                                           10,
                                           "false",
                                           "",
                                           "false",
                                           "",
                                           "latin1",
                                           "latin1");

print <<EOF;
<b>Query</b>: $result->{searchQuery}<br/>
<b>Showing results</b> $result->{startIndex} to $result-
>{endIndex} of $result->{estimatedTotalResultsCount}<br
/>
<b>Search time</b>: $result->{searchTime}<br/>
EOF

foreach my $item (@{$result->{resultElements}})
{
    $item->{title} = reformat($item->{title});
    $item->{snippet} = reformat($item->{snippet});

    print <<EOF;
<a href="$item->{URL}">$item->{title}</a><br/>
<p>$item->{snippet}</p>
<hr/>
EOF
}

sub reformat
{
    my ($text) = @_;
    $text =~ s/&lt;/</g;
    $text =~ s/&gt;/>/g;
    return $text;
}
```

The resulting output for the Perl example is actually HTML. Listing 4-2 outlines the main components of the returned structure (which contains the data that we know is returned) by showing a dump of the hash structure returned by the call to the remote procedure. I've shortened it and re-formatted the structure to make easier to read.

Listing 4-2: A Dump of the Google Web API Remote Procedure Call

```
$VAR1 = bless( {
  'searchTime' => '0.087767',
  'endIndex' => '10',
  'searchComments' => '',
  'documentFiltering' => 0,
  'searchTips' => '',
  'estimatedTotalResultsCount' => '997',
  'searchQuery' => 'MCslp',
  'startIndex' => '1',
  'resultElements' => [
  bless( {
    'relatedInformationPresent' => 1,
    'hostName' => '',
    'URL' => 'http://mcslp.com/',
    'snippet' => 'All of them are under the
&lt;b&gt;MCslp&lt;/b&gt; banner and all of them will,
&lt;b&gt;...&lt;/b&gt; As with this&lt;br&gt;  site, and indeed
all &lt;b&gt;MCslp&lt;/b&gt; sites, all of the new blogs are free
to use and &lt;b&gt;...&lt;/b&gt;',
    'directoryCategory' => bless( {
      'fullViewableName' => '',
      'specialEncoding' => ''
      }, 'DirectoryCategory' ),
    'summary' => '',
    'cachedSize' => '44k',
    'title' => '&lt;b&gt;MCslp&lt;/b&gt;',
    'directoryTitle' => ''
    }, 'ResultElement' ),
...
],
  'directoryCategories' => [],
  'estimateIsExact' => 0
}, 'GoogleSearchResult' );
```

The primary keys of the hash contain the information about the search, in other words, the base data, as described in Table 4-2. The resultElements value is an array of individual hashes. Each hash is an individual result, and the structure of each result matches the descriptions given in Table 4-3.

Printing out the information is, therefore, quite straightforward: You just dump out the information in the hash, and then progress through each item in the array and print out the individual result fields to get the information you want.

You can also see here that the title and snippet fields of each result are in encoded HTML. For example, the angle brackets (<>) that normally identify a tag are instead included in HTML-encoded format. The reformat function in Listing 4-1 uses a regular expression to convert these back into angle brackets so that they are correctly displayed as HTML.

Java

With Java, the easiest method is to use the Java class supplied with the Google API (see Listing 4-3).

Listing 4-3: A Java Code Example

```java
import com.google.soap.search.*;
import java.io.*;

public class GMapsAPISearch {
    public static void main(String[] args) {

        String Key = "XXX";

        GoogleSearch s = new GoogleSearch();
        s.setKey(Key);

        try {
            s.setQueryString(args[0]);
            GoogleSearchResult r = s.doSearch();
            System.out.println(" Results:");
            System.out.println(r.toString());
        } catch (GoogleSearchFault f) {
            System.out.println("Search failed:");
            System.out.println(f.toString());
        }
    }
}
```

The class is quite straightforward to use. You must first change the API key to the one provided to you in e-mail. Then, from the command line, specify the string you want to search for, for example:

```
$ java GMapsAPISearch Grantham
```

The results are dumped out, including the structure of the information returned, which includes data such as the URL, title, snippet, and size information.

Combining Offline and Online Information

The Google database allows you to extract information about businesses or locations that may be relevant to the Google Map you are creating.

However, you will likely want to combine information from your Google search with "offline" data. For example, you might want to combine a list of businesses you've already composed with the search information related to those businesses you've gleaned from the Google database.

Although how you merge this information is implementation- and data-specific (see the examples throughout the rest of this book), the best way to merge online and offline information is to relate data directly through an identifiable key such as the name, URL, or address.

For example, if you have a list of companies and their URLs, you can use the URL data you have on file (offline) with the Google search results and use the URL as the key between the online and offline source.

Another alternative is to incorporate the search string for a given business into the offline data, and then use this as the basis for a related search through the Google engine.

Be aware, though, that there is a limit to what you can sensibly merge together without the availability of a specific piece of key data. For example, having an offline list of plumbers for a particular city and combining it with an online search will not work if you have no way to merge the data together.

Wrapping Up

In this chapter you have seen how to extract data from the Google search database that could be used and combined with geographical information to extend the data that you provide within your Google Maps applications.

Although a lot of the information added to a Google Maps application will probably come from other personal sources, such as census data or photos that you have taken, you may also want to integrate some of the data contained in the rest of the Google Web database.

Understandably, usage of the Google Web API has its limitations. You can only obtain 1,000 items each day, and retrieving all 1,000 from a single set of criteria requires a number of web accesses. But if you are willing to work within these limits, you can glean an amazing amount of information to use in your own applications.

Storing and Sharing Information

G oogle Maps–based applications are rarely completely standalone. Sure, you can use them to merely embed information into the pages of your web site, but the power of Google Maps is found in the additional information and interfaces to the system that you can introduce by using dynamic components and data.

Most Google Maps applications are made up of a combination of some basic data embedded into the web page and data that is stored and supplied through an external interface. A good example of this is the basic Google Maps interface, which uses information from the Google database to overlay information on a Google Map.

The primary focus of this chapter is how to convert, store, and provide the information that you will ultimately be providing through your Google Maps applications.

Format Types and Uses

There are many different formats and methods of storing information. Using the right one for the Google Maps application you are building is critical to achieving the flexibility and ease of use that are key to the application's functionality.

For some applications, you want as simple a solution as possible to avoid the complexity of having to read and write files in various formats and keep them updated. For example, if all you are producing is a simple map of your organization, producing a static data file that contains the information you need will probably be more than sufficient.

However, if you want to create and work with more dynamic information (for example, if you want to create a map of properties for a realtor), you will probably already be dealing with data extracted from or directly available within a database. You'll need to convert and translate this information into XML for it to be effectively used within your Google Maps application.

Before the XML is generated, you need to store and retrieve information from your own databases for use with your applications. Choosing the right format for storing the data is, therefore, critical. The three potential solutions are flat-text files; Extensible Markup Language (XML); and database systems such as a Structured Query Language (SQL) Relational Database Management System (RDBMS) like MySQL, PostgreSQL, or SQL Server.

Using Flat-Text Files

A flat-text file is just a text file with some very basic formatting or organizational information. For example, the common format output by database or spreadsheet software is the comma-separated values (CSV) file, in which a carriage return separates individual records and a comma separates individual fields in each record. Another variation is the tab-delimited file (TDF), which uses tabs to separate field data. You can also use other formats and separators according to your needs and requirements.

Reading and extracting information from a flat-text file is easy, especially with the modern scripting languages often used within web development. You can use a scripting language to convert your original source flat-file text into XML, the format you need for Google Maps. You can also use flat-text as a method for extracting or transferring information from other sources (for example, an Excel spreadsheet) into a database for use or processing.

However, although adding information to the end of a text file is also relatively easy, deleting or editing the information in the file is difficult. The only way to delete or edit is to read the file up the point where you want to add or change the data, add the updated or new information, and then continue writing the remainder of the original data.

Of course, you may ask yourself, "If I have to use XML for Google Maps, why not just use XML to store the data in the first place, rather than converting the stored data to XML from another format?"

Using XML

Storing information in XML has its advantages from the perspective that, in its native format, you can use XML data with the Google Maps API to update and display information. Storing the data for your application in XML can, therefore, simplify the entire process.

However, XML is not a format that is easy to write by hand. Although converting most types of information from the source format to XML through a simple program or script is generally quite straightforward, the layout and format of XML information does not lend itself to easy manipulation. Even with efficient tools like XPath, which enables you to reference specific areas of a given XML file by working through the XML tags, updating the information still relies on the same basic methods as updating bare text files: You seek to the location you want to change, you modify the text, and then you write out the new version.

But although XML is not an ideal storage mechanism for the information on the server end, XML is the data format you'll use to exchange information with Google Maps. For this reason, you must examine more closely how to produce and parse XML documents with your application.

Using an RDBMS

The problem with both XML and text files is that you are limited to editing the files one at a time. Using these files in a Google Maps application is a not a problem if you are the only person editing and dealing with the data. If you want to offer interactivity or provide the facility for multiple people to store and edit the information you are using, however, you need to either consider using some sort of locking mechanism (to prevent multiple applications trying to update the same file) or take a look at a proper database solution that handles the locking and storage of the data.

An RDBMS provides the ability for multiple clients to update and access the information in the database at the same time. For this reason using an RDBMS makes it much easier to support a large Google Maps application with multiple users.

Most RDBMS solutions use SQL as the method for querying and updating information. Examples of SQL databases include commercial solutions such as Microsoft's SQL Server, Oracle, and free software solutions like MySQL, PostgreSQL, and Derby. All are capable examples of database software that you can use for storing vast quantities of information in a format that also makes it easy to retrieve the data when you want it.

If you support a SQL interface within your application, you can connect and interact with existing databases that you may have access to. For example, you might want to expose sales or customer information through your Google Maps application, and that will require combining location data with the information from the RDBMS that you already use to store this information.

Parsing and Generating Text Files

When you are developing Google Maps applications, you may be forced to work with existing text files that have been exported by other applications and environments, or you may want to use a flat-text file as an interface for exchanging information between applications.

Storing structured data in a standard text file means applying some simple rules about the format of the information. These are rules that you will need to know in order to be able to read the information back. Once you know the format, generating the file or parsing the content is comparatively easy. The two basic formats are as follows:

- Fixed-width files, in which the record and its content is of a fixed size.
- Delimited files, in which a special character is used to separate individual fields and records.

I don't recommend text files of either type for storing information, but you may often need to exchange data between other applications (like Excel) that use fixed-width files. For that reason, here's a quick look at how to read and write both delimited and fixed-width files.

Reading Delimited Files

Getting information out of a delimited file is generally straightforward, although there are a few oddities that can complicate matters. If the file is tab-delimited or uses some other delimiting character (colons, semicolons, and tildes [~] are common), fields are delimited by tabs and records are delimited by a carriage return and/or a linefeed character. To read the data, you read each line and split the line up by tabs to extract the individual fields.

Listing 5-1 shows an example of this technique in action with a Perl script. Most languages have some form of tokenizer (a function that converts lines according to a separation character or expression) that will split up the string on a given character; here, I use the split function to extract each field from the record.

Listing 5-1: Reading a Delimited File

```
open(DATA,$ARGV[0]) or die "Cannot open file: $!";

while(<DATA>)
{
    chomp;
    my ($id,$ref,$fname,$lname,$country) = split /\t/,$record;
    print "ID: $id\nRef: $ref\nFirst: $fname\nLast: $lname\nCountry:
$country\n";
}

close(DATA);
```

For comma-separated value (CSV) files, the process is slightly more complicated because a value in a CSV file is normally additionally qualified with double quotes to ensure that any data that may include a comma is not misunderstood during parsing. Although you could develop such a solution yourself, it's easier to use an existing module. In this case, I use the Text::CSV_XS module to do the parsing. Listing 5-2 shows an example of an application in action.

Listing 5-2: Reading a Comma-Separated Value File

```
use Text::CSV_XS;

open(DATA,$ARGV[0]) or die "Couldn't open file: $!";

my $csv = Text::CSV_XS->new();

while(<DATA>)
{
```

```
    chomp;
    $csv->parse($_);
    my ($id,$ref,$fname,$lname,$country) = $csv->fields;
    print "ID: $id\nRef: $ref\nFirst: $fname\nLast: $lname\nCountry:
$country\n";
}

close(DATA);
```

Writing Delimited Files

Writing delimited files is also easy. You only have to separate each field of data with the delimiting character and each record with a carriage return. In Perl, doing is this is as easy as combining a print statement with join to merge fields together with your delimiter. You can see a sample of writing to a tab-delimited file (TDF) in Listing 5-3.

Listing 5-3: Writing to a Tab-Delimited File

```
print(join("\t",145,1385674,'Martin','Brown','United Kingdom'),"\n");
```

When you are writing a CSV file, you should also quote each field of data in double quotes. Even though you may not need to quote the data in this way (it is only a requirement for fields that contain a comma), it won't do any harm if you do it anyway. Listing 5-4 shows an example of writing to a CSV file, again in Perl. In this example, I run a list of values through the map function to quote them, and then use join to merge the fields, separated by commas, together into the record.

Listing 5-4: Writing to a Comma-Separated Value File

```
use Text::CSV_XS;

open(DATA,$ARGV[0]) or die "Couldn't open file: $!";

my $csv = Text::CSV_XS->new();

while(<DATA>)
{
    chomp;
    $csv->parse($_);
    my ($id,$ref,$fname,$lname,$country) = $csv->fields;
```

Continued

Listing 5-4 *(continued)*

```
    print "ID: $id\nRef: $ref\nFirst: $fname\nLast: $lname\nCountry:
$country\n";
}

close(DATA);
```

Reading Fixed-Width Files

To extract the information from a fixed-width file, you must read an entire record (say 80 bytes) and then extract individual fields by reading that number of bytes from the file. For example, you could extract three fields of 20 bytes each and two of 10 bytes each. For the system to work, you have to "pad out" the fields with additional bytes to fill up the space (and remove them when you read them back). For example, you might pad out "Martin" with an additional 14 bytes to make up the 20 characters for the field width.

The basic operation is to read the number of bytes from the file according to the size of the record you are reading. In this case, I've calculated the record size by adding the width of each individual field. The unpack() function accepts a string that specifies how to "unpack" a string from its original format into a sequence of fields. For a fixed-width system, you specify the width of each field and the character type (in this case ASCII). Listing 5-5 shows a sample method for reading fixed-width records.

Listing 5-5: Reading Fixed-Width Files in Perl with Unpack

```
open(DATA,$ARGV[0]) or die "Cannot open file: $!";

my $reclength = 10+10+20+20+20;
my $record;

while(read(DATA,$record,$reclength))
{
    my ($id,$ref,$fname,$lname,$country) = unpack('a10a10a20a20a20',$record);
    print "ID: $id\nRef: $ref\nFirst: $fname\nLast: $lname\nCountry:
$country\n";
}

close(DATA);
```

The unpack() function in Perl is a great way of extracting the information, but Listing 5-6 shows how you can achieve the same result by using regular expressions.

Listing 5-6: Reading Fixed-Width Files in Perl with Regular Expressions

```
open(DATA,$ARGV[0]) or die "Cannot open file: $!";

my $reclength = 10+10+20+20+20;
my $record;

while(read(DATA,$record,$reclength))
{
    my ($id,$ref,$fname,$lname,$country)
        = ($record =~ m/(.{10})(.{10})(.{20})(.{20})(.{20})/);
    print "ID: $id\nRef: $ref\nFirst: $fname\nLast: $lname\nCountry:
$country\n";
}

close(DATA);
```

Either way of reading fixed-width files is equally effective, although with very large files you may find that the unpack() method is more efficient.

Note that in both examples the fields contain all the data—I haven't removed the padding zeros or spaces. You can fix that by using the int() function to convert the numbers into an integer; the function will automatically remove initial zeros for you because they do not add anything to the number. For the text fields, you can use a simple regular expression (embedded into a function for ease of use). Listing 5-7 shows the full script for this example.

Listing 5-7: Removing Padding Data

```
open(DATA,$ARGV[0]) or die "Cannot open file: $!";

my $reclength = 10+10+20+20+20;

my $record;

while(read(DATA,$record,$reclength))
{
    my ($id,$ref,$fname,$lname,$country) = unpack('a10a10a20a20a20',$record);

    $id = int($id);
    $ref = int($ref);
    $fname = despace($fname);
    $lname = despace($lname);
    $country = despace($country);

    print "ID: $id\nRef: $ref\nFirst: $fname\nLast: $lname\nCountry:
$country\n";
```

Continued

Listing 5-7 *(continued)*

```
}

close(DATA);

sub despace
{
    my ($text) = @_;
    $text =~ s/ *$//g;
    return $text;
}
```

Writing Fixed-Width Files

Writing a fixed-width file, like writing a delimited file, is very straightforward. Once you know the format of the file, your only real problem is choosing a padding character to use. An obvious solution in most situations is to use a zero for numerical values and a space for text values.

If your chosen language supports the `printf()` or `sprintf()` functions (both part of the standard C library), you can use the formatter to align the data for you. For example, you can output a record with two 10-character fixed-width numbers and three 20-character-wide fixed-width text fields with the line in Listing 5-8.

Listing 5-8: Writing a Fixed-Width Record

```
printf('%010d%010d%-20s%-20s%-20s',145,1385674,'Martin','Brown','United
Kingdom');
```

The code in Listing 5-8 will work in Perl and C (with the necessary headers and wrappers added).

Updating Text Files

As mentioned earlier in the chapter, updating a text file is a matter of either copying information up to the point where you want to update, or of inserting information before that point, writing the new information, and then copying the rest of the file. Once you get to this stage, however, it really is more effective to use an alternative method to store the information.

Generating and Parsing XML

Programmers familiar with HTML will understand the basic concept behind XML. Both are technically identical to the structure of Standard Generalized Markup Language (SGML). All three rely on the same basic structure.

When supplying information for use with Google Maps, you need to generate comparatively simple XML documents, with perhaps only a couple of nested levels of information. Generally, the key is to generate information that can easily be parsed by JavaScript to display information and provide a list of map points or additional data.

Before seeing the processes for creating and parsing XML, it is worth looking at the main points and key terms of the XML format. XML is a superset of the Standard General Markup Language (SGML), which is also the source for the HTML standard used for web pages. XML enables you to structure data in a neutral format that can be generated and understood by many different platforms and environments.

The basic component of XML is the tag. This is a single word enclosed in angle brackets. For example, you could create a tag for restaurant information using this:

```
<restaurant>
```

Tags are actually defined in pairs: the opening tag and the closing tag, which has the same text, but a leading forward slash:

```
</restaurant>
```

Within a tag is the tag data. This could be actual information, for example:

```
<restaurant>One on Wharf</restaurant>
```

Or it can be further tags:

```
<restaurant>
    <name>One on Whard</name>
    <city>Grantham</city>
</restaurant>
```

Finally, tags can also contain attributes (additional pieces of information that help to define further information about a tag or its contents). For example, you could rewrite the preceding code as

```
<restaurant name="One on Wharf" city="Grantham">A nice restaurant.</restaurant>
```

Because XML files are basic text, generating the files is quite straightforward, although care must be taken to ensure that the structure of the XML is correct. Parsing an XML document is more difficult, because you have to take into account the different parts of the structures. Fortunately there are techniques and extensions for both operations that make it easy to generate and parse the contents of an XML file.

Generating XML

You can generate XML very easily just by embedding data into suitable tags when you write out the information. Listing 5-9 shows an adaptation of the fixed record length parsing code that outputs the information from a fixed-width record file into XML.

Listing 5-9: Generating XML from Fixed Data

```
open(DATA,$ARGV[0]) or die "Cannot open file: $!";

my $reclength = 10+10+20+20+20;

my $record;

print '<staff>';

while(read(DATA,$record,$reclength))
{
    my ($id,$ref,$fname,$lname,$country) = unpack('a10a10a20a20a20',$record);

    $id = int($id);
    $ref = int($ref);

    $fname = despace($fname);
    $lname = despace($lname);
    $country = despace($country);

    print <<EOF;
<staffmember>
<td>$id</id>
<ref>$ref</ref>
<firstname>$fname</firstname>
<lastname>$lname</lastname>
<country>$country</country>
</staffmember>
EOF

}

close(DATA);

print '</staff>';

sub despace
{
    my ($text) = @_;

    $text =~ s/ *$//g;

    return $text;
}
```

You can see the resulting XML generated from this file in Listing 5-10.

Listing 5-10: An XML File Generated from Fixed-Width File Data

```
<staff><staffmember>
<td>145</id>
<ref>1385674</ref>
<firstname>Martin</firstname>
<lastname>Brown</lastname>
<country>United Kingdom</country>
</staffmember>
<staffmember>
<td>383</id>
<ref>4897947</ref>
<firstname>Mickey</firstname>
<lastname>Mouse</lastname>
<country>United States</country>
</staffmember>
<staffmember>
<td>384</id>
<ref>2349875</ref>
<firstname>Donald</firstname>
<lastname>Duck</lastname>
<country>United States</country>
</staffmember>
</staff>
```

In Listing 5-10, all of the data is stored within a `<staff>` tag, individual records are contained within a `<staffmember>` tag, and individual fields are contained by appropriate individual tags.

For a more flexible programmable interface for building XML files in Perl, you can use the `XML::Generator` module. The module provides a very flexible method for creating XML and even nested XML. You can see a sample of this in Listing 5-11.

Listing 5-11: Generating XML with XML::Generator

```
use XML::Generator;

my $gen = XML::Generator->new('escape' => 'always',
                              'pretty' => 2);

my $restaurants = {'One on Wharf' => {longitude => -0.64,
                                      latitude => 52.909444},
```

Continued

Listing 5-11 *(continued)*

```
                            'China Inn' =>   {longitude => -0.6391666,
                                             latitude => 52.911111},
                };

foreach my $name (sort keys %{$restaurants})
{
    my $xml
        = $gen->restaurant($gen->name($name),
                           $gen->points(
                                        {"longitude" => $restaurants
                                            ->{$name}
                                        ->{longitude},

                                        latitude => $restaurants
                                            ->{$name}
                                        ->{latitude}
                                    }));
    print $xml,"\n";
}
```

As you can see, to the XML::Generator object, function names become the tag name and the argument becomes tag data (or subtags). Attributes for a given tag can be inserted by supplying a hash reference; keys are used as the attribute name and the values are the attribute values. Listing 5-12 shows the generated output.

Listing 5-12: XML Generated through the XML::Generator Module

```
<restaurant>
  <name>China Inn</name>
  <points longitude="-0.6391666" latitude="52.911111" />
</restaurant>
<restaurant>
  <name>One on Wharf</name>
  <points longitude="-0.64" latitude="52.909444" />
</restaurant>
```

You won't always, however, be generating the information directly from other sources like the fixed-width record file or a database, as demonstrated here. Sometimes the information will be in XML format already (for example, as an export from another application), and that data will need to be parsed, extracted, and reformatted, either for importing into a database or an alternative XML format.

Parsing XML with Perl

You can deal with XML data within Perl in many ways. There are primarily two solutions within Perl that are useful when thinking about Google Maps applications: the XML::Simple module and the Document Object Model (DOM). The two systems have similar principles; understanding the DOM method within Perl will help you to understand the DOM method used within JavaScript.

The XML::Simple module parses an XML document and converts it into a Perl structure using hashes or arrays as appropriate. You can then access the XML data by using the name of each tag. For example, Listing 5-13 shows a simple XML::Simple parser script that dumps out the structure of the XML document it has just parsed.

Listing 5-13: Using XML::Simple for Parsing XML Documents

```
use XML::Simple;
use Data::Dumper;

my $xml = XMLin($ARGV[0]);
print Dumper($xml);
```

The result when parsing the restaurants XML document is shown in Listing 5-14.

Listing 5-14: The Perl Structure of an XML Document

```
$VAR1 = {
    'restaurant' => {
            'One on Wharf' => {
                    'points' => {
                        'longitude' => '-0.64',
                        'latitude' => '52.909444'
                          }
                 },
            'China Inn' => {
                    'points' => {
                            'longitude' => '-0.6391666',
                            'latitude' => '52.911111'
                         }
                 }
         },
    'restaurants' => {}
    };
```

Using this structure you can extract a list of restaurants by obtaining a list of the top-level tags with the key `'restaurant'`. For example, the following line would print this list:

```
print keys %{$xml->{'restaurant'};
```

The DOM method follows similar principles — you access the tags by name. The difference is that when you access a particular tag, the return value is another XML object. The DOM model therefore lets you walk through the document accessing different tags and different levels of information through the document.

A number of different functions within the DOM method enable you to obtain a list of XML tags with a particular name (for example, all of the `<restaurant>` tags) and also to extract the information contained within the tags or their attributes.

For example, when parsing the document from Listing 5-12, the longitude and latitude of each restaurant can be extracted using this method:

1. Get a list of restaurants (effectively, each restaurant is a subset of the tags in each `<restaurant>` tag).

2. Get the `<points>` tag from each restaurant.

3. Extract the longitude and latitude attributes from this `<points>` tag.

Alternatively, the same information could be extracted from the XML document using this method:

1. Get a list of the `<points>` tags.

2. Extract the longitude and latitude attributes from each `<points>` tag.

Both solutions work, but the latter is possible only because there is only one `<points>` tag within each restaurant definition.

Tip All Perl modules can be downloaded from CPAN (`http://cpan.org`) or through the CPAN module. For Windows users using the ActiveState Perl distribution, use the Perl Package Manager (PPM) or Visual Package Manager (VPM) if you have a commercial license.

The `XML::DOM` module for Perl provides an interface to the DOM methods for extracting information from XML documents in this way. Listing 5-15 shows a sample script that extracts the information using the second method described earlier.

Listing 5-15: Extracting Information from an XML Document Using DOM in Perl

```
use XML::DOM;

my $parser = new XML::DOM::Parser;
```

```
# First, parse the supplied file into an XML object
my $doc = $parser->parsefile ($ARGV[0]) or die "Couldn't parse $ARGV[0]";

# Extract a list of XML fragments enclosed by the <points> tag
my $nodes = $doc->getElementsByTagName ("points");
# Get the number of objects returned
my $n = $nodes->getLength;

# Now process through the list of <points> tags and extract the data
for (my $i = 0; $i < $n; $i++)
{
# Get a single <points> tag structure from the XML document
    my $node = $nodes->item ($i);
# Extract the value from <longitude>XXX</longitude>
    my $long = $node->getAttributeNode("longitude")->getValue();
# Extract the value from <latitude>XXX</latitude>
    my $lat = $node->getAttributeNode("latitude")->getValue();
    print "Longitude: $long, Latitude: $lat\n";
}
# Free up the structure
$doc->dispose;
```

These are the key elements in the script:

1. The XML document is loaded and parsed into a DOM object.

2. A list of points elements is extracted from the main document using the getElementsByTagName() function.

3. A loop is used to iterate through the list of points elements.

4. Each points element is extracted.

5. The values of the longitude and latitude attributes are obtained using the getAttributeNode() function on the points element object.

Parsing XML with JavaScript

Once you go beyond the statically created Google Maps examples and start working with more complicated sets of data, you must use XML as a method for exchanging information between your web server application and the Google Maps client-side application. All of this is achieved through JavaScript.

JavaScript, in its base form, is a fairly limited language designed with some strict rules and goals in mind. Although it doesn't contain a specific interface for working with XML documents, JavaScript can use the Document Object Model (DOM) to work with XML (and HTML) documents. Technically, the DOM is not part of JavaScript, but JavaScript does contain an interface to the DOM system. You may be familiar with the DOM interface, because the DOM enables you to access elements of an HTML document by name (for example, you can obtain the value of a form field by using the DOM to access the value by name).

Listing 5-16 shows an HTML fragment from which you can extract the information in each field by using the code in Listing 5-17.

Listing 5-16: A Simple HTML Form

```
<form name="personal" action="index.cgi">
<input type=text size=20 name=name>
<input type=text size=20 name=longitude>
<input type=text size=20 name=latitude>
</form>
```

Listing 5-17: Accessing the Form Data by Name Using DOM/JavaScript

```
document.personal.name
document.personal.longitude
document.personal.latitude
```

The term `document` refers to the entire HTML document (when used within JavaScript, it typically means the current HTML document). The term `personal` relates to the form (which was given the name `personal`), and `name`, `longitude`, and `latitude` refer to the field names within that form.

When working with XML, the basic rules for parsing the content through DOM are identical to the structures you saw earlier when processing documents in this format through Perl.

The key way in which you use XML and the DOM system within Google Maps is to expose data in XML format and use this data within your Google Maps application to create map points, vectors, and other information.

Google Maps provides an XML HTTP interface (`GXmlHttp`) that can load XML documents from a server. The resulting information is then accessible using the DOM interface, enabling you to extract the relevant data from the XML and use it within the JavaScript application and, ultimately, Google Maps.

Listing 5-18 shows the JavaScript model (and associated Google Maps commands) to add map points to a map when provided with the XML file generated in Listing 5-12.

Listing 5-18: Processing XML in JavaScript

```
var request = GXmlHttp.create();
request.open("GET", "/examples/xmlbasic2.xml", true);
request.onreadystatechange = function()
{
   if (request.readyState == 4)
   {
     var xmlDoc = request.responseXML;
     var points = xmlDoc.getElementsByTagName("points");
     for (var i = 0; i < points.length; i++)
     {
       var xmlpoint = new
GPoint(parseFloat(points[i].getAttribute("longitude")),

parseFloat(points[i].getAttribute("latitude")));
       var xmlmarker = new GMarker(xmlpoint);
       map.addOverlay(xmlmarker);
     }
   }
}
request.send(null);
```

This is just a fragment of the full HTML document that generates the map, but it demonstrates the DOM access methods built into JavaScript for processing XML documents.

The script works as follows:

1. A new GXmlHttp object is created.

2. The XML file is downloaded.

3. Once the file has been loaded (when the GXmlHttp object reaches readyState 4), the rest of the processing can begin.

4. The list of points elements from the document is extracted. The xmlDoc is the name of the object that contains the XML data. The getElements ByTagName() method to this object returns a list of XML objects that contain the data in each <points>...</points> tag.

5. A new GPoint object is created based on the attribute value of the longitude and latitude attributes for each points element. Attributes are extracted from a given tag (in this case one of the <points> tag objects) using the getAttribute() method.

6. The GPoint is used to create a new marker.

7. The marker is added to the Google Map.

Aside from the additional steps required to add the points to the map and the more complex process of loading the XML through an HTTP request to the web server, the basic structure of accessing the information contained in the XML file through DOM is the same within JavaScript as in the earlier Perl example.

Note This type of processing—loading XML, parsing the contents, and then displaying the information—is an example of AJAX (Asynchronous JavaScript and XML) in action. The entire process from loading to display is handled entirely within JavaScript and, therefore, happens without having to specifically reload the page. AJAX provides a dynamic interface within the scope of what is normally a static web page. See Chapter 9 for more information and examples on using AJAX with Google Maps.

More of this kind of XML processing is used throughout the rest of this book.

Working with SQL

Storing and retrieving information from SQL databases relies on creating a connection between your script or application and the SQL database. The exact method you use depends on the language and environment you are using with your web environment to extract information from the database.

The most likely scenario for using a SQL database is when storing information that you want to have displayed on the map. The information needs to be extracted from the SQL database and converted into an XML document that can be used by the Google Maps application. By using a SQL database, you can pick out the specific elements from the database that you want very easily. For example, you might want to extract all the restaurants, or maybe even all the restaurants within a particular town. To support this, you create a script that dynamically generates the XML from the SQL data and that is called directly through the GXmlHttp function supported by the Google Maps API.

Using SQL in this way adds these additional overheads to your application:

- You will need to create a suitable structure for the database.
- You will need to create a method for updating the information in the database (through the web or a desktop application).
- You will need to build the script that extracts the information and produces the XML.

Note If you are using MySQL (one of the more popular open source database solutions), the documentation available on the web site (http://dev.mysql.com/doc) provides one of the best all-around guides to both the SQL language and the MySQL extensions.

The structure, format, and scripts used to support these operations are application specific, but the basics are included here to enable you to get started.

Open Source Databases

Numerous open source databases are available that you can use while developing and deploying your Google Maps application. Many web host services provide access to a MySQL database, so it is probably a better solution while developing your application because it will present the least problems when you deploy.

Creating a Database Structure

Using a professional RDBMS for storage means that structured data can easily be created and stored. Through queries (using SQL), precise sets of data can be returned and then formatted into the XML required by a Google Maps application.

Obviously, the precise format of the database created will be entirely dependent on the information being stored, but you should be aware of the following tips and hints as you develop your application:

- Longitude and latitude are best represented as floating-point values. Both should be stored as floating-point values (the FLOAT or REAL type in most databases). It is best to store these two values in individual float fields in your database. Even though the RDBMS may support limited-precision floating-point values, you should not limit the precision of the values you want to store; the higher the precision, the more exact you can be about point placement.

- Store other data in appropriate individual fields. Don't embed the data and the XML tags in the field data; just store the data and have the application create the surrounding tags. This also allows the application to change the tags and formatting if necessary to suit the needs of the Google Maps application.

- Use a unique ID against individual records. This makes it easier to join information together and also to identify the correct row to update or delete.

- Structure data according to the information being stored. For example, a list of restaurants may be provided in one table with a list of the meals they provide in a separate table, linked to the original. Don't create multiple fields to store duplicate information (that is, meal_type_a, meal_type_b, and so on). Use the relational functionality of the database to relate the data and create an appropriate XML structure from the compound data.

Although most RDBMSs use SQL — a standard for creating database tables — differences in the underlying RDBMS can affect the exact statement used to create the table. Listing 5-19 shows the SQL statement to create a table for storing the restaurant data used in earlier examples in this chapter.

Listing 5-19: Creating a SQL Table

```
create table restaurants (id int auto_increment not null primary key,
                          lng float,
                          lat float,
                          name varchar(80));
```

The example in Listing 5-19 shows the creation of a table with an ID field with an `auto_increment` option. Each time a record is inserted into the database, the ID field will automatically be populated with the next ID in the sequence, providing a unique reference for that row in the database.

To create this table, add data to it, or retrieve previously stored data requires using a database interface.

Interfacing to the Database

Whether you are creating an interface for building the database or writing the script that extracts the information from the database in XML format for Google Maps to process, you will need to interface to the underlying RDBMS.

Depending on the language you are using, a number of different interfaces are available; generally, it is best to use the one with which you are most familiar or, if this is your first time, the one most widely supported, because this increases the available resources and support.

SQL Quick Guide

SQL statements for manipulating data can be divided into three types, SELECT, INSERT, and UPDATE:

- SELECT retrieves data from the database (selecting it). You must specify the fields you want to retrieve, the tables you want to retrieve the information from, an optional criteria statement (that is, specify the precise rows from the table you want), and the rules for matching data between tables (joins).

- INSERT adds rows to the table. You must specify the table and either a list of values to be inserted (according to the order of the fields in the database) *or* a list of the fields and their values.

- UPDATE modifies one or more rows in a table. You must specify the table, the updated fields and their values, and the criteria to use when selecting which existing rows should be updated.

With one or two exceptions, 99 percent of the interaction with an RDBMS will be through one of these three statements.

Connecting to a Database Using DBI and Perl

The DBI module in Perl provides access to database engines through a number of individual Database Drivers (DBDs). Although you need different DBDs for connecting to different databases, the basic interface to submitting queries and obtaining results remains the same. The approach means that you can develop your Google Maps application locally using MySQL but deploy it using PostgreSQL or Oracle without making any changes to the queries and interfaces in the application.

Tip Use CPAN, PPM, or VPM to install DBI and the DBD you need to use for your database environment. If you are using MySQL, you will need to install DBI and the DBD::mysql module.

To connect to a database through DBI, a data source name (DSN) must be assembled based on the information required by the DBD driver. For example, to connect to a MySQL database, you must specify the name of the database and the host on which the database can be found. To connect to the google_maps database on the host mysql.mcslp.pri, the DSN would be DBI:mysql:database=google_maps;host=mysql.mcslp.pri.

The DSN is supplied as an argument to the connect method, along with the username and password if required, to create a new database handle. All queries to the database then use this database handle as a way of communicating between your application and the MySQL database.

The entire process can be seen more clearly in the stub shown in Listing 5-20.

Listing 5-20: Connecting to a MySQL Database with Perl

```perl
#!/usr/bin/perl

use DBI;

my $dbh = DBI-
>connect("DBI:mysql:database=google_maps;host=mysql.mcslp.pri",'maps','maps');

if ($dbh)
{
    print "Connected to database\n";
}
else
{
    print "Couldn't connect\n";
}

#Do your stuff

$dbh->disconnect();
```

The object created in the example, $dbh, now becomes the method for communicating with the MySQL database. For example, to execute an arbitrary statement, you'd use the do() method. Some examples of this are demonstrated later in this chapter.

Connecting to a Database with PHP

PHP provides built-in support for communicating with a number of different databases, depending on how the application is compiled. MySQL support is usually included by default. Older versions of PHP used a suite of built-in methods for communicating with a MySQL database that were MySQL-specific. The interface has been improved since version 5.1, when an object-based solution similar to the DBI solution in Perl was introduced.

For the older version, connecting to a database is a question of calling the mysql_connect() function with the name of the host, username, and password. Once connected, you must select the database to use before submitting any queries.

Note The old PHP method more or less mirrors the structure of connecting to a MySQL database by hand through the command-line mysql tool and may make more sense to users familiar with that tool.

An example of the typical connection sequence is shown in Listing 5-21.

Listing 5-21: Connecting to a Database through PHP (Traditional)

```php
<?php

mysql_connect(localhost,'maps','maps');
@mysql_select_db('google_maps');

//Do your stuff

mysql_close();

?>
```

To execute a query through this interface, use the mysql_query() function.

PHP 5.1 supports an alternative method for communicating with a MySQL database or, indeed, any database using the PHP Data Object (PDO) interface. The approach is similar in style to the DBI approach used by Perl and is, therefore, more portable. However, it may take some time for your hosting service to update to PHP 5.1. Check what version is supported before choosing an interface type.

With PDO, you create a new object that provides connectivity to the RDBMS you are using, rather than the implied database connectivity supported through the older interface. You must, therefore, specifically create a new database connection object, as shown in Listing 5-22.

Listing 5-22: Connecting to a Database through PHP Data Objects (PDO)

```php
<?php

try {
    $dbh = new PDO('mysql:host=localhost;dbname=google_maps','maps','maps');
} catch (PDOException $e) {
    print "Error!: " . $e->getMessage() . "<br/>";
    die();
}

//Do your stuff

$dbh = null;

?>
```

Executing a query through the PDO method uses the exec() method to the database handle that was created (that is, $dbh->exec()).

Populating the Database

Populating an RDBMS with SQL relies on composing a suitable INSERT statement and then using the database interface to execute that statement in the database. To insert data into a table according to order of fields as they are created, you use a statement like the one shown in Listing 5-23.

Listing 5-23: Inserting the Data

```
insert into restaurants(0,-0.6391666,52.911111,"China Inn");
```

The zero for the ID is used to indicate that a new unique ID, automatically generated by the database (according to the table definition), should be used for this value.

To execute the SQL statement with a Perl/DBI interface, use the code in Listing 5-24; for traditional PHP, use Listing 5-25; and for PHP/PDO, use Listing 5-26.

Listing 5-24: Inserting Data with Perl

```perl
#!/usr/bin/perl

use DBI;

my $dbh = DBI-
>connect("DBI:mysql:database=google_maps;host=mysql.mcslp.pri",'maps','maps');

if ($dbh)
{
    print "Connected to database\n";
}
else
{
    print "Couldn't connect\n";
}

$dbh->do("insert into restaurants values(0,-0.6391666,52.911111,'China Inn');");

$dbh->disconnect();
```

Note   Text being inserted into a database must be quoted using single or double quotation marks. Which you use depends on what kind of quotation marks you have used to build the rest of the query. The DBD interface also provides the `quote()` method to the database handle, which will appropriately quote a given string of text, even if it already contains quotation marks.

Listing 5-25: Inserting Data with PHP (Traditional)

```php
<?php

mysql_connect(localhost,'maps','maps');

@mysql_select_db('google_maps');

mysql_query("insert into restaurants values(0,-0.6391666,52.911111,'China
Inn')");

mysql_close();

?>
```

Listing 5-26: Inserting Data with PHP (PDO)

```php
<?php

try {
    $dbh = new PDO('mysql:host=localhost;dbname=google_maps','maps','maps');
} catch (PDOException $e) {
    print "Error!: " . $e->getMessage() . "<br/>";
    die();
}

$dbh->exec("insert into restaurants values(0,-0.6391666,52.911111,'China
Inn')");

$dbh = null;

?>
```

Although more detailed examples of inserting and updating the database are beyond the scope of this book, examples are provided as part of the applications presented in the remainder of the book.

Extracting Data from the Database

When extracting data from the database, the typical procedure is to execute the SELECT statement and then iterate over the returned rows to extract the information required. The best way to achieve this is through the use of a prepared statement. This provides the most flexible method for extracting information from the database on a row-by-row basis.

An example of this through the Perl/DBD interface is shown in Listing 5-27.

Listing 5-27: Extracting Data on a Row-by-Row Basis

```perl
#!/usr/bin/perl

use DBI;
use Data::Dumper;

my $dbh = DBI-
>connect("DBI:mysql:database=google_maps;host=mysql.mcslp.pri",'maps','maps');

if ($dbh)
{
```

Continued

Listing 5-27 *(continued)*

```
    print "Connected to database\n";
}
else
{
    print "Couldn't connect\n";
}

my $sth = $dbh->prepare("select * from restaurants");

$sth->execute();

while(my $row = $sth->fetchrow_hashref())
{
    print Dumper($row),"\n";
}

$dbh->disconnect();
```

In Listing 5-27, a hash reference containing the row data is returned for each row in the table. The hash in each case contains the field names (in the keys) and the corresponding value (in the value). The Data::Dumper module is used to output a dump of the hash; the output generated after inserting a single row is shown in Listing 5-28.

Listing 5-28: Dumped Data from the Database with Perl

```
Connected to database
$VAR1 = {
          'lat' => '52.9111',
          'name' => 'China Inn',
          'id' => '1',
          'lng' => '-0.639167'
        };
```

Because the Google Maps API requires the information to be in XML format, Listing 5-29 shows an example of the same script returning an XML representation of each restaurant. Listing 5-30 contains the generated XML for reference.

Listing 5-29: Generating XML from Your SQL Database

```perl
#!/usr/bin/perl

use DBI;
use XML::Generator;

my $dbh = DBI-
>connect("DBI:mysql:database=google_maps;host=mysql.mcslp.pri",'maps','maps');

if ($dbh)
{
    print "Connected to database\n";
}
else
{
    print "Couldn't connect\n";
}

my $sth = $dbh->prepare("select * from restaurants");

$sth->execute();

my $gen = XML::Generator->new('escape' => 'always',
                              'pretty' => 2);

while(my $row = $sth->fetchrow_hashref())
{
    my $xml
        = $gen->restaurant($gen->name($row->{name}),
                           $gen->points({"longitude" => $row->{lng},
                                         latitude => $row->{lat}
                                        }));
    print $xml,"\n";
}

$dbh->disconnect();
```

Listing 5-30: XML Generated from Your SQL Database

```xml
<restaurant>
  <name>China Inn</name>
  <points longitude="-0.639167" latitude="52.9111" />
</restaurant>
```

Similar results can be achieved with PHP. In a real-world situation, the script would work as a CGI script and generate the information on the fly for the GXmlHttp object in the Google Maps API.

As with other basic examples earlier in this chapter, I will produce and develop more detailed applications and samples, starting with Chapter 9.

Wrapping Up

Without additional information, a Google Map is just that: a map of a location. The additional data supplied with the map is what turns the map into a useful application that provides specific, customized information on locations, photographs, statistical data, routes, and other interesting data points.

How you store and use that information is up to you and your application. As shown in this chapter, standard text files have their limitations, whereas an RDBMS supporting SQL provides the most flexibility. Both, however, need to be converted into XML to be compatible with the Google Maps API. And you can both generate and parse XML documents with ease by using the right tools. In the next chapter, you'll see some examples of how to determine location information for addresses and business that can then be used with a Google Map to create a Google Maps application.

Instant Gratification

Working with Existing Address Information

Often the information you want to use in your examples is based on your own knowledge and discovery of suitable latitude/longitude points for the information that you want to display. There are times, however, when you already have address information and want to take that address and convert it into the latitude and longitude data required by Google Maps for creating points and polylines. For this, the method you require is called *geocoding*. This chapter examines the role of geocoding, how to use geocoder services, and how to update your existing databases with location information so that you can use the data in your Google Maps applications.

Looking Up Geocode Information

Geocoding is the process of matching up an address, Zip/postal code, or city with the coordinates required to locate that place on a map. The geocoding system required depends on the information you require and the location of the original address. Within Google Maps you are looking for latitude and longitude information, and this is the most prolific of the services available.

Data about U.S. addresses is the easiest to look up, because more services provide the U.S.-based information than information for other countries. The situation is changing rapidly, and the services available for looking up information in a range of different countries and through a variety of methods are constantly expanding.

The basic methods of looking up information remain fairly constant. You must connect to a specific service, supply the information about the address that you have, and hope to get a response back. Different geocoding services expose their services in different ways. Some use web services, some use simple URL-based interfaces, and some are even available "offline" as part of a separate downloadable package.

Geocoding Priorities

Some readers will be surprised to see a detailed analysis of geocoding quite so late in this book. The simple reason for this is that the importance of geocoding depends entirely on the map you are generating.

As you will see in forthcoming chapters, the latitude and longitude information is critical to the way you use Google Maps. However, it is also clear that if you already have the latitude and longitude information or are using the Google Maps to locate and identify specific locations (as used in the community and photographic examples in earlier chapters), the requirement to look up information by address is actually a much lower priority.

Two of the more practical times to use geocoding are when converting your existing database to include the latitude and longitude data or when looking up the information dynamically while generating XML data for a given application.

If geocoding is not available for your country or needs, other solutions exist that can determine the information you need, such as the Google scraping method covered later in this chapter.

Looking Up U.S. Information

The easiest way to resolve U.S. geocoding is to use the service provided by the `geocoder.us` web site. The web site provides a number of different interfaces, including SOAP, XML-RPC, and a basic URL interface. The information returned can be in either object, XML, or CSV format, making it suitable for use within a wide range of applications and environments.

For example, to use the XML-RPC version of the service, use a script like the one shown in Listing 6-1.

Listing 6-1: Using XML-RPC with geocoder.us to Look Up Address Information

```
use XMLRPC::Lite;
use Data::Dumper;

my $address = XMLRPC::Lite->proxy('http://geocoder.us/service/xmlrpc')
    ->geocode(join(' ',@ARGV))
    ->result;

print Dumper($address),"\n";
```

The preceding script contacts the `geocoder.us` server and then dumps out the information returned. For example, with this script you can supply the address information on the command line:

```
$ geocoderus.pl Madison at 45th, New York, NY
$VAR1 = [
          {
            'type1' => 'Ave',
            'type2' => 'St',
            'lat' => '40.754951',
            'street1' => 'Madison',
            'suffix1' => '',
            'prefix2' => 'E',
            'suffix2' => '',
            'state' => 'NY',
            'zip' => '10017',
            'city' => 'New York',
            'prefix1' => '',
            'long' => '-73.978088',
            'street2' => '45th'
          }
        ];
```

You can see from the output that the latitude and longitude are in the `'lat'` and `'long'` keys of the returned hash. You can also see that the rest of the address information is returned as well, including the Zip code and the full street names of the intersection of 45th Street and Madison Avenue in New York (the location of the Roosevelt Hotel). If the returned information has not been populated with the latitude and longitude and Zip code information, the supplied string probably could not be understood.

The same basic principles can be used to geocode any U.S. address information. You could use a modified format of the preceding code to update your address database or the database used to hold specific information about map data.

Warning

The service provided by `geocoder.us` is free, but if you expect to use the site in a commercial environment with large numbers of requests, you should consider signing up for an account that enables you to bulk-purchase lookups. The money you pay goes toward supporting the service.

The `geocoder.us` service is probably the most practical solution for large-volume lookups. Although you can use it live, I've generally found the geocoding and interface to be more useful when you are encoding a lot of addresses, such as when updating an existing database.

Looking Up Global Information

If you are trying to look up information outside the larger and more popular territories of the United States and the U.K., you have a number of different options.

Within some limitations Google can be tricked to do the geocoding for you right across the world using the database that Google Local uses to look up and generate information. The way you do this is to send a request to the Google service that would normally look up the information for you within a web page. You then "scrape" the web page for the information you were looking for.

For example, if you visit Google Local and enter New York, you get the web page shown in Figure 6-1.

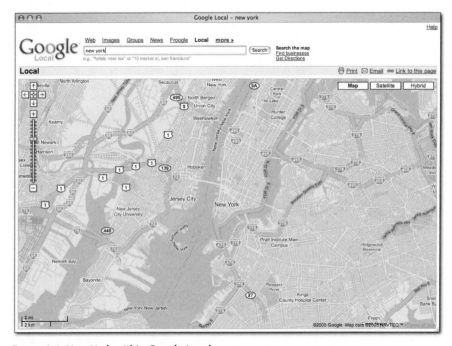

FIGURE 6-1: New York within Google Local.

If you examine the raw HTML from the page that was generated, the geocode information can be extracted from the JavaScript component of the page. Scraping for the data works because the page itself contains a map, and that includes the JavaScript that centers the map on the address entered. The relevant fragment from the page can be seen in Listing 6-2. The element you are looking for is the GLatLng() function call.

Listing 6-2: Scraping Information from Google

```
<html><head><title>Google Local - New York</title><script>
...
</style><script src="/maps?file=api&v=2&async=1&hl=en" ⟳
```

```
type="text/javascript"></script><script type="text/javascript"><!--
if (GBrowserIsCompatible()) {document.write('<div id="map"
style="width:600px;height:400px"></div>');
document.write('<style type="text/css">.staticmap{display:none}</style>');
window.loadMap = function() {
var zoom = 14;
var points= [];
var container = document.getElementById("map");
container.style.display = '';
var map = new GMap(container);
map.addControl(new GSmallMapControl());
map.addControl(new GMapTypeControl(true));
map.setCenter(new GLatLng(40.714167, -74.006389), zoom);
for (var i = 0; i < points.length; i++) {var
 icon = new GIcon(G_DEFAULT_ICON);
 var image = '/mapfiles/marker' + points[i][2] + '.png';icon.image =
image;map.addOverlay(new GMarker(new GLatLng(points[i][0],
points[i][1]),icon));}}}
//--></script><table cellpadding=0 cellspacing=0 border=0
class="staticmap"><tr><td><script type="text/javascript"><!--
if (!window.loadMap) {document.write('<img src="http://maps.google.com/
mapdata?latitude_e6=40714167&longitude_e6=4220960907&zm=9600&w=600&h=
400&cc=us&min_priority=2" style="border: 1px solid black;
position:relative" border=1 width="600" height="400">');}
//--></script><noscript><img src="http://maps.google.com/
mapdata?latitude_e6=40714167&longitude_e6=4220960907&zm=9600&w=600&h=
400&cc=us&min_priority=2" style="border: 1px solid black;
position:relative" border=1 width="600" height="400"></noscript>
...
```

To extract the information you can use Perl (or any other language) to send the query and then use a suitable regular expression on the returned data to extract the latitude and longitude information required. The key you are looking for in this case is the GLatLng fragment in the response:

```
map.setCenter(new GLatLng(40.714167, -74.006389), zoom);
```

Extracting that information with a regular expression is comparatively straightforward.

A simple script (using Perl) to perform the necessary steps is shown in Listing 6-3.

Listing 6-3: Using Google to Geocode Information

```
#!/usr/bin/perl

use strict;
use LWP::UserAgent;
```

Continued

Listing 6-3 *(continued)*

```perl
use URI::Escape;


my $ua = LWP::UserAgent->new(
                    agent => "Mozilla/5.0 ⤵
  (X11; U; Linux i686; en-US; rv:1.0.2) Gecko/20021120 Netscape/7.01",
                    );

# Send the query
my $response = $ua->get⤵
  ('http://maps.google.com/maps?q=' . uri_escape($ARGV[0]));

# Extract the content
my $var = $response->{_content};

# Extract the latitude and longitude
my ($lat,$lng) = ( $var =~ m/GLatLng\(([-\d.]+).*?([-\d.]+)\)/ms );
print "Lat: $lat - Lng: $lng\n";

if (!defined($lat)) # Show alternates if we can't find lat/lng
{
    # First remove any irrelevant data from the raw text
    $var =~ s/.*Did you mean:(.*)/$1/gmi;

    # Extract the query values
    my (@alternatives) = ($var =~ m/q=(.*?)[&"]/gm);
    print "Alternatives:\n";

    # Dedupe results
    my $alternates = {};
    foreach my $alt (@alternatives)
    {
        $alt =~ s/\+/ /g;
        $alternates->{$alt} = 1;
    }

    foreach my $alt (keys %{$alternates})
    {
        print "$alt\n";
    }
}
```

The script works by supplying a suitable query to the Google system. You then parse the output, first extracting the latitude and longitude (if you can find it). If the correct latitude and longitude cannot be found, you parse the raw HTML sent back to look for the alternatives suggested by the Google Maps system. To do this, the script effectively does the opposite of building a query—it looks for the query values, removes the + signs (which are spaces) and prints the results, removing duplicate results in the process.

The script is very basic. To use it, just supply the address and/or city and country that you want to look up. The more specific the information you provide the better; also, remember to use suitable conventions (such as "ave" in place of "avenue") where appropriate.

For example, to find Fifth Avenue in New York you might use the following:

```
$ find.pl "fifth avenue, New York, NY"
Lat:  - Lng:
Alternatives:
Grand Army Plz, New York, NY 10021
5th Ave, New York, NY
```

Here Google Maps is suggesting the use of the numeric form of the avenue name and the shorter form of avenue:

```
$ find.pl "5th Ave, New York, NY"
Lat: 40.765520 - Lng: -73.972100
```

Note Google is case sensitive when using this interface. Searching for "5th ave" returns only a list of alternatives, but "5th Ave" returns the latitude and longitude.

You can also locate U.K. addresses:

```
$ find.pl "Sheep Street, Bicester, UK"
Lat: 51.898116 - Lng: -1.151409
```

Find U.S. Zip codes:

```
$ find.pl "90210"
Lat: 34.090107 - Lng: -118.406477
```

Find U.K. Postcodes:

```
$ find.pl "OX9 2ED"
Lat: 51.745956 - Lng: -0.979953
```

Finally, Google will also return most major towns and cities across the world:

```
$ find.pl "Ronda, Spain"
Lat: 36.740001 - Lng: -5.159999
$ find.pl "tokyo"
Lat: 35.669998 - Lng: 139.770004
```

The Google solution, unlike the `geocoder.us` solution, is not really designed for large-volume situations, but it can be an excellent way to look up information for a smaller map.

The only issue with "scraping" for information in this way is that the format of the data that is extracted is not guaranteed. It is quite possible that the text extraction and regular expression matching process fails to find the information that you want after such a change, and that could render your software and application unworkable without redevelopment.

You should therefore use a geocoding service if it is available because these provide a more reliable interface to the information. Geocoding, rather than scraping, is also more suitable in large-volume situations, for example, when adding geocoding data to a very large customer database.

Wrapping Up

Geocoding your existing address data makes it significantly easier to use your existing location database with Google Maps. The techniques demonstrated in this chapter could be adapted to update an entire address database with latitude/longitude information, for example. The same techniques could also be used to introduce an additional step into a data update process that automatically looks up the information when an address is added to the system. How you use the information you have obtained is up to you and the needs of your application. Numerous examples throughout the book show how the information can be portrayed within a Google Map.

Extending the Google API Examples

chapter

7

in this chapter

☑ Add controls to your map

☑ Provide tools to help the user move about your map

☑ Add overlays and information windows to your map

☑ Use event listeners to add functionality to your map

The Google API documentation comes with a number of standard examples that show some of the basics of how the API can be used to build interactive maps. This chapter takes a closer look at the basic principles of the Google Maps system and environment in some basic examples showing the key functionality areas of the API.

Installing a Simple Example

The simplest map example is just to display a map centered on a particular location. All Google Maps are made up of the HTML of the page that contains the map and the embedded JavaScript component (supplied by Google Maps) that actually displays the map on the page.

Listing 7-1 shows a basic Google Maps sample, here centered on Grantham in Lincolnshire in the U.K.

Listing 7-1: Basic Map Example

```
<!DOCTYPE html PUBLIC "-//W3C//DTD XHTML 1.0 Strict//EN"
"http://www.w3.org/TR/xhtml1/DTD/xhtml1-strict.dtd">
<html xmlns="http://www.w3.org/1999/xhtml">
  <head>
  <meta http-equiv="content-type" content="text/html; charset=UTF-8"/>

  <title>Mcslp  Maps Chapter 7, Ex 1</title>
  <script src="http://maps.google.com/maps?file=api&v=1&key=XXX"
      type="text/javascript">
  </script>

  <script type="text/javascript">
  //<![CDATA[

  function onLoad() {
    if (GBrowserIsCompatible()) {
    var map = new GMap(document.getElementById("map"));
    map.centerAndZoom(new GPoint(-122.1419, 37.4419), 4);
    }
  }

  //]]>
  </script>
  </head>
  <body onload="onLoad()">

  <div id="map" style="width: 800px; height: 600px"></div>
  </body>
</html>
```

The code is split into a number of different parts and it is important to note, even at this stage, that the majority of the information here is HTML; the actual portion of the code that relates to the Google Maps API is comparatively small. This is generally true of most Google Maps–based applications: A lot of the interesting code is actually in the background or simply never seen at all.

Note Google advises that you use either XHTML (as in this example) or DHTML to ensure compatibility and portability.

The key component of the example is the installation of the Google Maps API JavaScript in this portion:

```
<script src="http://maps.google.com/maps?file=api&v=1&key=XXX"
    type="text/javascript">
  </script>
```

This section loads the Google Maps API. You must specify the Google Maps API key and the version of the API that you are using in this line to load the correct interface.

Once the Google Maps API is loaded, you can then call the API functions that introduce the map components into your web page. As shown in this example, you do this by creating a new local function, onLoad(), which is called when the page is loaded. The onLoad() function does three things:

- Checks that the browser is compatible and capable of running the Google Maps API.

- Creates a new map object. Within your XHTML, you've defined a <div> element with an id of 'map' and given it a size. When you create the new map object, you specify this element, which is where the map will appear within your site.

- Centers the map on a new GPoint. In this case, it points to my favorite local restaurant, One on Wharf.

You now have a simple map on a web page (see Figure 7-1). You can extend this to add some other functionality to the page.

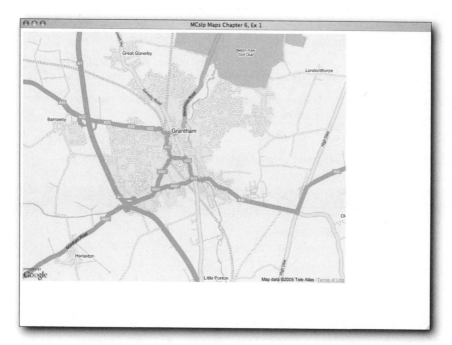

FIGURE 7-1: A simple Google Maps example.

Note Remember, all examples from the book can be tried online by using the chapter and listing reference. For example, you can view the map created by Listing 7-1 by visiting `http://maps` `.mcslp.com/examples/ch07-01.html`.

Adding Controls to the Map

Although you may at times want to limit how people interact with their maps, more often than not you will want to allow them to move and zoom freely through your map application.

The most effective way to do this is to add the standard Google Maps controls to your map application. You accomplish this by using the `addControl()` method to the map object. For example, you can add the map type control (for switching between Map, Earth, and combined modes) by using the following line:

```
Map.addControl(new GMapTypeControl());
```

Adding the controls when you first build the map, though, is not always useful. Sometimes the information your users really want to look at is actually hidden behind the controls.

Of course, in order to get around this, the display area of the map can be moved, but that's not any fun. Instead, you can extend the functionality by building in a simple clickable button or link that will switch the display of the controls on and off. Controls are actually objects, so when you add a control to a map you are in fact adding an object. Conveniently, the API provides methods on the map object to both add and remove control objects.

To achieve this, you must keep a record of the control objects you are creating before you add them to the map. That way, you can also remove them because you have a record of the object.

For convenience, you can also create a new <div> area on your page into which you can put an appropriate link that either enables or disables the controls, like this:

```
<div id="controller"></div>
```

Listing 7-2 shows the JavaScript code for this.

Listing 7-2: Adding Controls to a Google Map

```
<script type="text/javascript">
//<![CDATA[

var map;
var maptypecontrol = new GMapTypeControl();
var largemapcontrol = new GLargeMapControl();
var controller;
function onLoad() {

  if (GBrowserIsCompatible()) {
  map = new GMap(document.getElementById("map"));
```

```
    map.centerAndZoom(new GPoint(-0.64,52.909444), 4);
    }

    controller = document.getElementById('controller');

    addcontrols();
}

function addcontrols() {
  map.addControl(maptypecontrol);
  map.addControl(largemapcontrol);
  controller.innerHTML = '<a href="#" onClick="hidecontrols();">↵
Hide Controls</a>';
}

function hidecontrols() {
  map.removeControl(maptypecontrol);
  map.removeControl(largemapcontrol);
  controller.innerHTML = '<a href="#" onClick="addcontrols();">↵
Add Controls</a>';
}

//]]>
</script>
```

The following are the key areas of this example:

- The creation of the control objects at the start of the JavaScript section.

- The movement of the map object definition from the `onLoad()` function to the global area of the JavaScript (which means you can access the map object from other functions).

- The identification of the area where the add/remove controls button will be placed.

- The main `addcontrols()` and `hidecontrols()` functions.

The `addcontrols()` function calls the `addControl()` method on the map object to add the control objects that were created at the head of the script. Note that pre-existing instances of the objects are being added. This is important because the same principle will provide the ability to later remove them.

Once the controls have been added, you add HTML to the controller section of the document to provide a link for hiding them (by calling `hidecontrols()`). The `hidecontrols()` function does the opposite; it removes the controls and then sets the HTML to add controls to the map by calling the `addcontrols()` function.

Figure 7-2 shows the map in its initial state, with the controls displayed and the link for hiding the controls at the bottom of the screen. Figure 7-3 shows the result when you click the `hidecontrols()` link: The controls are gone and the link has changed to show a link for adding the controls. Click that link to return to the state in Figure 7-2.

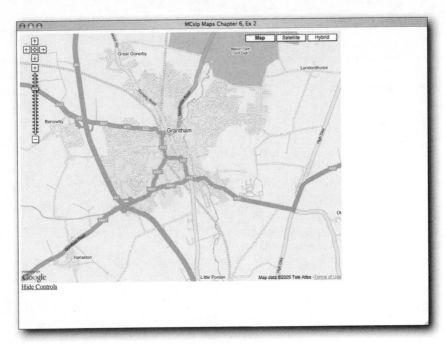

FIGURE 7-2: Adding controls and providing a hide link.

FIGURE 7-3: Hiding controls and providing a show link.

Moving about a Map

Often you'll let people move around the map at will, but more than likely you will want to provide some quick methods for taking your users to particular places on the map. Three methods are useful in this situation:

- The first, which you have already used, is `centerAndZoom()`. It centers the map on a supplied GPoint and zooms to a specific level on the map. The move is instantaneous and is best used when initializing the map for the first time and centering (and zooming) on a specific area. For example:

  ```
  map.centerAndZoom(new GPoint(-122.1419, 37.4419), 4);
  ```

- The second method is `centerAtLatLng()`, which centers the map on the supplied GPoint. The movement is instantaneous, but does not change the zoom level. For example:

  ```
  map.centerAtLatLng(new GPoint(-122.1419, 37.4419));
  ```

- For a smoother sequence, use the third method: `recenterOrPanToLatLng()`. This smoothly moves the map to the new point, if the map data is available to do a smooth pan to the new point. This is most effective in maps in which you are redirecting users to different points within a reasonable locale (such as places within the same borough or city).

For example, Listing 7-3 shows some sample code that provides quick links to four of my favorite restaurants. In this case, I'm using `recenterOrPanToLatLng()`. For the first two restaurants that are both in Grantham, you should get a smooth movement when clicking the two links. But click to the restaurants in Seattle, or even Ambleside, and the distance is so great that a smooth pan to the new location is out of the question.

Listing 7-3: Moving Users about a Map

```
<!DOCTYPE html PUBLIC "-//W3C//DTD XHTML 1.0 Strict//EN"
"http://www.w3.org/TR/xhtml1/DTD/xhtml1-strict.dtd">
<html xmlns="http://www.w3.org/1999/xhtml">
  <head>
  <meta http-equiv="content-type" content="text/html; charset=UTF-8"/>

  <title>MCslp Maps Chapter 7, Ex 3</title>
  <script src="http://maps.google.com/maps?file=api&v=1&key=XXX"
      type="text/javascript">
  </script>

  <script type="text/javascript">
```

Continued

Listing 7-3 *(continued)*

```
//<![CDATA[

var map;

function onLoad() {
if (GBrowserIsCompatible()) {
  map = new GMap(document.getElementById("map"));
  map.centerAndZoom(new GPoint(-0.64,52.909444), 2);
  }
}

function movemap(x,y) {
    map.recenterOrPanToLatLng(new GPoint(parseFloat(x),parseFloat(y)));
}

//]]>
</script>
</head>
<body onload="onLoad()">

<div id="map" style="width: 800px; height: 600px"></div>
<ul>
<li><a href="#" onClick="movemap(-0.64,52.915423);">China Inn, Grantham</a></li>
<li><a href="#" onClick="movemap(-0.64,52.909444);">One on Wharf, ⏎
Grantham</a></li>
<li><a href="#" onClick="movemap(-2.9638,54.4334);">Glass House, ⏎
Ambleside</a></li>
<li><a href="#" onClick="movemap(-122.3346,47.6133);">Dragonfish ⏎
Asian Cafe, Seattle</a></li>
</ul>
  </body>
</html>
```

The movemap() function does all the work, accepting two arguments that are used to gener-ate a GPoint and move the map by calling recentOrPanToLatLng() on the map object.

Straightforward links, which call the function, are then added as HTML to the end of the page. Clicking a link recenters the map to that location. Figure 7-4 shows the initial display. To best understand how this works, I highly recommend that you try this application for yourself.

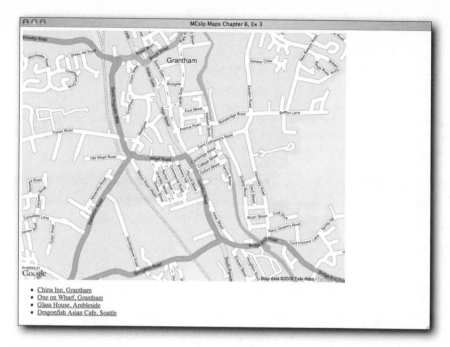

FIGURE 7-4: Providing links for moving around a map.

Adding Overlays

In the previous example, the ability to move the user about the map was added to the map. However, although the map has moved to show a different location, the exact point you are highlighting is not clear. For example, although the map may move to One on Wharf, the restaurant's exact location is not really clear from just looking at the map.

There are two types of overlays: the marker and the polyline. The former is an icon or map point that can be used to identify a specific point (for example, a restaurant). The latter is just a line with start and end points (based on latitude/longitude) and a width specification.

Adding a Single Marker

The GMarker() object creates a simple icon based on a given GPoint and can be used to highlight a specific location, like a restaurant. To add a GMarker to the map, add an overlay (using addOverlay()) to place the marker object on the map.

In short, to add a marker:

1. Create a GPoint().

2. Create a new GMarker using the GPoint.

3. Add the GMarker to the map using addOverlay().

The movemap() function from the previous example can be adjusted so that it adds a marker to the map when a restaurant is clicked. Listing 7-4 shows an updated movemap() function with the added steps, and Figure 7-5 shows the results.

Listing 7-4: Adding a Marker to the Map Movement Function

```
var marker;

function movemap(x,y) {
    if (marker)
    {
        map.removeOverlay(marker);
    }
    var point = new GPoint(parseFloat(x),parseFloat(y));
    map.recenterOrPanToLatLng(point);
    marker = new GMarker(point);
    map.addOverlay(marker);
}
```

For convenience, the marker object is created globally, and the existing marker is removed before moving the map and creating the new marker for the selected restaurant. This latter operation is handled by checking whether the marker variable has already been configured. If it has, you can remove it from the map by calling the removeOverlay() method. Because the object holding the marker is created globally, you can easily call it from the method to remove it.

Adding Multiple Markers

Highlighting one location, as in the previous example, is useful, but it's not really very handy if you want to show users all of the potential restaurants or locations that are available on a map. In the restaurant example, what would be really useful is to show the location of a number of potential restaurants that the user might be interested in.

If you don't actually want to keep or update the markers, the movemap() can be further simplified to create a marker each time the user clicks a restaurant. Listing 7-5 shows an altered movemap().

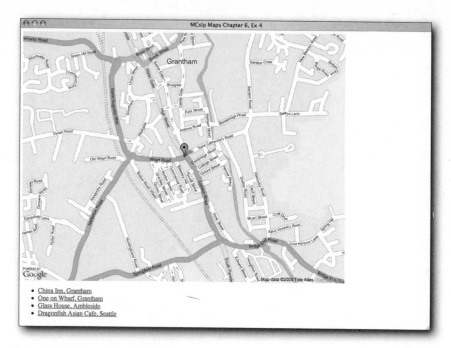

FIGURE 7-5: Adding a simple marker.

Listing 7-5: Adding Markers from Points

```
function movemap(x,y) {
    var point = new GPoint(parseFloat(x),parseFloat(y));
    map.recenterOrPanToLatLng(point);
    map.addOverlay(new GMarker(point));
}
```

In this case, each time the user clicks the restaurant link, an appropriate marker will be added. Existing markers are not removed. Figure 7-6 shows the application after the user has clicked two links.

Another alternative is to change the `onLoad()` code and create multiple markers when the web page is first loaded, as shown in Listing 7-6.

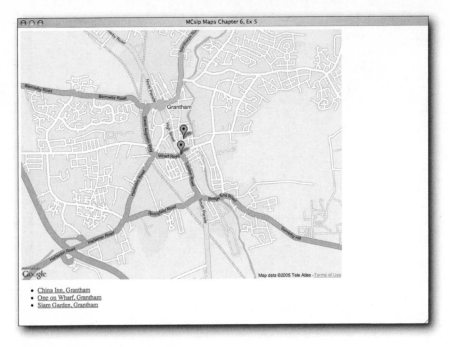

FIGURE 7-6: Adding multiple markers.

Listing 7-6: Creating Markers during Startup

```
<script type="text/javascript">
//<![CDATA[

var map;

function onLoad() {
  // The basics.
  //
  // Creates a map and centers it on Palo Alto.
  if (GBrowserIsCompatible()) {
  map = new GMap(document.getElementById("map"));
  map.centerAndZoom(new GPoint(-0.64,52.909444), 3);
  addmarker(-0.6394,52.9114);
  addmarker(-0.64,52.909444);
  addmarker(-0.6376,52.9073);
  }
}

function addmarker(x,y) {
```

```
    var point = new GPoint(parseFloat(x),parseFloat(y));
    map.addOverlay(new GMarker(point));
}

//]]>
</script>
```

This time, the code defines a new function, addmarker(). This function creates a new point and marker and then adds this to the active map. Calls to the function are then added at the end of the onLoad() function to create the markers when the web page is loaded.

The result is shown in Figure 7-7.

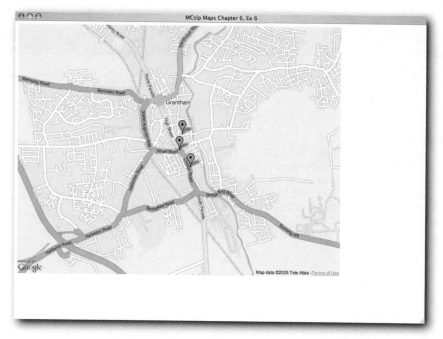

FIGURE 7-7: Adding multiple markers during startup.

Adding Lines

Individual map markers are a great way of highlighting a particular point on a map, but sometimes you want to indicate an area or locale, rather than a specific point. You could create an icon that highlights this information, but a more effective approach is to use the built-in line drawing system provided by the Google Maps API to draw a polyline.

Using a single polyline, you can map a distance or length, or show the relationship between two points. With multiple polylines, you can draw a variety of different shapes, routes, and paths.

The GPolyline class creates a line or series of lines from a supplied list of GPoints. Obviously, you need a minimum of two points (the start and end points), and lines are drawn in the order of the points stored in the array. If you supply three points, a line is drawn from Point 1 to Point 2, and then from Point 2 to Point 3. It follows that you will get one line less than the number of points provided. So to draw a box, you need to supply five points: the top left, top right, bottom right, bottom left, and the top left again to complete the box.

Adding a Bounding Box

Listing 7-7 shows how to use polylines to add a bounding box to your display. The goal is to show the key areas that are covered by the map of Grantham restaurants. To achieve this, you need to add five points to an array and then supply this array to create a new GPolyline object and add this as an overlay to the map.

Listing 7-7: Adding a Bounding Box to the Map

```
<script type="text/javascript">
//<![CDATA[

var map;

function onLoad() {
if (GBrowserIsCompatible()) {
  map = new GMap(document.getElementById("map"));
  map.centerAndZoom(new GPoint(-0.64,52.909444), 2);
  addmarker(-0.6394,52.9114);
  addmarker(-0.64,52.909444);
  addmarker(-0.6376,52.9073);
  boundingbox(-0.6488,52.9157,-0.6292,52.9027);
  }
}


function boundingbox(tlx,tly,brx,bry) {
    var box = [];
    box.push(new GPoint(tlx,tly));
    box.push(new GPoint(brx,tly));
    box.push(new GPoint(brx,bry));
    box.push(new GPoint(tlx,bry));
    box.push(new GPoint(tlx,tly));
    map.addOverlay(new GPolyline(box));
}

function addmarker(x,y) {
    var point = new GPoint(parseFloat(x),parseFloat(y));
```

```
        map.addOverlay(new GMarker(point));
}

//]]>
</script>
```

As you can see, the core of the process is a function, `boundingbox()`, which takes the location of the top-left and bottom-right points of the box. With this information, you can determine the location of all four corners and build an array with the five points (the four corners and the first corner again to complete the line).

 Note Although it is tempting to use the size and zoom level of a map to show the precise area you are concentrating on, this also limits the utility of your map. In an example like the restaurant map, if you display a wider map area but highlight a smaller focus area, it gives your users context and the ability to identify how they might reach or approach a location, while still indicating the core of your map content.

Figure 7-8 shows the results of the code in Listing 7-7: a nice box surrounds the town center of Grantham and shows the basic limits of your guide.

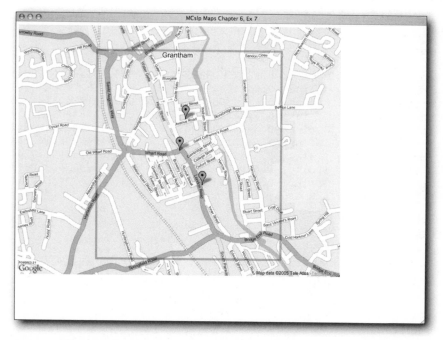

FIGURE 7-8: Adding a bounding box to a map.

Adding a Route

Adding a route is much the same as adding a bounding box: You build an array into which you place list of points and then get the GPolyline function to plot those points and add them as an overlay to your map. Unlike with a bounding box or other shape, you don't try to complete the circuit.

Listing 7-8 shows an example of how to add a route to a map by hard-coding a series of points. In this case, I'm demonstrating a route, by road, for getting from one of the larger parking lots in Grantham to Siam Garden.

Listing 7-8: Adding a Route

```
<script type="text/javascript">
//<![CDATA[

var map;

function onLoad() {
  if (GBrowserIsCompatible()) {
  map = new GMap(document.getElementById("map"));
  map.centerAndZoom(new GPoint(-0.64,52.909444), 2);
  addmarker(-0.6394,52.9114);
  addmarker(-0.64,52.909444);
  addmarker(-0.6376,52.9073);

  var route = [];

  route.push(new GPoint(-0.6467342376708984, 52.91519081031524));
  route.push(new GPoint(-0.6466054916381836, 52.915527220441405));
  route.push(new GPoint(-0.6440305709838867, 52.916122401186186));
  route.push(new GPoint(-0.6434726715087891, 52.91578599568332));
  route.push(new GPoint(-0.6442880630493164, 52.915294321401625));
  route.push(new GPoint(-0.6411123275756836, 52.9104807941625));
  route.push(new GPoint(-0.6398248672485352, 52.90952320075754));
  route.push(new GPoint(-0.638279914855957, 52.90778912639283));
  route.push(new GPoint(-0.6376361846923828, 52.90716794854011));
  map.addOverlay(new GPolyline(route));
  }
}

function addmarker(x,y) {
    var point = new GPoint(parseFloat(x),parseFloat(y));
    map.addOverlay(new GMarker(point));
}

//]]>
</script>
```

Obviously, this is a less-than-efficient method of adding a route to the map, but it does demonstrate the basic principle. As with the bounding box, the sequence is to add points to an array and then construct the polyline and overlay it on your map.

Note Remember that polylines are plotted according to the sequence of points. If you want to draw two shapes, you must create two arrays and two polylines; otherwise, you will have a line connecting the two shapes.

Note that the `GPolyline` class creates a new object, so just as with the markers you created earlier, the polyline route could be recorded in a variable and added, modified, or hidden on the map at will.

The resulting route is shown in Figure 7-9.

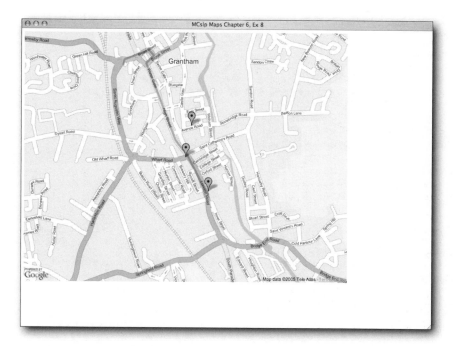

FIGURE 7-9: Adding a route to a map.

Note Polylines can have different colors, sizes, and opacities (or transparencies, depending on your preferred start position!). However, specification of these colors is made at the time the `GPolyline` object is instantiated, which means that to create a box with sides of different colors or opacities actually requires the creation of different polylines.

Opening an Info Window

When you added markers to the map to indicate the location of different restaurants, you actually lost the ability to identify which marker relates to which restaurant.

To resolve this issue, you can add an information window that is displayed when the marker is clicked. The window can contain any amount of HTML and can incorporate pictures, text formatting, or whatever you need to display the information you want.

Listing 7-9 is a modification of Listing 7-5; it displays the three markers and adds a small title to the information window, based on a new argument to the addmarker() function.

Listing 7-9: Adding Information Windows

```
<script type="text/javascript">
//<![CDATA[

var map;

function onLoad() {
  // The basics.
  //
  // Creates a map and centers it on Palo Alto.
  if (GBrowserIsCompatible()) {
  map = new GMap(document.getElementById("map"));
  map.centerAndZoom(new GPoint(-0.64,52.909444), 2);
  addmarker(-0.6394,52.9114,'China Inn');
  addmarker(-0.64,52.909444,'One on Wharf');
  addmarker(-0.6376,52.9073,'Siam Garden');
  }
}

function addmarker(x,y,title) {
    var point = new GPoint(parseFloat(x),parseFloat(y));
    var marker = new GMarker(point);
    GEvent.addListener(marker,
                       'click',
                       function() {
        marker.openInfoWindowHtml('<b>' + title + '</b>');
    }
                       );
    map.addOverlay(marker);
}

//]]>
</script>
```

The key to the example is the use of GEvent. This function makes the Google Maps application respond to a specific event. The next section of this chapter covers events in a bit more detail, but the principle is similar to adding a response to a mouse click or key press within any other type of application.

In Listing 7-9, you are configuring a new type of event on the marker that is triggered when you click the marker. The result of the click is the inline function that you have designed. It calls the openInfoWindowHtml method on the marker to display the HTML supplied as an argument, with the title embedded into a set of bold tags.

Once the marker has been configured, it can be added as an overlay object to the map. Figure 7-10 shows the map in its initial state: just showing the configured markers. Figure 7-11 shows the result when the marker for One on Wharf is clicked: a small information window with the name of the restaurant.

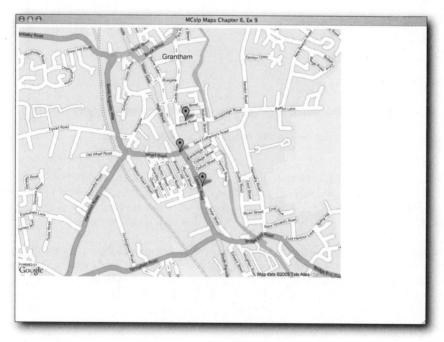

FIGURE 7-10: A map with markers configured for info windows.

Note You cannot have more than one info window open at a time. If you click a different marker, the existing info window is closed before the new one is opened.

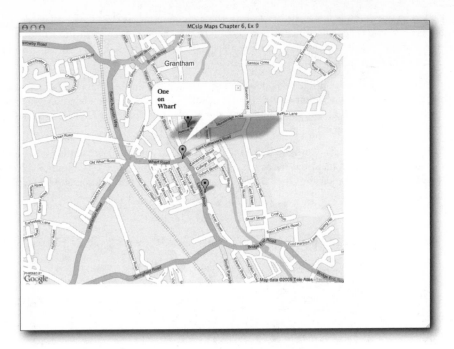

FIGURE 7-11: An info window after a user has clicked a marker.

Because the information in the info window is HTML, you could easily add the address, a link to the restaurant web site, and even a picture of the restaurant. There is no limit to what can be displayed in this info window, although there are some obvious limitations to the size and quantity of information that be effectively displayed in such a small window.

Note

The method option (which automatically attaches the info window to the marker and the point that triggers it) has been used in the example, but you can also create info windows separately by using openInfoWindowHtml() and supplying the point and HTML to be displayed. As an alternative to displaying HTML embedded into the call to openInfoWindowHtml(), you can also use openInfoWindow(), which takes an HTML DOM reference of the information to display, and openInfoWindowXslt(), which translates the supplied XSLT reference and XML into HTML for display.

The entire map also has an info window that can be used to display information about the map in general.

Event Listeners

Events can be used to add interesting effects to a map. There are a number of events, such as when

- The user clicks on the map.

- The user moves the map (there are separate event types for when the user moves the map, one before the redraw and one after the move has been completed).

- The map zooms for any reason.

- An info window is displayed or closed.

- An overlay is added to or removed from the map.

Monitoring Movement

One of the simplest events you can monitor is the movement of your map. If a user moves a map and either moves off the limits of your mapping area, or moves to a point where different overlays and information should be displayed, you will want to know about the movement.

For a very simple demonstration of this movement in operation, look at Listing 7-10. Here you create two maps: One is a typical map, the other the satellite view. The two maps are the same size and dimension, and you initialize them with the same zoom level and location.

Listing 7-10: Synchronizing Two Maps

```
<!DOCTYPE html PUBLIC "-//W3C//DTD XHTML 1.0 Strict//EN"
"http://www.w3.org/TR/xhtml1/DTD/xhtml1-strict.dtd">
<html xmlns="http://www.w3.org/1999/xhtml">
  <head>
  <meta http-equiv="content-type" content="text/html; charset=UTF-8"/>

  <title>MCslp Maps Chapter 7, Ex 10</title>
  <script src="http://maps.google.com/maps?file=api&v=1&key=XXX"
      type="text/javascript">
  </script>

  <script type="text/javascript">
  //<![CDATA[

  var map;
  var earth;

  function onLoad() {
    if (GBrowserIsCompatible()) {
```

Continued

Listing 7-10 *(continued)*

```
        map = new GMap(document.getElementById("map"));
        map.centerAndZoom(new GPoint(-0.64,52.909444), 4);
        earth = new GMap(document.getElementById("earth"));
        earth.centerAndZoom(new GPoint(-0.64,52.909444), 4);
        earth.setMapType(G_SATELLITE_TYPE);
        GEvent.addListener(map,'moveend',function() {
            var center = map.getCenterLatLng();
            earth.recenterOrPanToLatLng(center);
        });
        GEvent.addListener(earth,'moveend',function() {
            var center = earth.getCenterLatLng();
            map.recenterOrPanToLatLng(center);
        });
    }
}

//]]>
</script>
</head>
<body onload="onLoad()">
<table cellspacing="0" cellpadding="0" border="0">
<tr>
<td><div id="map" style="width: 400px; height: 600px"></div></td>
<td><div id="earth" style="width: 400px; height: 600px"></div></td>
</tr>
</table>
</body>
</html>
```

Two events are configured, one for each map. On the default map, a listener is added that responds to the movement event. When the map is moved, you also move the satellite map to be at the same position. The other listener does the opposite when the satellite map moves (that is, it moves the map to the same location). You can see a screenshot of the two maps in action in Figure 7-12, although this is definitely an example where you need to try out the map for yourself to see it in action.

 Note Remember, all examples from the book can be tried online by using the chapter and listing reference. For example, you can view the map created in Listing 7-10 by visiting `http://maps .mcslp.com/examples/ch07-10.html`.

The effect of the two listeners is to keep the two maps in synch with each other. Move one map, and the other moves to the same location. Although you can view the map and satellite image using the hybrid map type, sometimes the separate layout is useful.

FIGURE 7-12: Synchronizing map display using listeners and events.

The example also shows two other key elements:

1. You can determine the current center point of your map by using the getCenterLatLng() method on the map object. You can also determine the map size, the span of the map (the span of the latitude and longitude being displayed), and the bounds (edges) of the displayed map.

2. The example demonstrates how to adjust your map display type. Remember that you can choose between three types (map, satellite, and hybrid) and that you can change the map type at any time. You can also, by adding movement controls to your map, allow users to choose the type of map that is displayed.

Adding Markers to Multiple Maps

Of course, if you have two maps like those shown in Listing 7-10, you might also want to display the same overlays and markers. This is where the use of objects to store your overlay items is useful. To add a marker to both maps, all you have to do is call the addOverlay() method on each displayed map object. Listing 7-11 gives you an example of this by merging the code from Listing 7-9 and Listing 7-10 to provide two maps with marker and information windows.

Listing 7-11: Adding Overlays to Multiple Maps

```
<!DOCTYPE html PUBLIC "-//W3C//DTD XHTML 1.0 Strict//EN"
"http://www.w3.org/TR/xhtml1/DTD/xhtml1-strict.dtd">
<html xmlns="http://www.w3.org/1999/xhtml">
  <head>
  <meta http-equiv="content-type" content="text/html; charset=UTF-8"/>

  <title>MCslp Maps Chapter 7, Ex 11</title>
  <script src="http://maps.google.com/maps?file=api&v=1&key=XXX"
      type="text/javascript">
  </script>

  <script type="text/javascript">
  //<![CDATA[

  var map;
  var earth;

  function onLoad() {
    if (GBrowserIsCompatible()) {
        map = new GMap(document.getElementById("map"));
        map.centerAndZoom(new GPoint(-0.64,52.909444), 4);
        earth = new GMap(document.getElementById("earth"));
        earth.centerAndZoom(new GPoint(-0.64,52.909444), 4);
        earth.setMapType(G_SATELLITE_TYPE);
        GEvent.addListener(map,'moveend',function() {
            var center = map.getCenterLatLng();
            earth.recenterOrPanToLatLng(center);
        });
        GEvent.addListener(earth,'moveend',function() {
            var center = earth.getCenterLatLng();
            map.recenterOrPanToLatLng(center);
        });
    addmarker(-0.6394,52.9114,'China Inn');
    addmarker(-0.64,52.909444,'One on Wharf');
    addmarker(-0.6376,52.9073,'Siam Garden');
    }
  }

  function addmarker(x,y,title) {
      var point = new GPoint(parseFloat(x),parseFloat(y));
      var marker = new GMarker(point);
      GEvent.addListener(marker,
                         'click',
                         function() {
          marker.openInfoWindowHtml('<b>' + title + '</b>');
      }
                         );
      map.addOverlay(marker);
      earth.addOverlay(marker);
```

```
   }

   //]]>
   </script>
   </head>
   <body onload="onLoad()">
<table cellspacing="0" cellpadding="0" border="0">
<tr>
<td><div id="map" style="width: 400px; height: 600px"></div></td>
<td><div id="earth" style="width: 400px; height: 600px"></div></td>
</tr>
</table>
</body>
</html>
```

The difference between the two scripts (aside from the code for adding the markers in the first place) is this line:

```
earth.addOverlay(marker);
```

This line simply adds the marker to the Earth map, as well as to the Maps map. An example of the application is shown in Figure 7-13.

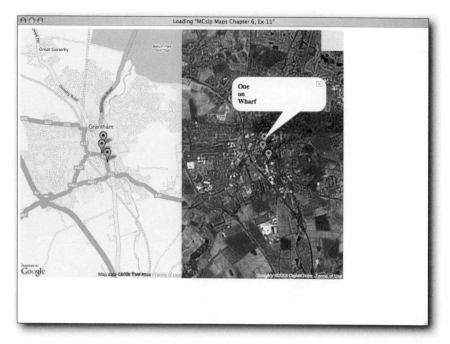

FIGURE 7-13: Adding markers to multiple maps.

Clicking either marker will bring up an info window. However, the listener for opening the window is displayed only in the latter map.

Monitoring Location

The last script in this quick overview of extending the basic examples given by Google Maps demonstrates what is probably the most useful map in the map developer's arsenal.

One of the problems with developing maps is that, as you build data and add markers, polylines, and other information, you need to be able to find out your exact location on the map. You must know this information in order add the latitude and longitude information to your own applications. Listing 7-12 shows the code for this application.

Listing 7-12: Finding Your Location

```
<!DOCTYPE html PUBLIC "-//W3C//DTD XHTML 1.0 Strict//EN"
"http://www.w3.org/TR/xhtml1/DTD/xhtml1-strict.dtd">
<html xmlns="http://www.w3.org/1999/xhtml">
  <head>
  <meta http-equiv="content-type" content="text/html; charset=UTF-8"/>

  <title>MCslp Maps Chapter 7, Ex 12</title>
  <script src="http://maps.google.com/maps?file=api&v=1&key=XXX"
      type="text/javascript">
  </script>

  <script type="text/javascript">
  //<![CDATA[

  var map;

  function onLoad() {
    if (GBrowserIsCompatible()) {
    map = new GMap(document.getElementById("map"));

    GEvent.addListener(map, 'click', function(overlay,point) {
      var latLngStr = '(' + point.x + ', ' + point.y + ')<br/>';
      var message = document.getElementById("message");
      message.innerHTML = latLngStr;
      });

    map.centerAndZoom(new GPoint(-0.64,52.909444), 2);
    }
  }


  //]]>
```

```
    </script>
    </head>
    <body onload="onLoad()">

    <div id="map" style="width: 800px; height: 600px"></div>
    <div id="message"></div>
<ul>
</ul>
</body>
</html>
```

The application works by adding a listener to the map. Each time the user clicks on the map, the latitude and longitude will be displayed in the message area of the display (identified by the <div> tag immediately after the map). The embedded function that is called each time the map is clicked just updates the HTML content of the message area.

Now you can click on the map and get a precise value to locate your position when creating markers. See Figure 7-14 for an example.

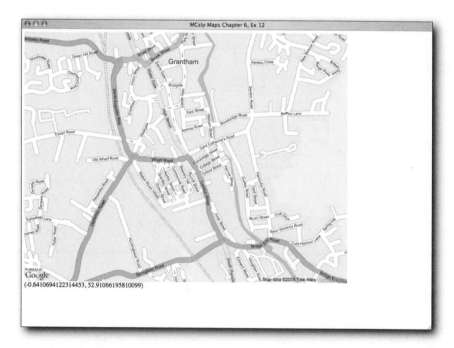

FIGURE 7-14: Finding your latitude and longitude in a map.

Note This application is incredibly useful. In fact, it was invaluable to me when preparing this chapter because it provided the information needed for the examples.

As an extension of that principle, a minor change to the function called by the listener shows each point clicked, and also draws the polyline that would be created with each click. Listing 7-13 shows the updated code for the application. This system is also useful for building routes, boxes, and other shapes.

Listing 7-13: Dynamically Building Polylines while Getting Location Data

```
var map;
var points = [];
var route;

function onLoad() {
  if (GBrowserIsCompatible()) {
  map = new GMap(document.getElementById("map"));

  GEvent.addListener(map, 'click', function(overlay,point) {
      var latLngStr = '(' + point.x + ', ' + point.y + ')<br/>';
      var message = document.getElementById("message");
      message.innerHTML = message.innerHTML + latLngStr;
      if (route) {
          map.removeOverlay(route);
      }
      points.push(point);
      if (points.length > 1) {
          route = new GPolyline(points);
          map.addOverlay(route);
      }
  });

  map.centerAndZoom(new GPoint(-0.64,52.909444), 2);
  }
}
```

The application works by creating a global array to hold each point, and a variable to hold the polyline that is generated each time.

Each time the user clicks on the map, the application adds a point to the array. If the length of the array of points is greater than one, there is enough information to build a polyline. If the polyline is created, it is recorded and the overlay is deleted and redrawn with each click. So that a record of each point clicked is included, the message displayed at the bottom of the map is also updated with each point.

You can see a screenshot of the application in action in Figure 7-15, although — again — this is an application that you need to try out in order to really appreciate how it works.

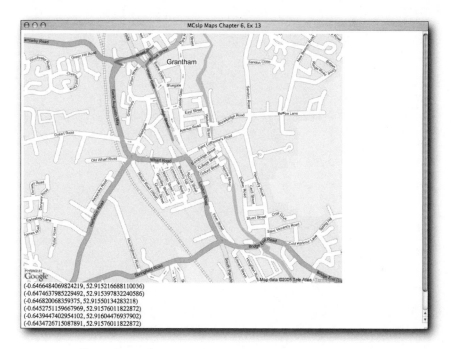

FIGURE 7-15: Collecting points and mapping polylines dynamically.

Wrapping Up

The examples in this chapter give you some quick ideas as to how you can modify the basic map environment to turn a basic map display into a more useful interactive map system that shows detail and information about a specific topic.

All Google Maps applications are based on the principles covered in this chapter. You provide a map, zoom to the locality, overlay data and information that extends the utility of the map, and allow the user to interact with that information. The next step is to make the information and data that is displayed more dynamic, rather than using the statically created markers, routes, and information that you used in this chapter. Before you look at specifics, the next chapter covers some examples of Google Maps–enabled sites that other people have developed.

Discovering Overlays and Mash-ups

Two common techniques for increasing functionality in Google Maps applications are overlays and mash-ups. In an overlay, information is placed on top of a "hot" map, which is an interactive and controllable map of a particular area. For instance, you can layer restaurant location data on top of a Google street map. In a mash-up, a variety of information is combined to create an entire application. For example, you can overlay transit maps onto a Google street map and then provide additional information and functionality, such as route guides.

This chapter presents some excellent examples of existing applications that use overlays and/or mash-ups to enhance the usefulness of a particular web site. Not only are these web sites convenient, practical, and fun to navigate, but you can also use them as inspiration when you begin to create your own applications.

Traffic Solutions

For maps that include road data, providing interactive information on the traffic situation or better ways of finding your way around are excellent ways to extend the utility of the map beyond a basic overview of the surrounding environment.

Toronto Transit Commission (TTC) Map

Toronto has an excellent public transit system, but some elements of the underground system are less than clear. There are, of course, plenty of maps and guides to how to get around, but they are not always easy to use. For starters, working out the precise location of the station compared to the street on which it is located is difficult. The maps of the subway are either named explicitly or stylized to the point that street names are not a critical part of the identification. Even if you are looking at a combined street map and transit map, the detail may be so small that what you are looking for is difficult to identify.

Integrating the original street map with an overlay of the transit map can make understanding the information much easier. Figure 8-1 shows an example of a Google Map overlaid with the TTC subway map. You can find this example online at `http://crazedmonkey.com/ ttcgooglemap/`. It provides route and station information for the whole of the Toronto subway system.

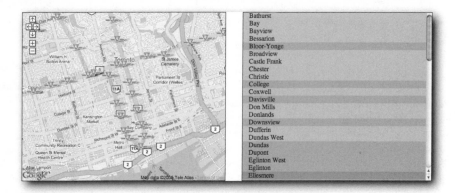

FIGURE 8-1: A Google Map overlaid by the TTC subway map.

The map is split into two parts. On the left is a map, which is (obviously) the Google Maps component. You can see the markers showing the individual stations and their locations on the map. You can also see the route of the transit line, in an appropriate color, behind the stations. On the right is the list of stations, colored according to the color of the line on the official TTC map.

Because the map is interactive, you can zoom right in to the location of the station to find out exactly where the station is located, and you can find out the precise details by clicking on one of the stations, as shown in Figure 8-2.

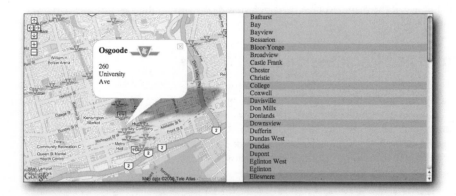

FIGURE 8-2: Viewing station information.

You can also jump directly to a station by clicking its name in the list on the right. A simple, straightforward Google Map displays a single set of information in a format that makes it easy to find information that is already otherwise available on a static map.

Toronto Traffic Cameras

The city of Toronto has traffic cameras set up at various points around town. These cameras take pictures periodically, allowing viewers to evaluate the state of traffic and road conditions year-round.

The Toronto Star helpfully provides a Google Map–enabled page for viewing traffic camera information at `http://www.thestar.com/static/googlemaps/gtatraffic .html?xml=trafficcams.xml`. Each of the markers on this map of Toronto (see Figure 8-3) is an individual traffic camera.

FIGURE 8-3: Toronto Star traffic camera locations.

To see a traffic-camera view of a particular site, click that site's marker (see Figure 8-4).

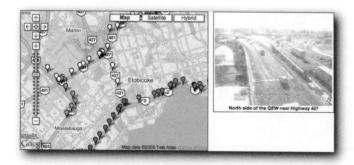

FIGURE 8-4: Toronto Star traffic camera view.

U.K. Speed Cameras

Speed cameras are seen as something of a menace in the U.K. Although the majority of drivers understand the need to control the speed of some individuals, the placement of the some of the cameras can be considered somewhat suspect. There are rules and regulations about the locations of cameras, but some seem placed purely to generate revenue rather than to prevent accidents.

For a long time, many cameras seemed to be deliberately hidden in order to catch the unaware driver; there are rules against that now, but it is still possible to be unaware of the location of a camera and get caught. Even worse, some cameras are placed in a zone where there is no indication of the speed limit, which makes it even more likely that you will be caught speeding.

As such, U.K. citizens have begun something of a grass-roots campaign to make the cameras more visible, make the speed limit for that region more visible, and for the locations of the cameras to be made public.

You can buy books with this information, and many of the car-based route finders and GPS navigation systems now come with information about speed cameras and traps. Even better, though, is the publication of camera locations on a Google Map mash-up.

The speed camera location map (at `http://spod.cx/speedcameras.html`) is shown in Figure 8-5. The map is simple but functional, showing the location of each camera on a standard driving map.

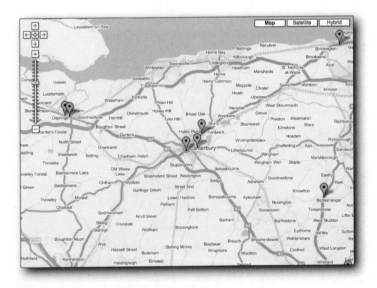

FIGURE 8-5: U.K. speed cameras.

Trackers and Locators

Maps can be used to provide both active information about an event (for example, live feeds of hurricane and weather activity) and also a historical view of that information. You only have to watch the TV weather reports to see how this information can be used. Sometimes, using the information extracted from the map can be just as useful. The photos taken and used for the Google Maps satellite imagery are real photos, and occasionally that means that objects are photographed and incorporated into the data. Some users are using this information to watch and study different objects. Some are examining the details of well-known landmarks, such as Area 51, while others look out for "capture" objects, like the photos of planes in flight or similar events. Where that information is missing, the markers and icons in Google Maps can be used to add the information to the map.

This section looks at two examples, one providing live and historical information about hurricanes, and the other showing photos and the locations of one of the most famous aircraft ever made.

Hurricanes

As I noted in Chapter 1, my wife and I were in New York the weekend Hurricane Katrina hit the Gulf Coast of the United States. Predicting, and then tracking, the path of the hurricane went a long way to help individuals, organizations, and companies determine where the hurricane was likely to hit and what sort of effects it could have on them.

At the time, numerous sites providing the hurricane's path and the forecast route popped up, both from official sources and from individuals who had built Google Maps applications to show the information.

One of the most extensive hurricane-tracking applications available is the Hurricane Path Tracking & Storm Status Information page for the Atlantic Ocean (at `http://compooter` `.org/sandbox/code/google/hurricane/atlantic/`). This tool provides historical hurricane data for more than 150 years for the Atlantic region. Similar applications are available for the East and West Pacific.

The starting interface for this application combines a simple layout with an advanced application that enables you to load hurricane information in a hurry. From the pop-up in the upper-right corner, you can select one of the years to view. I've selected 2005 so that the page shows the path of Hurricane Katrina (see Figure 8-6).

The application then provides you with a list of hurricanes for the year, sorted by name. Clicking a hurricane name loads up all the data for that hurricane, including the path it took and data points for the storm's severity and classification. You can see the route and a sample information window in Figure 8-7.

You can even combine multiple hurricanes to compare the paths and severity at different points, as you can see in Figure 8-8 (which shows hurricanes Katrina and Wilma). Katrina is the S-shaped route from just above Cuba that snakes up through Louisiana and on land up toward New York State. Wilma starts south of Cuba and snakes up across the tip of Florida and heads out to sea, following the coastline of the eastern seaboard.

FIGURE 8-6: Choosing a hurricane.

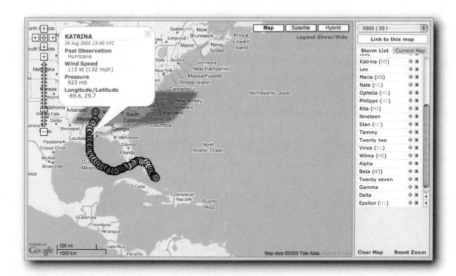

FIGURE 8-7: Viewing the hurricane path and data points.

What impresses most about the map is the combination of the quality of the interface and the level of detail and information provided in the map. The comprehensive data goes back to 1851. Although this tool may not be an officially recognized source for information, it is by far one of the best looking.

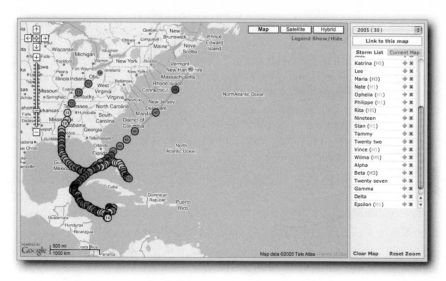

FIGURE 8-8: Viewing multiple hurricanes.

Satellites

If you've ever looked up at the sky to view the stars and the constellations, you may be surprised to know that one of those stars may have been the International Space Station (ISS). With a large enough telescope — or even one of the hobby scopes — you can actually see the ISS from the ground.

But how do you know where to look?

The Space Station Tracker (located at `http://gmaps.tommangan.us/spacecraft_tracking.html`) shows the location in the sky of the International Space Station and the Hubble Space Telescope as they pass over different part of the world (see Figure 8-9).

The site shows a very simple overlay of information on top of a Google Earth Map. If you leave the site open, the application will actually create a trail of the path taken by the satellites, as you might be able to see more clearly in Figure 8-10.

Blackbirds

Blackbird is the nickname given to the Lockheed SR-71, a spy plane that first took flight in the 1960s. Thirty-two were built, and 12 of these were lost in flying accidents (remarkably, no SR-71 has ever been shot down). Some of the remaining planes now reside in museums, and others are technically still in service and can be found at airfields across the U.S.

The Lockheed SR-71

When I was a kid, I had posters on my wall of the Lockheed SR-71 reconnaissance aircraft, otherwise known as the Blackbird. The design of the airplane had a number of purposes, not least of which was to allow the plane to fly very, very fast. The cruising speed of the SR-71 was Mach 3.3 (that's 3.3 times the speed of sound), and it still holds the record for the fastest production aircraft (2,193.167 miles per hour). The plane flew not only fast, but also at very high altitudes: The original design reached 80,000 feet, with a record altitude just short of 85,069 feet (which was later broken by the Russian MiG-25).

To put those speeds into perspective, the Blackbird holds the U.S. coast-to-coast speed record of just 68 minutes, and the New York-to-London speed record of just under 1 hour and 54 minutes. As though you needed any further proof of the speed, in case of missile attack, the standard operating procedure was to simply accelerate and outrun it.

The Blackbird was also one of the first aircraft to be designed not to show up on radar—an astonishing feat for a plane that is more than 107 feet in length and more than 55 feet wide. The effect was to create a plane that appeared, on radar, to be about the size of a barn door rather than the size of a barn.

With all of this in mind, it is easy to see why the Blackbird has garnered such a cult following. The plane and its fictional derivatives have even appeared in numerous films, although not always in a factual or believable environment.

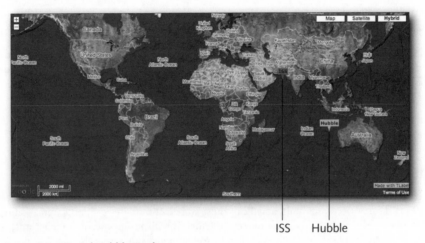

ISS   Hubble

FIGURE 8-9: ISS and Hubble Tracker.

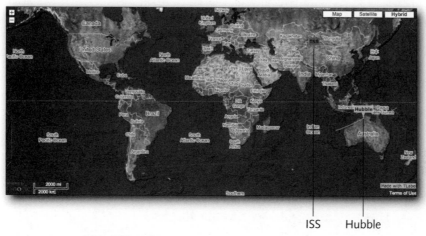

ISS   Hubble

FIGURE 8-10: ISS and Hubble paths.

To find the locations of all remaining Blackbirds and the crash points of those lost in service, you can visit the Blackbird-spotting Google Map (see Figure 8-11).

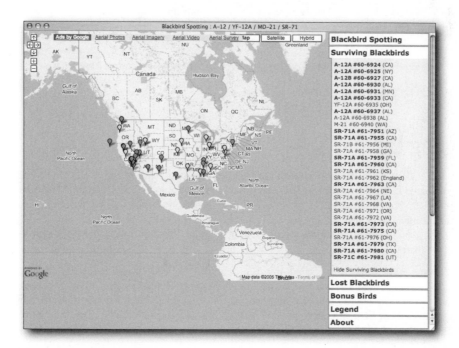

FIGURE 8-11: Blackbird spotter.

If you click on the list of available Blackbirds or one of the icon points, you get detailed information about the plane. The map will hone right in on the Google Earth photo of the plane so that you can see its precise location. Figure 8-12 shows the Blackbird on the USS *Intrepid*.

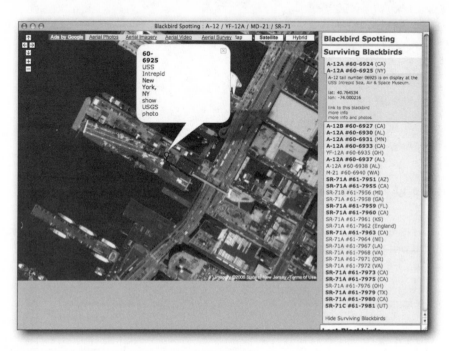

FIGURE 8-12: Spotting the SR-71 on the USS *Intrepid*.

Wrapping Up

Google Maps can be used to create a variety of different applications, from the most basic icon-based highlights right up to complex, interactive sites where information from a variety of sources is merged into a format that does more than simply overlay information onto a map. In this chapter, you've seen some examples of a wide range of map-based applications. Next you look at a simple way of building an information-driven application that is browser-driven rather than web site–driven.

With the information in this chapter, you should have some ideas and inspiration for your own maps, as well as a good idea of what the Google Maps system is capable of doing. Often, as demonstrated by the examples in this chapter, it is not just the map that helps to provide information. Outside data and alternative representations of information in combination with the Google Maps API demonstrate the power and flexibility for providing information.

Google Maps Hacks

part

in this part

Using Overlays

The overlay is the most basic piece of additional layout information that you can add to a Google Map, but it is also very powerful. By creating multiple Google Maps markers, you provide an effective way of highlighting different points on your map. With the addition of more detailed data about the point using an info window, you can provide a fully interactive experience.

This chapter shows how you can extend and improve upon the basic marker through a combination of the information that is displayed, how the marker is shown, and how additional information about the marker is displayed.

Building in Multiple Points

Chapter 7 covered the basic processes behind extending the basic Google Maps examples into your own custom maps, highlighting the points you wanted. It is the JavaScript within an HTML page that actually creates the points on the map, so any system that adds multiple points must be part of the JavaScript process.

How you add the additional points that you want to a map will largely depend on the complexity of the information, how dynamic you want the map to be, and the capabilities of your environment. For very simple maps and layouts, for example, you may simply want to extend the information in the HTML file for your map. In a more dynamic environment, you may want to generate the HTML dynamically. Both solutions are covered here, before more complex, completely dynamic solutions are covered later in this chapter.

Extending the Source HTML

The simplest method of adding more points to your map is to embed them into the HTML for your map. You cannot display a Google Map without some form of HTML component to encapsulate the JavaScript that defines the map parameters and properties.

Adding points in this way is therefore a case of adding the necessary JavaScript statements to the HTML. To extend the basic functionality a bit further than simply adding points, you'll also add a list of the points and create a small function that will move to a particular point when the highlighted point is clicked.

Listing 9-1 shows the entire HTML for an example demonstrating this process. The map shows a list of restaurants in Grantham in the U.K., and the remainder of the chapter demonstrates how to extend and improve on this original goal.

Note You can view this example, and all the examples from all of the chapters, online by using the chapter number and listing number. For example, to view the map generated by Listing 9-1, use the URL `http://maps.mcslp.com/examples/ch09-01.html`.

Listing 9-1: A More Complex Multiple Marker HTML Example

```
<!DOCTYPE html PUBLIC "-//W3C//DTD XHTML 1.0 Strict//EN"
"http://www.w3.org/TR/xhtml1/DTD/xhtml1-strict.dtd">
<html xmlns="http://www.w3.org/1999/xhtml">
<head>
<meta http-equiv="content-type" content="text/html; charset=UTF-8"/>

<title>MCslp Maps Chapter 9, Ex 1</title>
<script src="http://maps.google.com/maps?file=api&v=1&key=XXX"
    type="text/javascript">
</script>

<script type="text/javascript">


var map;

var points = [];
var index = 0;

var infopanel;

function onLoad() {
  if (GBrowserIsCompatible()) {
      infopanel = document.getElementById("infopanel");
      map = new GMap(document.getElementById("map"));
      map.centerAndZoom(new GPoint(-0.64,52.909444), 2);
      addmarker(-0.6394,52.9114,'China Inn');
      addmarker(-0.64,52.909444,'One on Wharf');
      addmarker(-0.64454,52.91066,'Hop Sing');
      addmarker(-0.642743,52.9123959,'Nicklebys');
      addmarker(-0.6376,52.9073,'Siam Garden');
  }
}

function addmarker(x,y,title) {
    var point = new GPoint(parseFloat(x),parseFloat(y));
    points.push(point);
    var marker = new GMarker(point);
    map.addOverlay(marker);
```

```
        infopanel.innerHTML = infopanel.innerHTML +
            '<a href="#" onClick="movemap(' + index + ');">' +
            title +
            '</a><br/>';
        index++;
}

function movemap(index) {
    map.recenterOrPanToLatLng(points[index]);
}


</script>
</head>
<body onload="onLoad()">
<table cellspacing="15" cellpadding="0" border="0">
<tr valign="top">
<td><div id="map" style="width: 800px; height: 600px"></div></td>
<td><h1>Restaurants</h1><div id="infopanel"></div></td>
</tr>
</table>
</body>
</html>
```

The key to the example is the `addmarker()` function. The function performs two operations:

- It creates the marker, based on the supplied longitude (x) and latitude (y) and title. The marker-creation process is three steps: create the point, create the marker, add the marker to the overlay.

- It creates an HTML link that runs the `movemap()` function each time the name of the marker is clicked. To achieve this, the document reference for the information window is generated during the `onLoad()` function. HTML is then appended to the doc reference by updating the content of the `innerHTML` property.

Each time a new point is created you add it to the global points array and then explicitly reference the index of that point into the HTML that is generated for each restaurant. That way, when each restaurant is clicked, it loads the previously created point from the array and recenters the map. The reason for using this method is that it reduces the amount of complex information that is referenced in different areas of the system. By standardizing where the information is kept, the application can also standardize how the information is referenced, which will have more relevance as the complexity of the examples increases.

The example can be seen in action in Figure 9-1. The info window can be seen on the right. Clicking the restaurant name recenters the map on the given marker. Clicking a marker does nothing, for the moment.

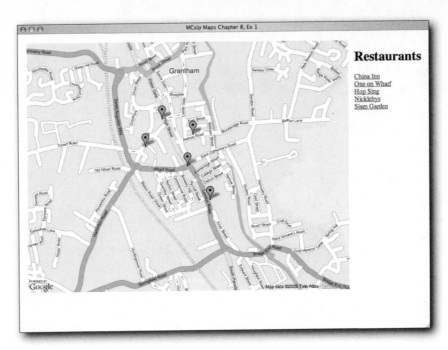

FIGURE 9-1: A basic multi-point HTML-only example.

Warning

Remember that coordinates are generally referenced using latitude and longitude in that order, although many of the built-in functions within the Google Maps API use the terms X and Y (or horizontal and vertical). Latitude is the vertical (Y) measure; longitude is the horizontal (X) measure.

Making the Generation Dynamic with a Script

The previous example used a static HTML file to generate the map. The static method has some limitations, including the most obvious one, that changing or editing the content means making modifications directly to the HTML.

Technically there is no problem with this approach, but you do not always want users to be able to edit the HTML on a live web server. It is better to use a method that dynamically generates the HTML and JavaScript required for the map based on a source of data separate from the map points and information on the screen.

The simplest way to dynamically create a Google Map is to change from using the static HTML method to a script-based method that generates the necessary HTML and JavaScript to build the map. The system is dynamic in that the script can be updated and the source for the information can be any reliable data source, such as static files or a database.

Listing 9-2 demonstrates the generation of a set of HTML identical to that generated in Listing 9-1. The difference is that this listing is a Perl script designed to run as a CGI. The information source is an embedded hash structure containing the X, Y, and title information for each restaurant. The script generates the necessary text when the script is called.

Listing 9-2: Generating a Google Map HTML File from a Script

```perl
#!/usr/bin/perl

use CGI qw/:standard/;

print header(-type => 'text/html');

my $points = [
              {x =>      -0.6394,
               y =>      52.9114,
               title => 'China Inn'},
              {x =>      -0.64,
               y =>      52.909444,
               title => 'One on Wharf'},
              {x =>      -0.64454,
               y =>      52.91066,
               title => 'Hop Sing'},
              {x =>      -0.642743,
               y =>      52.9123959,
               title => 'Nicklebys'},
              {x =>      -0.6376,
               y =>      52.9073,
               title => 'Siam Garden'},
              ];

page_header();
js_addmarker();
js_movemap();
js_onLoad();
page_footer();

sub page_header
{

print <<EOF;
<!DOCTYPE html PUBLIC "-//W3C//DTD XHTML 1.0 Strict//EN"
"http://www.w3.org/TR/xhtml1/DTD/xhtml1-strict.dtd">
<html xmlns="http://www.w3.org/1999/xhtml">
  <head>
  <meta http-equiv="content-type" content="text/html; charset=UTF-8"/>

  <title>MCslp Maps Chapter 9, Ex 2</title>
  <script src="http://maps.google.com/maps?file=api&v=1&key=XXX"
     type="text/javascript">
  </script>

  <script type="text/javascript">
```

Continued

Listing 9-2 *(continued)*

```perl
    var map;
    var points = [];
    var index = 0;
    var infopanel;
EOF
}


sub js_onLoad
{
    my @markers;

    foreach my $point (@{$points})
    {
        push @markers,sprintf("addmarker(%f,%f,'%s');",
                              $point->{x},
                              $point->{y},
                              $point->{title});
    }

    my $template = <<EOF;
  function onLoad() {
    if (GBrowserIsCompatible()) {
        infopanel = document.getElementById("infopanel");
        map = new GMap(document.getElementById("map"));
        map.centerAndZoom(new GPoint(-0.64,52.909444), 2);
        %s
    }
  }
EOF

    printf($template,join("\n",@markers));

}

sub js_addmarker
{
    print <<EOF;
  function addmarker(x,y,title) {
      var point = new GPoint(parseFloat(x),parseFloat(y));
      points.push(point);
      var marker = new GMarker(point);
      map.addOverlay(marker);
      infopanel.innerHTML = infopanel.innerHTML +
          '<a href="#" onClick="movemap(' + index + ');">' +
          title +
          '</a><br/>';
      index++;
  }
```

```
   EOF

   }

   sub js_movemap
   {

       print <<EOF;
     function movemap(index) {
         map.recenterOrPanToLatLng(points[index]);
     }
   EOF

   }

   sub page_footer
   {
       print <<EOF;
   </script>
   </head>
   <body onload="onLoad()">
   <table cellspacing="15" cellpadding="0" border="0">
   <tr valign="top">
   <td><div id="map" style="width: 800px; height: 600px"></div></td>
   <td><h1>Restaurants</h1><div id="infopanel"></div></td>
   </tr>
   </table>
   </body>
   </html>
   EOF

   }
```

Although Listing 9-2 is dynamic, it is only dynamic in that the information is being generated on the fly. It generates a static HTML page that works identically to the first example. The map itself and the information it portrays are not dynamic; the content and highlights on the map will be modified when the page is reloaded. This is essentially the same behavior as seen in the previous example. In short, though it technically is dynamically generating the information, it really isn't a dynamic map.

Using AJAX

For a dynamic map you need to use Asynchronous JavaScript and XML, or AJAX for short. AJAX is a methodology for loading information dynamically within a web page using JavaScript. With AJAX, the HTML page that is used to load the map and other information is static, but the JavaScript that is embedded within that page is capable of loading its own data and information, which it can then use to alter the information and operations on the map or the data displayed within the HTML.

For example, in the previous examples in this chapter the information generated when the page is loaded essentially creates a blank page. It is only when the JavaScript embedded into the page is loaded that the content of the page is altered, first by loading the Google Maps API and displaying the map, and second through the JavaScript generating HTML to be updated within an element of the HTML body.

AJAX works on the same basic principle. When the HTML of a page is loaded, it starts the JavaScript that loads additional information to be displayed. Alternatively, the trigger for loading additional information and then displaying that information on the screen can be a link or form embedded within the HTML.

The JavaScript function triggered then loads the data in XML format from the server, parses the XML content, and extracts the components it wants before updating the page. This entire process occurs without the page having to reload (because the user hasn't accessed a different page; the JavaScript is accessing data in the background).

In some ways this is similar to the way an image is loaded into a web page — the information is displayed inline within the realms of the page that you originally accessed; it is the browser that extracts the reference to the image and displays it onscreen. The difference with AJAX is that the information can be loaded from a variety of sources and the information and how it is shown is highly configurable.

Using AJAX relies on two elements:

- An HTML page with JavaScript that is capable of loading and parsing XML information to extract the data that it contains. Most browser implementations of JavaScript include the ability to load XML using a given URL and to then parse the content. For convenience, and to cope with different browser implementations, the Google Maps API includes a wrapper interface that will automatically use either the browser implementation or its own to handle the loading and parsing of content.

- An XML source that contains the information that you want to parse and display. The XML that is loaded can come from either a static file or a CGI script.

Before describing the methods for loading and parsing the XML, take a brief look at how the XML to be loaded can be generated.

Generating a Static XML File

Generating XML is not difficult, but there are some tricks to generating XML that is easily parsed and usable within JavaScript and Google Maps. For the majority of metadata about a particular map point, it is generally easier to extract information from attributes in a tag than it is to extract the data constrained by a tag. Using this method you can create a number of XML tags, and then within the JavaScript obtain a list of tags and extract the appropriate attributes from the tag, and generate the information.

For example, you might specify the latitude, longitude, and title data used in the earlier examples into a single XML tag:

```
<marker lat="52.9114" lng="-0.6394" title="China Inn"/>
```

A script to generate XML information based on the information previously stored within a hash in an earlier example can be adjusted to generate suitable XML, as shown here in Listing 9-3.

Listing 9-3: An XML Version of the Data

```perl
#!/usr/bin/perl

my $points = [
            {x =>      -0.6394,
             y =>      52.9114,
             title => 'China Inn'},
            {x =>      -0.64,
             y =>      52.909444,
             title => 'One on Wharf'},
            {x =>      -0.64454,
             y =>      52.91066,
             title => 'Hop Sing'},
            {x =>      -0.642743,
             y =>      52.9123959,
             title => 'Nicklebys'},
            {x =>      -0.6376,
             y =>      52.9073,
             title => 'Siam Garden'},
            ];


print '<marker>';

foreach my $point (@{$points})
{
    printf('<marker lat="%f" lng="%f" title="%s"/>',
           $point->{y},
           $point->{x},
           $point->{title});
}

print '</marker>';
```

Running this script will generate an XML document to the standard output, which you can redirect into a suitable file.

Note You might want to use an XML library to generate the XML that is used in your Google Maps applications. Although generating the XML by hand is an acceptable way to generate the data, it can lead to problems because of a simple typographical error. That said, some XML generation libraries can make the process more complicated and in some cases may simply be unable to create the complexity of document that you want if you are generating information from a database or non-linear data source.

Loading and parsing the file is a multi-stage process, starting with creating a suitable GXmlHttp object — a class exposed by the Google Maps API for loading remote HTTP:

```
var request = GXmlHttp.create();
```

To download an item you send a request for the specified file, in this case `ch09-04.xml`:

```
request.open('GET','ch09-04.xml', true);
```

Rather than blocking the execution of the rest of the JavaScript within the HTML until the load has been completed (which could be a long delay), instead you define a function that will be called when the status of the download object changes. You can do this inline; state 4 indicates a successful retrieval, so you can then start parsing the document:

```
request.onreadystatechange = function() {
if (request.readyState == 4) {
   var xmlsource = request.responseXML;
```

The `responseXML` field of the request contains a DOM representation of the XML data, which in turn means that you can use the same functions and methods that you use to manipulate HTML in the document. Thus you can use a list of the XML tags with a specific name using `getElementsByTagName`:

```
var markerlist = xmlsource.documentElement.getElementsByTagName("marker");
```

This generates an array of the individual tag elements. You can extract the information embedded into the attributes of a tag within each element by using the `getAttribute()` method on that element, specifying the attribute name. For example:

```
markerlist[i].getAttribute("lng")
```

You can repeat the same process on the same tag multiple times to get information out of multiple attributes.

Putting this together, and replacing the earlier `addmarker()` elements in the previous HTML-only examples with a model that dynamically loads the XML and then generates the markers, is shown in Listing 9-4.

Listing 9-4: Parsing Your XML File into Information

```
function onLoad() {
    if (GBrowserIsCompatible()) {
        infopanel = document.getElementById("infopanel");
        map = new GMap(document.getElementById("map"));
        map.centerAndZoom(new GPoint(-0.64,52.909444), 2);

        var request = GXmlHttp.create();
        request.open('GET','ch09-04.xml', true);
        request.onreadystatechange = function() {
            if (request.readyState == 4) {
                var xmlsource = request.responseXML;
                var markerlist = ⟳
xmlsource.documentElement.getElementsByTagName("marker");
                for (var i=0;i < markerlist.length;i++) {
                    addmarker(parseFloat(markerlist[i].getAttribute("lng")),
                            parseFloat(markerlist[i].getAttribute("lat")),
                            markerlist[i].getAttribute("title"));
```

```
                }
            }
        }
        request.send(null);
    }
}
```

The basic process is as listed earlier — the page is loaded, and during the `onLoad()` function the JavaScript requests the XML, loads it, parses the contents, and then generates the markers. The `addmarker()` function does not change; it doesn't need to.

You can see the results in Figure 9-2. The basic operation of the map has not changed; no additional information is being shown and, in reality, there is no interactivity built into the map, but the information that is generated is now more dynamic. Changing the XML (rather than the HTML) would change the information shown on the map.

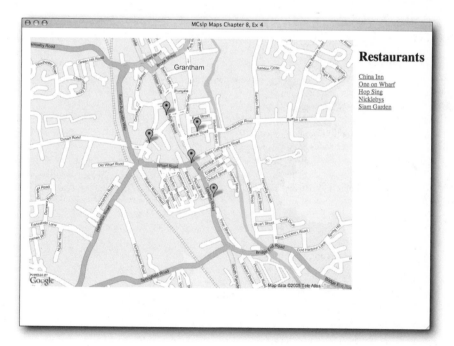

FIGURE 9-2: Generating a map by dynamically loading XML.

Tip   Always make sure that any numerical information that you load into JavaScript for use with your map, particularly when specifying latitude or longitude, is first parsed with the `parseFloat()` function (or `parseInt()`) to ensure that the string is correctly identified as a number.

Generating an XML File Dynamically

In the previous example a static XML file was generated by adapting an earlier script. Ultimately, though, the map interface was loading static XML. Loading XML that is generated on the fly is the next phase toward building a truly dynamic interface. Listing 9-5 shows an adaptation of the earlier XML generating example that runs as a CGI and returns the XML based on the earlier requirements.

Listing 9-5: Generating the XML File with Perl on the Fly

```perl
#!/usr/bin/perl

use CGI qw/:standard/;

print header(-type => 'text/xml');

my $points = [
            {x =>      -0.6394,
             y =>      52.9114,
             title => 'China Inn'},
            {x =>      -0.64,
             y =>      52.909444,
             title => 'One on Wharf'},
            {x =>      -0.64454,
             y =>      52.91066,
             title => 'Hop Sing'},
            {x =>      -0.642743,
             y =>      52.9123959,
             title => 'Nicklebys'},
            {x =>      -0.6376,
             y =>      52.9073,
             title => 'Siam Garden'},
            ];

print '<marker>';

foreach my $point (@{$points})
{
    printf('<marker lat="%f" lng="%f" title="%s"/>',
           $point->{y},
           $point->{x},
           $point->{title});
}

print '</marker>';
```

The script uses the CGI module, a standard module within the Perl distribution, to generate the information.

Note The most important line in this script is the one that outputs the HTTP header. When supplying XML you must specify the correct header for the returned data to ensure that it is correctly identified as XML and not HTML.

You also need to update the URL of the XML file you want to load to reference the new CGI script. However, in all other respects the main HTML interface developed for the earlier example is still entirely valid. Updating the URL is a simple case of changing the appropriate line to the request object:

```
request.open('GET','/examples/ch09-05.cgi', true);
```

The map output will be the same, but the way the map gets the information to be displayed has changed. You could replace the static information within the script with a system that generates the same XML structure, but from a different source, such as directly from a database.

Pulling the Data from a Database

The previous examples have concentrated on the production of information that is largely static. Even when the XML content was generated dynamically, the source for that XML data was actually just a hash within a Perl script that generated the information.

Although it would be trivial to update the information within the script, it still lacks the flexibility of updating a database of information that in turn generates the necessary XML.

Creating a Suitable Database Structure

To load the information from a database, there must be a suitable database structure in place that can be accessed through a CGI script, which can then reformat the information from the database to the XML format required by Google Maps.

The examples here are in Perl, which can access a database using the DBI module through a number of different databases, including local files, MySQL, PostgreSQL, and Oracle. Other environments, such as PHP, Java, or Ruby, have similar interfaces and systems. Depending on the database system in use, you will also probably need to create a database to hold the table being used for your information.

Whichever system you use, the first step should be to create a suitable table structure to hold the information. To replicate the same structure for the restaurants used in earlier examples, only three fields are required: the latitude, longitude, and restaurant name. With most systems, tables are created by using a suitable SQL statement. The following statement would create a suitable table:

```
create table ch09_simple (lat float,lng float,title varchar(80))
```

Note Remember latitude and longitude can be represented in a number of different ways, but the method used internally by the Google Maps system is a floating-point value, so you will need to use floating-point fields in your database.

Listing 9-6 demonstrates a simple script that connects to the database and creates the table.

Listing 9-6: Creating the Table Structure

```perl
#!/usr/bin/perl

use DBI;

my $dbh = DBI->connect( 'dbi:mysql:database=mapsbookex;host=db.maps.mcslp.com',
                        'mapsbookex',
                        'examples',
                        );

if (defined($dbh))
{
    $dbh->do('create table ch09_simple ⊃
(lat float,lng float,title varchar(80))');
}
else
{
    die "Couldn't open connection to database\n";
}
```

Converting existing data and inserting that information into the database is a common task. Listing 9-7 is a script that translates a colon-separated version of the restaurant information (in title, longitude, latitude order) into the database and table that you created in Listing 9-6.

Listing 9-7: Populating the Database with Information

```perl
#!/usr/bin/perl

use DBI;

my $dbh = DBI->connect( 'dbi:mysql:database=mapsbookex;host=db.maps.mcslp.com',
                        'mapsbookex',
                        'examples',
                        );

if (!defined($dbh))
{
    die "Couldn't open connection to database\n";
}

open(DATA,$ARGV[0]) or die "Couldn't open file; did you forget it?";

my $counter = 0;

while(<DATA>)
{
    chomp;
```

```perl
    my ($title,$lng,$lat) = split /:/;

    $dbh->do(sprintf('insert into ch09_simple values(%s,%s,%s)',
                     $dbh->quote($lat),
                     $dbh->quote($lng),
                     $dbh->quote($title),
                     ));
    $counter++;
}
close(DATA);

print "$counter records inserted\n";
```

With the information correctly inserted the table, the rows in the table can be used to generate the XML information that is required by the HTML interface to load the data.

Generating XML from that Information

With a slight modification to an earlier script, a script that loads the information from the database table and generates the information as XML is shown in Listing 9-8. Instead of inserting data, a SELECT statement is used to extract the data from the database, and then the script reformats the data into XML ready for a Google Maps application.

Listing 9-8: Generating XML from Database Source Data

```perl
#!/usr/bin/perl

use DBI;
use strict;

my $dbh = DBI->connect( 'dbi:mysql:database=mapsbookex;host=db.maps.mcslp.com',
                        'mapsbookex',
                        'examples',
                        );

if (!defined($dbh))
{
    die "Couldn't open connection to database\n";
}

my @lines;

my $sth = $dbh->prepare('select title,lat,lng from ch09_simple');
$sth->execute();

while (my $row = $sth->fetchrow_hashref())

{
```

Continued

Listing 9-8 *(continued)*

```perl
    push(@lines,
        sprintf('<marker lat="%f" lng="%f" title="%s"/>',
                $row->{lat},
                $row->{lng},
                $row->{title}));
}
$sth->finish();

if (scalar @lines > 0)
{
    print("<marker>\n",
          join("\n",@lines),
          "</marker>\n");
}
```

The script in Listing 9-8 can also be adapted into Listing 9-9 so that the information is generated dynamically, through a CGI, into the XML required by the HTML interface. The only difference is the addition of the correct HTTP header type.

Listing 9-9: Generating the XML from a Database through CGI

```perl
#!/usr/bin/perl

use DBI;
use strict;
use CGI qw/:standard/;

print header(-type => 'text/xml');

my $dbh = DBI->connect( 'dbi:mysql:database=mapsbookex;host=db.maps.mcslp.com',
                        'mapsbookex',
                        'examples',
                        );

if (!defined($dbh))
{
    die "Couldn't open connection to database\n";
}

print("<marker>\n");

my $sth = $dbh->prepare('select title,lat,lng from ch09_simple');
$sth->execute();

while (my $row = $sth->fetchrow_hashref())
{
```

```
    printf('<marker lat="%f" lng="%f" title="%s"/>',
           $row->{lat},
           $row->{lng},
           $row->{title});

}
$sth->finish();

print("</marker>\n");
```

Now that the information is located within a database, further restaurants can be added to the map by adding rows to the database. There could be a potentially unlimited number of restaurants in the database, and the method in which the database is updated (from another web interface or desktop application, or even a feed from another database or application) becomes immaterial. The source does not matter.

What does matter is that the basic script and HTML page that was developed to display a map of restaurants in a particular location has not changed. Only the source of information driving the data displayed on the map has changed.

Note A sample of the map using information loaded from a database through the script in Listing 9-9 is available online at `http://maps.mcslp.com/examples/ch09-09.html`.

Extending the Information Pane

Back in Chapter 7, a logical extension of the basic map marker was to add an information window to the marker when the user clicks the marker. The idea of the information pane is to show relevant information for a map point.

There are many ways of populating the pane with information, but the most practical, because the map is now being built up using an XML source, is to continue using XML to generate the content. This will require changes to the database to store more information such as the address and phone number of the restaurant.

The HTML that generates the map will also need to be adapted so that the map marker and information window are displayed when the user clicks the marker.

Formatting Information Panes

As shown in Chapter 7, an information pane is added to a marker by adding an event listener to the marker that triggers one of the `openInfoWindow*()` functions to create an information window. The `addmarker()` function within the JavaScript in the HTML can be modified so that it adds the necessary event listener at the time when the marker is generated.

Listing 9-10 contains such a modification. Obviously, how the information is loaded that generates this information has not changed; the same principles can be used with either the static or dynamic samples. For the moment, it is the information window trigger that is interesting.

Listing 9-10: Adjusting the JavaScript to Create an Information Window

```
function addmarker(x,y,title) {
    var point = new GPoint(parseFloat(x),parseFloat(y));
    points.push(point);
    var marker = new GMarker(point);
    GEvent.addListener(marker,
                       'click',
                       function() {
        marker.openInfoWindowHtml('<b>' + title + '</b>');
    }
                       );
    map.addOverlay(marker);
    infopanel.innerHTML = infopanel.innerHTML +
        '<a href="#" onClick="movemap(' + index + ');">' +
        title +
        '</a><br/>';
    index++;
}
```

The limitation of the preceding solution is that you have to format the HTML that is contained within the panel by hand, although as you can see from Figure 9-3, the result is quite effective.

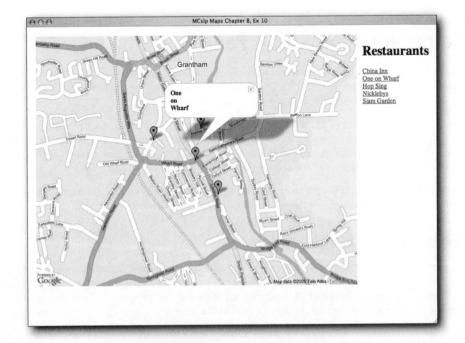

FIGURE 9-3: A basic information window.

Creating More Detailed Windows from XML and XSLT

The Extensible Stylesheet Language (XSL) provides a method for converting XML data into different formats through an XSL Transformation (XSLT). Google Maps includes a routine for formatting XML data through an XSL file into the HTML that is displayed within an info window. The HTML layout and format can be changed by altering the XSL without making any changes to the JavaScript. In addition, because the HTML is generated from the XML generated, the information that is displayed can be extended by adding information to the generated XML.

The first step toward that process is to generate the XML. For XSL, you normally generate the XML information where the data is contained within appropriate XML tags. For example, you might add phone information to the XML with this fragment:

```
<phone>0123456789</phone>
```

In addition, for your JavaScript-based parser, for ease of extraction you should put the entire block of XML data into an enclosing tag; for example, `infowindow`.

Listing 9-11 shows the generation (as a CGI script directly to XML) of suitable data from an adjusted database table based on the table created earlier in this chapter (Listing 9-7).

Listing 9-11: Creating the XML

```perl
#!/usr/bin/perl

use DBI;
use strict;
use CGI qw/:standard/;

print header(-type => 'text/xml');

my $dbh = DBI->connect( 'dbi:mysql:database=mapsbookex;host=db.maps.mcslp.com',
                        'mapsbookex',
                        'examples',
                        );

if (!defined($dbh))
{
    die "Couldn't open connection to database\n";
}

print("<marker>\n");

my $sth = $dbh->prepare('select * from ch09_cplx');
$sth->execute();

while (my $row = $sth->fetchrow_hashref())
```

Continued

Listing 9-11 *(continued)*

```
{
    printf('<marker lat="%f" lng="%f" title="%s"><infowindow> ↵
<title>%s</title><address>%s</address><city>%s</c\ity> ↵
<postcode>%s</postcode><phone>%s</phone></infowindow></marker>',
            $row->{lat},
            $row->{lng},
            $row->{title},
            $row->{title},
            $row->{street},
            $row->{city},
            $row->{postcode},
            $row->{phone},
            );

}
$sth->finish();

print("</marker>\n");
```

The result is an XML file where each restaurant is defined through XML containing the latitude, longitude, and full address information:

```
<marker lat="52.911400" lng="-0.639400" title="China Inn">
<infowindow>
<title>China Inn</title>
<address>4 Avenue Road</address>
<city>Grantham</city>
<postcode>NG31 6TA</postcode>
<phone>01476 570033</phone>
</infowindow>
</marker>
```

To translate the embedded XML file, an XSL file is required. Describing the specifics of XSL is obviously beyond the scope of this book, but you should be able to identify the basic structure of the document. Basically, the XSL in Listing 9-12 defines a structure that will convert the embedded XML information into an HTML table.

Note A good source for more information on XSL is *XSL Essentials* by Michael Fitzgerald (Wiley, ISBN 0-471-41620-7).

Listing 9-12: The XSL

```
<?xml version="1.0" encoding="ISO-8859-1" ?>
  <xsl:stylesheet version="1.0" ↩
xmlns:xsl="http://www.w3.org/1999/XSL/Transform">
  <xsl:template match="/">
        <xsl:apply-templates select="info" />
  </xsl:template>
  <xsl:template match="infowindow">

        <table width="215" cellspacing="15">
        <tr>
        <td style="font-size:14pt;text-align:Left;" colspan="2">
                <xsl:value-of select="title" />
        </td>
        </tr>
        <tr valign="top">
        <td style="font-size:12pt;font-weight:bold;text-align:Left;">
                Address
        </td>
        <td style="font-size:12pt;text-align:Left;">
                <xsl:value-of select="address" /> <br/>
                <xsl:value-of select="city" /> <br/>
                <xsl:value-of select="postcode" /> <br/>
        </td>
        </tr>
        <tr>
        <td style="font-size:12pt;font-weight:bold;text-align:Left;">
                Phone
        </td>
        <td style="font-size:12pt;text-align:Left;">
                <xsl:value-of select="phone" />
        </td>
        </tr>
</table>
</xsl:template>
</xsl:stylesheet>
```

Listing 9-13 shows the necessary changes to the JavaScript to create the information window.

Listing 9-13: Creating an Info Window from XML and XSLT

```
function onLoad() {
    if (GBrowserIsCompatible()) {
        infopanel = document.getElementById("infopanel");
        map = new GMap(document.getElementById("map"));
        map.centerAndZoom(new GPoint(-0.64,52.909444), 2);

        var request = GXmlHttp.create();
```

Continued

Listing 9-13 *(continued)*

```
        request.open('GET','/examples/ch09-11.cgi', true);
        request.onreadystatechange = function() {
            if (request.readyState == 4) {
                var xmlsource = request.responseXML;
                var markerlist = ↩
xmlsource.documentElement.getElementsByTagName("marker");
                var infowindow = ↩
xmlsource.documentElement.getElementsByTagName("infowindow");
                for (var i=0;i < markerlist.length;i++) {
                    addmarker(parseFloat(markerlist[i].getAttribute("lng")),
                              parseFloat(markerlist[i].getAttribute("lat")),
                              markerlist[i].getAttribute("title"),
                              infowindow[i]);
                }
            }
        }
        request.send(null);
    }
}

function addmarker(x,y,title,info) {
    var point = new GPoint(parseFloat(x),parseFloat(y));
    points.push(point);
    var marker = new GMarker(point);
    GEvent.addListener(marker,
                       'click',
                       function() {
        marker.openInfoWindowXslt(info,"/examples/ch09-12.xsl");
    }
                       );
    map.addOverlay(marker);
    infopanel.innerHTML = infopanel.innerHTML +
        '<a href="#" onClick="movemap(' + index + ');">' +
        title +
        '</a><br/>';
    index++;
}
```

When parsing the XML, the onLoad() function extracts the data contained within the XML tag infowindow and places each occurrence into an array, in exactly the same way as the original marker tags were extracted.

A further argument is then added to the addmarker() function that incorporates the XML contained within the infowindow tag, which in turn is used with the openInfoWindowXslt() method on each marker. This method takes the XML (or an object containing the XML) and URL of the XSL stylesheet (see Listing 9-12). The remainder of the code is identical to the other examples.

You can see the resulting information window in Figure 9-4. The information displayed is much more extensive, and you could add and extend that information even further simply by updating the database with more data, the XML with that data, and the XSL with a suitable transformation to turn it into the structure you want.

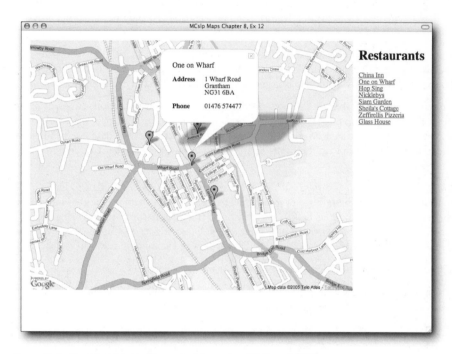

FIGURE 9-4: Creating information windows using XML and XSLT.

Everything is now in place to extend the example and make the map truly interactive and dynamic.

Making Your Example Truly Dynamic

The examples in this chapter have made use of static, dynamic, and ultimately XML generation techniques to allow the information within a map to be controlled through the data stored within a database. However, the map is still static, from the perspective that although markers and points are being generated dynamically from XML, they are being generated when the page loads, rather than in true response to user requirements. To make the system truly dynamic, the interface to the database needs to be adjusted so that you load specific information based on the user requirements.

Dividing the Application into Components

Before the specific scripts and elements are described, take a closer look at the elements that make up a dynamic map.

Previous examples have been dynamic when loading the XML, but the XML that was generated, although generated on the fly, was based on a static SQL statement pulling out every record from the table.

For your dynamic example, the HTML file (and the JavaScript that supports it) will be the only component that you load. Everything else about the page will be based entirely on JavaScript loading XML and making modifications to the HTML and the Google Map.

To start with, the database will be extended to show data about restaurants in towns and cities other than Grantham. Instead of initially showing Grantham on the map, the whole of the U.K. will be displayed instead, and a list of all the unique cities in the database will be listed in the information window on the right. That list of cities will need to be requested from the database.

Once the database has returned a list of cities, the application will provide this list in a method that in turn triggers the JavaScript to list the restaurants from that specific city and display them in the same manner as before. In addition to the information window being triggered when the user clicks an information marker, you will also trigger the information window when the user clicks the restaurant name in the list (as opposed to moving the map to that marker).

Finally, the user will be able to return to a list of the available cities.

The entire process, and the interaction between the main HTML page and the server that provides the data to be used on the page, can be seen in Figure 9-5.

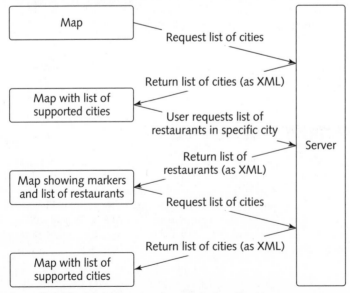

FIGURE 9-5: The interactive map operations in action.

The final system relies on three components:

- An HTML file with embedded JavaScript that provides the methods for loading and formatting data in a suitable structure.

- A CGI script that can return information about the available cities and restaurants within a specific city in XML format.

- An XSL file to format the information window for a restaurant and marker.

The JavaScript is the main component.

The JavaScript Component

The bulk of the HTML for a page does not change, but the JavaScript that loads the city, hotel, and other information in response to different triggers needs to be heavily updated.

Setting Up the Environment

The JavaScript will rely on the global variables in Listing 9-14 to hold the information that is required throughout the rest of the script.

Note Most languages frown on the heavy use of global variables, but in JavaScript the active, and inactive, elements make it difficult to communicate and share information across the different components without using global variables.

Listing 9-14: Global Variables

```
var map;
var points = [];
var index = 0;
var cities = [];
var markers = [];
var markerinfo = []
var infopanel;
var message;
```

The arrays are used to hold information about the main components of the application — points on the map, cities, markers, and the contents of information windows. These variables will need to be populated as different information is loaded by the JavaScript so that you can select other information to be displayed onscreen.

Loading a City List

Loading a list of cities to be displayed on the default page for the map is based on the same principles as loading a list of restaurants, except that a different XML document is parsed. To get the different XML document, you supply some arguments to the GET request through the script that provides an interface to the database. The CGI script is asked for a list of cities, which it collects from the database and returns as XML, placing the name of each city into a suitable attribute in an appropriate tag.

Listing 9-15 shows the showcitylist() function. This function is responsible for connecting to the CGI script, requesting a list of cities, and formatting that list of cities as a list of clickable links that will in turn trigger the loading of restaurants in a city.

Listing 9-15: Showing a List of Cities

```
function showcitylist() {
    map.clearOverlays();
    index = 0;
    points = [];
    markers = [];
    markerinfo = [];
    cities = [];    message.innerHTML = 'Select a City';
    infopanel.innerHTML = '';
    var request = GXmlHttp.create();
    request.open('GET','/examples/ch09-16.cgi?m=citylist', true);
    request.onreadystatechange = function() {
        if (request.readyState == 4) {
            var xmlsource = request.responseXML;
            var citylist = ⊃
xmlsource.documentElement.getElementsByTagName("city");
            for (var i=0;i < citylist.length;i++) {
                cities.push(citylist[i].getAttribute("cityname"));
                infopanel.innerHTML = infopanel.innerHTML +
                    '<a href="#" onClick="loadcity(' +
                    i +
                    ');">' +
                    citylist[i].getAttribute("cityname") +
                    '</a><br/>';
            }
        }
    }
    request.send(null);
}
```

Although when the script is initially executed all of the global variables will effectively be empty, the showcitylist() function can also be called once a list of restaurants in a given city have been listed, effectively resetting the application. The first step therefore is to reset the contents of all the variables. You then format the HTML information window with a list of available cities by loading the data from the CGI script as XML and creating a list of suitable links.

When the user clicks an individual city, the loadcity() function is triggered (see Listing 9-16). On the whole, this function is almost identical to the previous examples in this chapter; it asks the CGI script for a list of restaurants in a given city.

Listing 9-16: Loading Markers for a City

```
function loadcity(index) {
    map.clearOverlays();
    message.innerHTML = 'Restaurants in ' + cities[index];
    infopanel.innerHTML = '';
    var latpoints = [];
    var lngpoints = [];
    var request = GXmlHttp.create();
    request.open('GET','/examples/ch09-16.cgi?m=getmarkers&city='+ ⮐
cities[index], true);
    request.onreadystatechange = function() {
        if (request.readyState == 4) {
            var xmlsource = request.responseXML;
            var markerlist = ⮐
xmlsource.documentElement.getElementsByTagName("marker");
            var infowindow = ⮐
xmlsource.documentElement.getElementsByTagName("infowindow");
            for (var i=0;i < markerlist.length;i++) {
                addmarker(parseFloat(markerlist[i].getAttribute("lng")),
                          parseFloat(markerlist[i].getAttribute("lat")),
                          markerlist[i].getAttribute("title"),
                          infowindow[i],
                          i);
                latpoints.push(parseFloat(markerlist[i].getAttribute("lat")));
                lngpoints.push(parseFloat(markerlist[i].getAttribute("lng")));
            }
            var newcenter = calccenter(latpoints,lngpoints);
            map.centerAndZoom(newcenter,2);
            infopanel.innerHTML = infopanel.innerHTML +
                '<br/>' +
                '<a href="#" onClick="showcitylist()">Back to ⮐
city list</a><br/>';
        }
    }
    request.send(null);
}
```

The main differences are the rebuilding of the information window, a modified call to the CGI script, and some additional steps to be executed when the markers have been added to the map.

The URL used to load the XML from the CGI script now builds a suitable request that includes the name of the city. This will provide the CGI script with the information it requires to return a list of restaurants in the specified city.

As each marker is added to the map, an array of the latitude and longitude points is updated. You will use this information to relocate the map over the center point of the all of the restaurants for the city.

As a final step, you add a link to the city loading function so that the user can go back and select a city again.

Moving the Map and Adding Information

When the user clicks a restaurant in the information window, the map recenters on the marker and then shows the information window. For convenience, the information window XML was placed into a global array, and each element of the array should have the same index as the points for the restaurant. You can open the window by calling the `openInfoWindowXslt()` method on the appropriate marker with the same window information that is triggered by the click event for the marker. The two lines of the `movemap()` function are shown in Listing 9-17.

Listing 9-17: Moving the Map and Displaying the Info Window

```
function movemap(index) {
    map.recenterOrPanToLatLng(points[index]);
    markers[index].openInfoWindowXslt(markerinfo[index], ⤳
"/examples/ch09-12.xsl");
}
```

The `markers`, `points`, and `markerinfo` arrays are built each time the `addmarker()` function is called.

Adding a Marker to Your Map

Listing 9-18 is a small modification to the `addmarker()` function that updates the arrays necessary for `movemap()`, in addition to configuring the point, marker, and event and the information window.

Listing 9-18: Creating a New Marker

```
function addmarker(x,y,title,info,index) {
    var point = new GPoint(parseFloat(x),parseFloat(y));
    points.push(point);
    var marker = new GMarker(point);
    markers.push(marker);
    markerinfo.push(info);
    GEvent.addListener(marker,
                       'click',
                       function() {
        marker.openInfoWindowXslt(info,"/examples/ch09-12.xsl");
    }
                       );
    map.addOverlay(marker);
    infopanel.innerHTML = infopanel.innerHTML +
        '<a href="#" onClick="movemap(' + index + ');">' +
        title +
        '</a><br/>';
    index++;
}
```

Calculating Where to Center the Map

The final stage of moving the map to the location of the city that is being displayed is to determine a suitable point that can be used as the new center point for the map.

You could choose to display one of the restaurants as the new center point, but a much more effective method is to calculate the middle point between the extremes of latitude and longitude for the displayed markers. Essentially what you are after is the average, or more specifically the median, of the range of points.

There is no simple way of achieving this, although you could potentially ask the database to determine the information. Because this would imply further processing of data that you already have, it is just as easy to calculate it from that data. You can find the midpoint by determining the difference between the highest and lowest value and adding half the difference to the lower value. To determine the lowest and highest values, use the following logic: If the latitude and longitude points for each marker are added to an array and the array is sorted, the minimum and maximum values will be the first and last values in the array, respectively.

Listing 9-19 performs these operations, returning a new `GPoint()` to the caller that can be used to recenter the map.

Listing 9-19: Determining a New Center Point

```
function calccenter(latpoints,lngpoints) {
    latpoints.sort();
    lngpoints.sort();
    var newlat = latpoints[0] + ⏎
((latpoints[latpoints.length-1] - latpoints[0])/2);
    var newlng = lngpoints[0] + ⏎
((lngpoints[lngpoints.length-1] - lngpoints[0])/2);
    var newpoint = new GPoint(parseFloat(newlng),parseFloat(newlat));
    return newpoint;
}
```

The last stage to the process is initializing the entire system so that the application is in a state ready to start accepting user clicks.

Initializing the Map

In previous examples, the `onLoad()` function has been quite complex. For this example, the main part of the initialization in terms of providing interactivity now resides in the `showcitylist()` function. The main role of the `onLoad()` function, shown in Listing 9-20, is to initialize the map and obtain the location of the HTML elements that will be used to show information about the application, such as the message and information window.

Listing 9-20: Updating the onLoad() Function

```
function onLoad() {
    if (GBrowserIsCompatible()) {
        infopanel = document.getElementById("infopanel");
        message = document.getElementById("message");
        map = new GMap(document.getElementById("map"));
        map.centerAndZoom(new GPoint(-2.944336,53.644638), 10);
        map.addControl(new GSmallZoomControl());
        showcitylist();
    }
}
```

That completes the JavaScript functionality. The next part of the application is the CGI script that generates the XML used by this application.

Generating the XML on the Backend

Listing 9-21 is an adaptation of the earlier XML generation scripts. Remember that the script now needs to return two different pieces of information: a list of cities and a list of restaurants within a given city. Both operations are triggered through certain CGI parameters specified by the URL reference in the JavaScript component that wants to load the XML.

Listing 9-21: Generating the Necessary XML

```
#!/usr/bin/perl

use DBI;
use strict;
use CGI qw/:standard/;

print header(-type => 'text/xml');

my $dbh = DBI->connect( 'dbi:mysql:database=mapsbookex;host=db.maps.mcslp.com',
                        'mapsbookex',
                        'examples',
                        );

if (!defined($dbh))
{
    die "Couldn't open connection to database\n";
}

if (param('m') eq 'citylist')
{
    citylist();
```

```perl
}
elsif(param('m') eq 'getmarkers')
{
    getmarkers(param('city'));
}

sub citylist
{
    my $sth = $dbh->prepare('select distinct(city) from ch09_cplx');
    $sth->execute();

    print "<cities>";
    while (my $row = $sth->fetchrow_hashref())
    {
        printf('<city cityname="%s"/>>',$row->{city});
    }
    print "</cities>";
}

sub getmarkers
{
    my ($city) = @_;

    print("<markers>\n");

    my $sth = $dbh->prepare(sprintf('select * from ch09_cplx where city = %s',
                                    $dbh->quote($city)));
    $sth->execute();

    while (my $row = $sth->fetchrow_hashref())
    {
        printf('<marker lat="%f" lng="%f" title="%s">
<infowindow><title>%s</title><address>%s</address><city>%\
s</city><postcode>%s</postcode><phone>%s</phone></infowindow></marker>',
                $row->{lat},
                $row->{lng},
                $row->{title},
                $row->{title},
                $row->{street},
                $row->{city},
                $row->{postcode},
                $row->{phone},
                );

    }
    $sth->finish();

    print("</markers>\n");
}
```

There are two elements here, both in separate functions. The `citylist()` function uses a SQL statement to select a list of distinct cities from the database. The other function, `getmarkers()`, returns the list of restaurants. This function is based on the earlier example, only the SQL statement that selects the list of cities now requests only restaurants that are located within a specific city.

Using the New Map

You can see the new map, in its initial state, in Figure 9-6. You can see here that the initial mode is for the window to show a list of available cities. The database has been updated to also include the restaurants for a town in the Lake District in the U.K., Ambleside, so the default city list now includes both options.

Note   The final application is available online at `http://maps.mcslp.com/examples/ch09-14.html`.

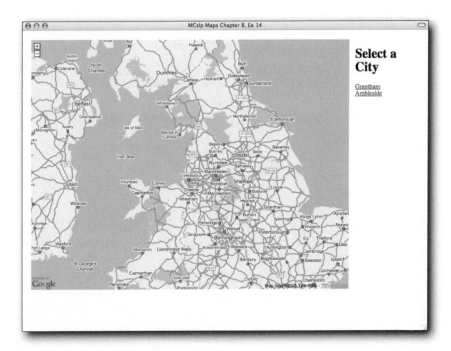

FIGURE 9-6: A dynamic application in its initial state.

If you click a city, the JavaScript loads the XML for the specific city by asking the CGI script to supply it with new XML. The XML is loaded, the markers are added to the map, and the map is recentered in the middle of all the markers. You can see a representation of restaurants in Ambleside in Figure 9-7.

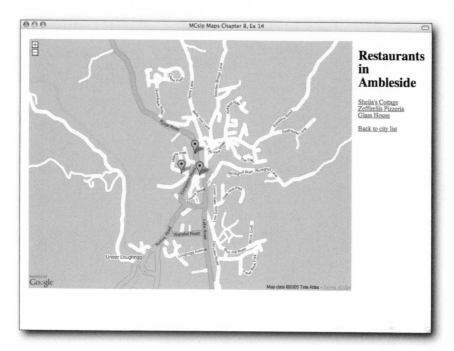

FIGURE 9-7: Restaurants in Ambleside.

Finally, clicking a marker or restaurant name shows the information window, as shown in Figure 9-8.

Clicking "Back to city list" would show the list of cities again (see Figure 9-9). The entire process has taken place without having to load any different pages, and all of the information is loaded from a database.

Extending the Content

The real power of the preceding solution is that you can easily extend the information and data provided on the map — even the list of supported cities — just by updating the database backend. By entering more restaurant titles, address information, map points, and other data into the database, you can add cities, restaurants, and contact information to the map without ever making any changes to either the HTML or the JavaScript demonstrated in this section.

It is possible, for example, to extend the basic interface so that the user could select entity types (restaurants, pubs, doctors, shops, and so on) from within the interface in addition to being able to choose a city to display. It is also not hard to imagine how you might extend this further to display an array of different information on the same map just by loading different selections of information. After all, it is the database query that loads the information that is to be displayed; a different query could load and display different information.

It is the combination of database-driven content, the CGI script that provides this information in XML format, the AJAX components that load this data, and the Google Maps API that enable you to lay all of this information out onscreen that provides you with power and flexibility.

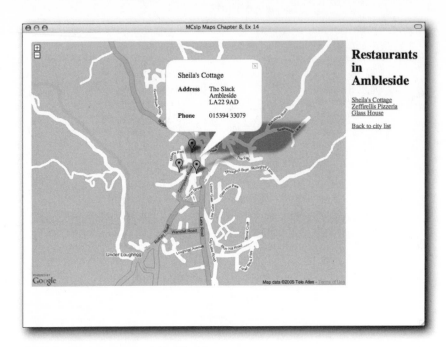

FIGURE 9-8: Sheila's Cottage in Ambleside.

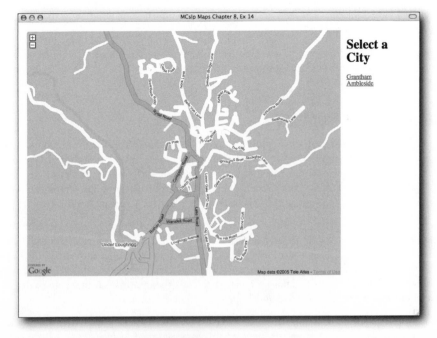

FIGURE 9-9: Going back to a list of cities.

Wrapping Up

As you have seen in this chapter it is the combination of the JavaScript, dynamic data, and the ability to parse and lay out this information in a dynamic environment that makes using Google Maps so much fun. Although the code is comparatively complex if you are not familiar with JavaScript, many of the basic principles should be straightforward.

Thanks to what you've learned in this chapter, you should now be able to build your own dynamic marker-based Google Maps. Populating a database with the information and then highlighting the right points onto the map is comparatively straightforward when you break down the system into manageable steps. With the basic techniques here, you could also show different businesses or cities and even build a worldwide map of highlighted points using the same basic structure that is shown in this chapter.

Now that the basics of a dynamically driven mapping environment are in place, it is time to extend the functionality. The next chapter covers the display and portrayal of statistical information and introduces new techniques that include polylines and different display icons.

Overlaying Statistical Data

With a map and some appropriate geographical information, you can plot statistical information (that is, information that has some sort of quantity across a range of different points) onto a Google Map. For example, you could plot the number of accidents at different intersections in a city, or highlight the number of sporting events in different cities across an entire country.

Viewing statistical information in a graphical form often makes the information significantly easier to understand. For example, in this chapter the population data of cities in the U.S. is used, and although a tabular form of the information is helpful, the graphical representations shown in this chapter make it much easier to understand the relationship and relative size of the different cities across the U.S.

Fortunately, as you'll see in this chapter, there are many ways in which statistical information can be overlaid on top of a Google Map. Polylines (the lines that Google Maps uses to show maps and routes) are one way, and you can alter their behavior slightly to give some other alternatives. A better solution, though, may be to use a custom icon.

Generating/Obtaining Statistical Information

There is a wealth of statistical information available if you start looking. The key element for displaying the information on a Google Map is that it has some kind of geographical relevance. Secondary to this consideration is how you want to represent that information.

For example, throughout this chapter the U.S. Census data on population is used (using the data from http://www.census.gov/). The information is available on a year-by-year basis. It is also available on a city-by-city (and state-by-state) basis. With these two combinations of information it is possible to show the population data both according to its location and to its year, and, by combining the two, the population growth over time can also be demonstrated.

First, the raw data.

The U.S. Census Data

For the examples in this chapter the population of different cities in the U.S. is used to provide the statistical information that is displayed on the map. The information used comes from the U.S. Census data and is based on questionnaires completed by the public. Looking at a table of that information (Table 10-1) is not a clear way to view the data. The table has been deliberately sorted alphabetically so there isn't any order to the population statistics.

Table 10-1   U.S. Census City Population Data

City	2004	2000	1990
Chicago, Ill.	2,862,244	2,896,016	2,783,726
Columbus, Ohio	730,008	711,470	632,910
Dallas, Tex.	1,210,393	1,188,580	1,006,877
Detroit, Mich.	900,198	951,270	1,027,974
Houston, Tex.	2,012,626	1,953,631	1,630,553
Indianapolis, Ind.	784,242	781,870	741,952
Jacksonville, Fla.	777,704	735,617	635,230
Los Angeles, Calif.	3,845,541	3,694,820	3,485,398
New York, N.Y.	8,104,079	8,008,278	7,322,564
Philadelphia, Pa.	1,470,151	1,517,550	1,585,577
Phoenix, Ariz.	1,418,041	1,321,045	983,403
San Antonio, Tex.	1,236,249	1,144,646	935,933
San Diego, Calif.	1,263,756	1,223,400	1,110,549
San Francisco, Calif.	744,230	776,733	723,959
San Jose, Calif.	904,522	894,943	782,248

With a little work it is possible to pull out key points, such as the number of people living in New York is obviously quite high, but making comparisons can be quite difficult.

Two columns were added to the table: the latitude and longitude of each city shown. Otherwise, the data used is exactly as shown here.

Converting the Source Data to XML

The preceding table was saved as a tab-delimited text file and then processed through the following simple script. The script is designed to handle as many years (identified by extracting the years from the "header" row in the text file), even though the data used throughout this chapter consists of just the three years shown, 1990, 2000, and 2004.

```perl
#!/usr/bin/perl -w

use strict;

open(DATA,$ARGV[0]) or die "Couldn't open file; did you forget it?";

my $counter = 0;

print "<citypop>";

my @popyears;

while(<DATA>)
{
    next unless (m/[a-z]/i);
    $_ =~ s/\"//g;
    $counter++;
    if ($counter == 1)
    {
        my ($city,$lat,$lng);
        ($city,$lat,$lng,@popyears) = split /\t/;
        $counter++;
        next;
    }
    chomp;

    my ($city,$lat,$lng,@pop) = split /\t/;

    printf('<city title="%s" lat="%f" lng="%f">',$city,$lat,$lng);
    print("\n");
    for(my $i=0;$i < scalar(@pop);$i++)
    {
        $pop[$i] =~ s/,//g;
        next unless (defined($pop[$i]));
        printf('<pop year="%s" value="%d"></pop>',$popyears[$i],$pop[$i]);
        print("\n");
    }

    print("</city>\n");
}
close(DATA);

print "</citypop>";
```

The script is comparatively straightforward. The data is extracted and a little cleaning up is performed (you remove double quotes from all lines and commas from population numbers) before generating a suitable XML file. Following is a sample of the generated file:

```
<citypop>
<city title="New York, N.Y." lat="40.714170" lng="-74.006390">
<pop year="2004" value="8104079"></pop>
<pop year="2000" value="8008278"></pop>
<pop year="1990" value="7322564"></pop>
</city>
```

```
<city title="Los Angeles, Calif." lat="34.052220" lng="-118.242780">
<pop year="2004" value="3845541"></pop>
<pop year="2000" value="3694820"></pop>
<pop year="1990" value="3485398"></pop>
...
<city title="San Francisco, Calif." lat="37.775000" lng="-122.418300">
<pop year="2004" value="744230"></pop>
<pop year="2000" value="776733"></pop>
<pop year="1990" value="723959"></pop>
</city>
<city title="Columbus, Ohio" lat="39.961100" lng="-82.998900">
<pop year="2004" value="730008"></pop>
<pop year="2000" value="711470"></pop>
<pop year="1990" value="632910"></pop>
</city>
</citypop>
```

The XML file is used in all of the examples in this chapter to demonstrate the different styles of statistical data representation available within a Google Map. The information could just as easily have been inserted into a database and then loaded dynamically; however, with static data like this (the population of New York in 2004 is unlikely to change now!) a static file is a suitable format for the information.

Using Polylines

In earlier chapters, the Google Maps polyline was used to show and highlight information on the map. The polyline is a simple line-drawing tool provided by the Google Maps software that draws a line between two points (or between pairs of points if there are more than two). However, because the definition of the polyline is so flexible, you can use that flexibility to your advantage and adapt it for other uses. Following is the definition for a new `GPolyline` object (question marks indicate optional arguments):

```
GPolyline(points, color?, weight?, opacity?)
```

The first argument is the array of points, the second the color (as specified using the HTML `#ff0000` format), the third the weight (that is, the width in pixels of the line) and the opacity of the line drawn (as a float between 0 and 1).

By adjusting the argument values and the array of points you can achieve a number of different techniques for highlighting data.

Basic Point Map

Using XML it is possible to create a very simple map with a marker showing each of the cities. Because this is a basic process (first covered in Chapter 8), I won't provide too much detail on the process, but the base code used and described here will be modified and expanded to work as the base for plotting the information onto a Google Map.

As with other examples, the trigger for the code is the `onLoad()` function, which is called when the page loads. As you can see in the following code for that function, you can parse the

XML document, picking out the city information, latitude and longitude of each city, and then use this when generating a marker for the city on the map:

```
function onLoad() {
    if (GBrowserIsCompatible()) {
        infopanel = document.getElementById("infopanel");
        map = new GMap(document.getElementById("map"));
        map.centerAndZoom(new GPoint(0,0), 2);

        var request = GXmlHttp.create();
        request.open('GET','ch10-01.xml', true);
        request.onreadystatechange = function() {
            if (request.readyState == 4) {
                var xmlsource = request.responseXML;
                var markerlist =
xmlsource.documentElement.getElementsByTagName("city");
                for (var i=0;i < markerlist.length;i++) {
                    addmarker(parseFloat(markerlist[i].getAttribute("lng")),
                              parseFloat(markerlist[i].getAttribute("lat")),
                              markerlist[i].getAttribute("title"));
                }
            }
            recenterandzoom(points);
        }
        request.send(null);
    }
}
```

Two other functions in that function are required for it to work, addmarker() and recenterandzoom().

Adding Markers

The addmarker() function is identical to examples shown in Chapter 7. It just accepts the latitude and longitude of a point, generates the GPoint() variable, pushing each value onto a stack for later use, and then creates a GMarker and updates the global information panel with the supplied title. The purpose of the panel is to provide a simple method of centering the map on each of the markers.

```
function addmarker(x,y,title) {
    var point = new GPoint(parseFloat(x),parseFloat(y));
    points.push(point);
    var marker = new GMarker(point);
    map.addOverlay(marker);
    infopanel.innerHTML = infopanel.innerHTML +
        '<a href="#" onClick="movemap(' + index + ');">' +
        title +
        '</a><br/>';
    index++;
}
```

The movemap() function referenced here performs a pan to the point's longitude and latitude when the city name is clicked.

Centering and Deciding on a Zoom Level

One of the problems with any map is ensuring that the view the user gets (initially, at least) contains all of the information you are trying to portray. Chapter 9 showed centerAndZoom(), a simple function that calculates the center point of all of the points being displayed. The limitation of this function is that it relies on using a generic zoom level, which may or may not be suitable for the points and markers being displayed on the map.

The recenterandzoom() function performs the same centering process, but this time it accepts a single argument, an array of points. To determine the midpoint, the latitude and longitude of each point are extracted and then added to their own array, which is then sorted, and the same calculation as before determines the center-point of all the supplied points for centering the map.

By comparing the span of the points (the difference between the maximum and minimum values), the function can determine an ideal zoom level by trying out zoom levels until a level that encompasses the span of the points is found. To do this, it iterates from the highest zoom level to the lowest and uses the getSpanLatLng() method to compare the point span with the span displayed on the active map. If the displayed span is smaller than the required span, the map zooms out by one level and the values are re-checked until a zoom level and span combination are determined.

To ensure that the span incorporates a small buffer (so points don't appear on the edges of the map), the actual span required is increased by 25 percent before the determination is made:

```
function recenterandzoom(points) {
    var latpoints = [];
    var lngpoints = [];

    var idealzoom = 1;
// Do nothing if no points supplied
    if (points.length == 0) {
        return;
    }
// Zoom right in if just one point is supplied
    if (points.length == 1) {
        map.centerAndZoom(points[0],idealzoom);
        return;
    }

    for(var i=0;i<points.length;i++) {
        latpoints.push(points[i].y);
        lngpoints.push(points[i].x);
    }
// Sort, enforcing a numerical comparison
    latpoints.sort(function(x,y) { return x-y });
    lngpoints.sort(function(x,y) { return x-y });

    var newlat = latpoints[0] + ((latpoints[latpoints.length-1] - ⊃
latpoints[0])/2);
```

```
    var newlng = lngpoints[0] + ((lngpoints[lngpoints.length-1] - ⤴
lngpoints[0])/2);

    var newpoint = new GPoint(parseFloat(newlng),parseFloat(newlat));

    var idealspan = new GSize ⤴
  (parseFloat((Math.abs(lngpoints[lngpoints.length-1]-
                                      lngpoints[0]))*1.25),
                        parseFloat ⤴
  ((Math.abs(latpoints[latpoints.length-1]-
                                      latpoints[0]))*1.25));

    map.zoomTo(idealzoom);

    for(var i=1;i<16;i++) {
        var currentsize = map.getSpanLatLng();
            if ((currentsize.width < idealspan.width) ||
            (currentsize.height < idealspan.height)) {
            map.zoomTo(i);
            idealzoom = i;
        }
        else {
            break;
        }
    }

    map.centerAndZoom(newpoint,idealzoom);
}
```

Warning

JavaScript treats more or less all values as text, even if the values are numerical. This can happen even in some logical and comparison operations and calculations. To force a numerical comparison (as in the `sort()` on the array of points) you have to trick JavaScript into performing a numerical comparison by explicitly defining the sort comparison function (x-y). See the Mozilla JavaScript guide (`http://developer.mozilla.org/en/docs/Core_JavaScript_1.5_Reference`) for more information.

Most JavaScript and Google Maps implementations even perform the span and zoom calculation without redisplaying the intervening zoom levels, making the process feel instantaneous. Using it in this application ensures that all the markers for each city on the map are displayed simultaneously.

The Basic Non-Statistical Map

You can see the result of the basic marker map and the recentering of the map onto the array of points in Figure 10-1.

You can see the basic map is exactly that, a basic representation of the list of cities. Now the map can be extended to incorporate the statistical data of the individual city population.

Note

The basic example is available at `http://maps.mcslp.com/examples/ch10-01.html`.

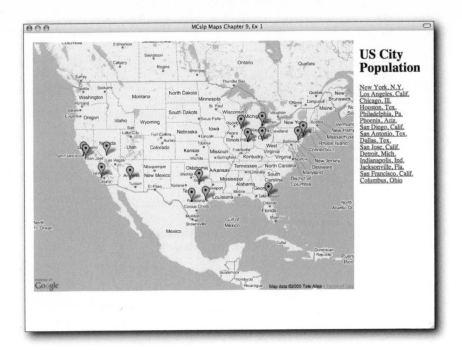

FIGURE 10-1: A simple city marker map.

Building an Internal Data Representation

Before the statistical data is plotted onto the map, the application must account for the different years for which the data is available. The information about the population data is stored in a single XML file, but the file does not need to be parsed multiple times to extract the information that is required.

The associative array in JavaScript enables data to be stored by text reference, instead of numerical reference. By combining a textual reference (the year of the data) with an array of population data (with the same numerical index as each city and associated map point and marker) it is possible to select and display the population information.

To achieve this, change the code for parsing the XML file to extract the data and build the necessary file. The core of processing remains the same:

```
if (request.readyState == 4) {
    var xmlsource = request.responseXML;
    var markerlist = xmlsource.documentElement.getElementsByTagName("city");
    for (var i=0;i < markerlist.length;i++) {
        addmarker(parseFloat(markerlist[i].getAttribute("lng")),
                parseFloat(markerlist[i].getAttribute("lat")),
                markerlist[i].getAttribute("title"));
```

Then, create an associative array at the same index for your map pointer/marker:

```
        popdata[i] = new Array();
```

Now the population data can be extracted from the XML. A separate associative array is also populated with a list of the years. Because the year is used as the text reference (instead of a numerical reference), you should end up with a unique list of the available years.

```
var poplist = markerlist[i].getElementsByTagName("pop");
for (var j=0;j<poplist.length;j++) {
    popdata[i][poplist[j].getAttribute("year")]
        = parseInt(poplist[j].getAttribute("value"));
    years[poplist[j].getAttribute("year")] = 0;
}
}
```

Finally, for convenience, you create a list of the available years (using the year associative array) as links so that the user can pick the year of population data to be displayed:

```
for (var i in years) {
    yearpanel.innerHTML = yearpanel.innerHTML +
        '<a href="#" onClick="addgraph(' + i + ')">' + i + '</a><br/';
}
recenterandzoom(points);
}
```

The preceding will create a structure like the following one:

```
popdata[0]['2004'] = 8104079
popdata[0]['2000'] = 8008278
popdata[0]['1990'] = 7322564
...
popdata[14]['2004'] = 730008
popdata[14]['2000'] = 711470
popdata[14]['1990'] = 632910
```

To select the population data for a city, you need only know the city reference (as embedded into the list of cities shown in the information panel on the right). To pick out the population for a specific year, you need the city reference and year string. To show the population data for all cities for a given year, you need to iterate through the list and then extract the population for a given year from a particular index. An example of this is the creation of a bar graph of that information on the map.

Adding a Bar Graph

To draw a bar graph of the population against each city, a starting point for the base of each graph must be determined. The location of the city is a good starting point. Then the height of the bar graph should also be determined. The height should be consistent across different values. For example, if New York had a population of 500,000 and Los Angeles a population of 250,000, the height of the bar for L.A. should be half that of New York.

With a Google Map there is no flexibility to draw arbitrary lines. The line must be drawn based on the longitude and latitude of the start and end points. To draw a vertical bar, the longitude remains the same; only the latitude changes according to a value. To calculate that value, obtain the height of the map in latitude and then use a factor of that for each increment of the bar. The value will be consistent irrespective of the size of the actual map.

To keep the height of each bar consistent, you need a baseline to work from. Using a percentage value, rather than the real value, keeps the height of the bars consistent across different data values. You can use the combination of the current map view and the percentage value of the data point to keep the bar height consistent within the available view. Because that value is a percentage, the size of the map can be divided by 100 and then by a further value (to ensure the graph is displayed within the map) to determine the latitude increment to use when drawing each bar.

The code for this is called when a user clicks a specific year in the list of available years. The code performs a number of steps to achieve the goal. The first is to calculate the increment to be used for drawing each tick on the bar graph:

```
function addgraph(year) {
    var currentsize = map.getSpanLatLng();
    var increment = (parseFloat(currentsize.height)/2.0)/100;
    var maxsize = 0;
    var graphdata = [];
```

The existing data and overlays are cleared from the map, and the information panel is also emptied because the data in the panel will be regenerated to include the population data:

```
    map.clearOverlays();
    polylines = [];
    markers = [];
    infopanel.innerHTML = '';
```

Now the `graphdata` for the selected year is extracted into a single array, and the maximum size of the data is determined. A marker for each city is generated (using a modified `addmarker()` function) that also embeds the city name and population value into an `InfoWindow` for each marker:

```
    for(var i=0;i<popdata.length;i++) {
        graphdata.push(popdata[i][year]);
        if (popdata[i][year] > maxsize) {
            maxsize = popdata[i][year];
        }
        addmarker(points[i].x,points[i].y,titles[i] + '; Pop: ' +
                popdata[i][year] + ' in ' + year);
    }
```

Finally, each bar is created by creating an array of points, with just two elements. The starting point is the location of each city, which is held in the global points array. The second point is the longitude of the city (which does not change). The latitude value is used to create the height of the bar. That value can be calculated, first, by multiplying the percentage of the data point by the increment calculated for the map. If you then add that value to the latitude of the city, you get a new latitude that represents bar size. The resulting two-point array is used to create a polyline, where the color is explicitly specified along with a wider than normal point width so that the bar shows up clearly on the map:

```
    for(var i=0;i<graphdata.length;i++) {
        var pointpair = [];
        pointpair.push(points[i]);
        var secondlatinc =  ((parseFloat(graphdata[i])*100)/maxsize)*increment;
        var secondlat = (parseFloat(points[i].y)*1)+secondlatinc;
```

```
pointpair.push(new GPoint(points[i].x,
                          secondlat));
var line = new GPolyline(pointpair,"#ff0000",20);
map.addOverlay(line);
polylines.push(line);
    }
}
```

Note The bar graph example is available at `http://maps.mcslp.com/examples/ch10-02` `.html`.

The resulting display is shown in Figure 10-2. You can see the polylines for each city overlaying each city location, with standard markers highlighting the precise location. It is also clearer from this display that the population of New York is large compared to the others.

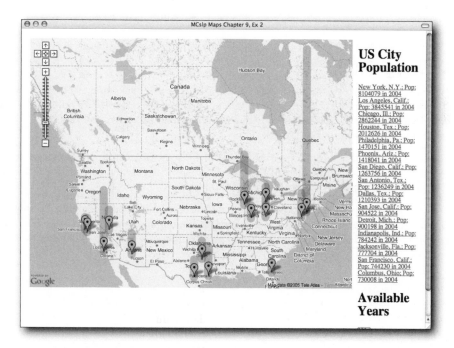

FIGURE 10-2: Bar graphs of population data.

Conveniently, polylines are also transparent, so you can see the information from multiple cities even when the data overlaps. Also, as polylines, the information remains displayed on the map even when the map is zoomed or moved, as shown in Figure 10-3.

FIGURE 10-3: A close up of California population data for 2000.

Adding a Circle

Polylines, by their very definition, must have at least two, non-equal points in order for them to be drawn on the map. By calculating the difference between the original data point and a destination data point, you can *almost* create a circle (although in reality it is probably closer to an oval or a rectangle with rounded edges).

To achieve this, a cue about the size of the circle that is to be created can be taken from the current longitude and latitude span of the map. In fact, you can use the same basic calculation you use when determining the bar graph interval size.

Instead of modifying only the latitude, you adjust both the latitude and longitude. To show the population values, the width of the line is adjusted according to the same rules as before. The code is almost identical, aside from the second point in the array for the polyline and the volume specification:

```
function addgraph(year) {
    var currentsize = map.getSpanLatLng();
    var increment = (parseFloat(currentsize.height)/10.0)/100;
    var maxsize = 0;
    var graphdata = [];

    map.clearOverlays();

    polylines = [];
    markers = [];
    infopanel.innerHTML = '';

    for(var i=0;i<popdata.length;i++) {
        graphdata.push(popdata[i][year]);
        if (popdata[i][year] > maxsize) {
            maxsize = popdata[i][year];
```

```
        }
        addmarker(points[i].x,points[i].y,titles[i] + ': ' + popdata[i][year]);
    }

    for(var i=0;i<graphdata.length;i++) {
        var pointpair = [];
        pointpair.push(points[i]);
        var volume =  parseInt((parseFloat(graphdata[i])*100)/maxsize);
        pointpair.push(new GPoint(points[i].x+increment,
                                  points[i].y+increment));
        var line = new GPolyline(pointpair,"#ff0000",volume);
        map.addOverlay(line);
        polylines.push(line);
    }
}
```

Note The circle example is available at `http://maps.mcslp.com/examples/ch10-03.html`.

The same population data shown in Figure 10-2 is shown here in Figure 10-4 as circles of varying sizes. Again, you can see from the transparency of the graph data that it doesn't matter if multiple population data is overlaid on different parts of the map. Figure 10-5 shows California again where the transparency of the overlaid data may be clearer.

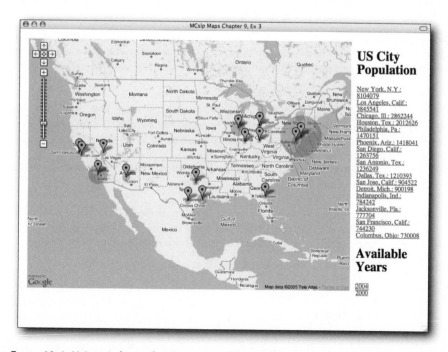

FIGURE 10-4: Using circles to demonstrate statistical data.

FIGURE 10-5: California's population data.

Plotting Multiple Data Sets

An alternative to plotting all the data for one year across multiple cities is to show the population data for a single city but across multiple years. This can be achieved with the circle trick in the previous section by overlaying the data for different years in different circles (which should be represented by different sizes, as the data changes).

For plotting that information there are a few things to consider. First, the data for different years must be represented in different colors for it to be distinguishable. Also, although by default polylines are transparent, the transparency will need to be adjusted slightly to ensure the information is properly visible.

Note   It also worth considering the visibility of the information for those with disabilities, especially those with color blindness. Using contrasting colors that color blind users cannot see will completely hide or even confuse the information you are trying to portray. Use the color charts available at the Colors for the Color Blind web site (`http://www.toledo-bend.com/colorblind`), which even includes guides for Web colors and combinations that are safe to use.

The color issue can be fixed by defining an array of colors as the HTML string used by the Google Maps API to color a polyline. You know there are only three values in your dataset, so you can specify that number of colors. For clarity, each color is one of the primary colors:

```
var colors = ['#ff0000','#00ff00','#0000ff'];
var colorsindex = 0;
```

When parsing the list of years, instead of providing a link to select the dataset to be loaded, the list will become a key for the colors used to highlight the population data. Meanwhile, the list of cities will be the method for triggering the population data to be displayed. Generating the key is a simple case of modifying the year panel information:

```
for (var i in years) {
    yearpanel.innerHTML = yearpanel.innerHTML +
        '<font color="' + colors[colorindex] + '">' + i + '</font><br/>';
    years[i] = colorindex++;
}
```

Meanwhile, the `addgraph()` function, now triggered by the `movemap()` function that is called when a user clicks the city name in the info panel, is modified to draw multiple circles, one for each population data point:

```
function addgraph(city) {
    var currentsize = map.getSpanLatLng();
    var increment = (parseFloat(currentsize.height)/4.0)/100;
    var maxsize = 0;
    var graphdata = [];

    map.clearOverlays();

    for(var i in popdata[city]) {
        graphdata.push(popdata[city][i]);
        if (popdata[city][i] > maxsize) {
            maxsize = popdata[city][i];
        }
    }

    for(var i=0;i<graphdata.length;i++) {
        var pointpair = [];
        pointpair.push(points[city]);
        var volume =  parseInt((parseFloat(graphdata[i])*100)/maxsize);
        pointpair.push(new GPoint(points[city].x+increment,
                                  points[city].y+increment));

        var line = new GPolyline(pointpair,colors[i],volume,0.25);
        map.addOverlay(line);
        polylines.push(line);
    }
}
```

The important line is the one that constructs the `GPolyline()` for each population set:

```
var line = new GPolyline(pointpair,colors[i],volume,0.25);
```

The last argument specifies the opacity of the line drawn, which is lowered to 25 percent. This amount will make the information on the map visible while making multiple overlays of the information recognizable.

The result can be seen in Figure 10-6. You can see how the information is overlaid, one circle on top of the other to show the population growth. Of course, the dramatic contrast of shade and color can be better seen on the book's web site (http://maps.mcslp.com).

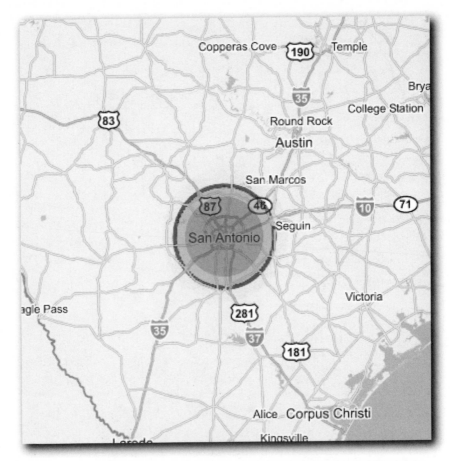

FIGURE 10-6: Showing the multiple population data using a polyline to simulate circles.

Note The circle example is available at http://maps.mcslp.com/examples/ch10-03.html.

Using Custom Icons

Polylines are an efficient way of representing information, but they are limited in that the amount of information they can represent is small in comparison to the amount of the work that is required to build the information displayed. With work, you could draw a 3D bar or use alternative methods to draw different diagrams to highlight the content, but the more lines you have to draw, the more work is required. That probably isn't an efficient way of representing the information.

Another alternative is to use custom icons to show the information onscreen. An icon is used when a marker is placed on the map, and it is possible to change the icon to almost any image that you like. By changing the image or altering its size, the marker icon can be used to show the volume and value of statistical information in the same way the polylines were employed earlier in this chapter.

Before choosing and setting an image, you should consider how that image is specified and defined.

Building Your Own Icon

Good icons consist of two elements: the icon and its shadow, although the shadow is technically an optional element. You can either build your own icon or copy an image from another location and turn it into an icon. The key issue is to ensure that your icon makes sense as an icon and can be easily placed onto a map.

Choosing an Icon Style

The most important aspect of your icon is that it should have an anchor point that can be associated with the precise point on your Google Map. You can see from the sample markers used in Google Maps applications that they generally have a pushpin or tack feel that provides a pinpoint that can be attached to the latitude and longitude of the point you are highlighting.

Tips for creating or choosing good Google Maps icons include the following:

- It should have an identifiable anchor point, which is usually exactly that: a point, pin, or other element that points to the location on the map you want.

- It should be relatively small. The icon is designed to highlight a point on the map, not dominate it.

- It ideally should not be used to provide information, short of marking the point on the map. Use an InfoWindow or other display element to show the information.

That doesn't mean you can't use other images, but it does mean that you should give some consideration to the icon you choose.

Creating the Icon

There is only one required element for a Google Maps icon: the icon itself. However, for clarity (and style) icons normally also include a shadow. Both elements should have the following attributes:

- They should be in the PNG format. Most graphics applications (including Adobe PhotoShop and GIMP) support PNG. PNG is used because it provides 24-bit color support and transparency. Transparency enables the icon to appear on the map as the icon, effectively hiding the square image that you generate.

- They should have the same height, although they can have different widths.

- The left edge of images should be identical. It is the combination of the height and the left-hand edge that allows the icon image to be overlaid on the shadow image.

- They must be placed on a transparent background.

- Ideally the width of the icon should be an odd number so that the middle pixel is precisely in the center.

- The basic size of the icon should be appropriate to the map size. Designing an icon with an image size of 400x400 pixels is not efficient when the image will probably be only 40x40 pixels on the final map. The exception is when adjusting the icon for larger sizes (as in the statistics example) where better resolution will make a better icon when it is scaled up.

The height and left edge requirements are important because Google Maps aligns images from the top left. If the icon and shadow were different heights or had different left edge orientations, the bottom and left edges would never line up.

Putting the process in practice, you can build a simple icon and shadow to use on your map. Figure 10-7 shows the basic layout of the icon and its shadow and why the left-hand edge and height are so important.

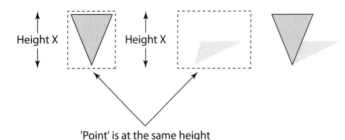

'Point' is at the same height
and distance from left edge

FIGURE 10-7: Understanding the icon/shadow overlay.

Building the Original Image

Building the original image is really about choosing (or creating) an image and then saving the file in the PNG format with a transparent background. For the icon in the example, you can build an icon similar to the pushpin provided by Google Maps.

Figure 10-8 shows the basic components used to build the pushpin. I used OmniGraffle on Mac OS X, but just about any image or drawing program can be used to build the icon. If the elements shown are combined into a single graphic, the topmost element is the one on the left, the bottommost is on the right, with a little spatial adjustment you can build a very good icon. Some elements were also adjusted for line width to make them more visible.

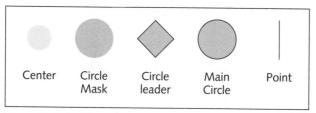

FIGURE 10-8: Building an icon.

The final icon can be seen in Figure 10-9.

FIGURE 10-9: The final icon.

Once the basic icon is complete, save it as a PNG with a transparent background, or copy the icon to Photoshop or a similar graphics program and do the same. The transparent background is vital to ensure that the pushpin appears as a pushpin, not a square graphic on the map.

Adding a shadow makes the icon look better onscreen and the gives the pushpin the feeling that it has, literally, just been pushed into the map.

Building a Shadow

Building a shadow is more complicated. For the item to look like a shadow, it needs to be skewed and the color altered (to black). You also need to be careful and ensure that you do not adjust the left-hand edge and distance of the point, because it is the point distance and height that allow the icon and shadow to be overlaid on one another to generate the final icon.

In Photoshop, first copy the original icon into a new document.

Figure 10-10 shows the canvas size adjustment screen. Double the width of the icon, but make sure that the expansion is on the right-hand side, so that the size and placement of the graphic on the left is not altered.

Now change the icon to solid black, and then use the Free Transform option to halve the height and skew the image. As with adjusting the image size, make sure you select the bottom of the image as the anchor. Then set the height to 50 percent and the horizontal skew to 135 degrees. You can see the settings and the effects in the final image in Figure 10-11.

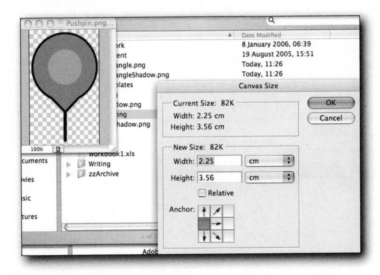

FIGURE 10-10: Setting the shadow size.

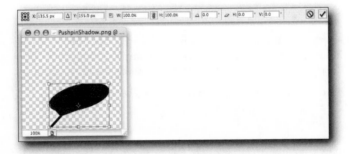

FIGURE 10-11: The final shadow.

Finally, change the opacity of the shadow to between 35 percent and 50 percent to ensure that the shadow looks like a shadow and not an image in its own right.

You now have an icon and shadow to display on your map.

Creating a Google Map Icon

Actually creating the icon within the Google Map is straightforward, provided the rules for the icon are understood. The GIcon() class is used to specify the icon detail and you should, at a minimum, specify the following:

- The URL of the icon image.
- The URL of the shadow image.
- The icon size width, then height (in pixels).
- The shadow size width, then height (in pixels).
- The anchor point (the point in the image that will be placed directly over the latitude and longitude for the marker).
- The anchor point for the info window.
- The anchor point for the info window shadow.

The different values are explained in Figure 10-12.

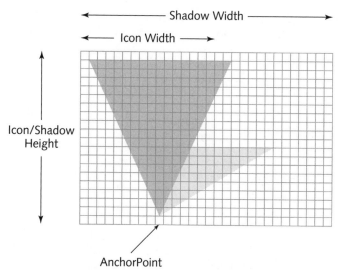

FIGURE 10-12: Understanding icon parameters.

Warning

Remember that image sizes are specified in pixels, not latitude and longitude. Also remember that you should scale your icon and shadow by the same value to retain the correct aspect ratio. For example, if your icon image is 210 pixels high but you want it to be just 22 pixels high on the map, you should also divide the width of the image by the same factor to get the icon widths.

To create the icon within Google Maps, specify each of these parameters for a new `GIcon` object. For example:

```
baseIcon = new GIcon();
baseIcon.image = "/examples/Pushpin.png";
baseIcon.shadow = "/examples/PushpinShadow.png";
baseIcon.iconSize = new GSize(31,33);
baseIcon.shadowSize = new GSize(57,33);
baseIcon.iconAnchor = new GPoint(16,33);
baseIcon.infoWindowAnchor = new GPoint(31,38);
baseIcon.infoShadowAnchor = new GPoint(31,38);
```

Note

The shadow image specification is not required, although Google has suggested in the past that it might become a compulsory element. You can actually omit either the shadow or the original icon, which can lead to some interesting effects, without any error being raised. If you want an icon without a shadow but the shadow becomes compulsory, just use a completely transparent image for the shadow.

Putting the Icon on a Map

Putting the icon onto a statistical map is relatively easy. The first stage is to modify the `addmarker()` function to accept an icon object as an argument. Then you use this icon when a marker is added to the map:

```
function addmarker(x,y,title,icon) {
    var point = new GPoint(parseFloat(x),parseFloat(y));
    points.push(point);
    var marker = new GMarker(point,icon);
    map.addOverlay(marker);
    markers.push(marker);
    titles.push(title);
    infopanel.innerHTML = infopanel.innerHTML +
        '<a href="#" onClick="movemap(' + index + ');">' +
        title +
        '</a><br/>';
    index++;
}
```

Specifying an icon to `GMarker()` places that icon on the map at the anchor point you defined when the icon was created at the latitude and longitude defined by the marker.

Using Icon Size to Represent Data

To represent statistical information, you can duplicate the original icon and then alter its size to represent the volume of the statistic that is being displayed. The map demonstrating this is an adaptation of the third example, displaying the population for all of the cities when a year is selected. The modifications to the map application take place in `addgraph()`, where instead of drawing a line or circle, the icon is drawn instead. The introductory portion of the functions remains consistent, although because the icons are measured in pixels, not longitude/latitude, you no longer have to calculate an increment:

```
function addgraph(year) {
    var maxsize = 0;
    var graphdata = [];

    map.clearOverlays();

    polylines = [];
    markers = [];
    infopanel.innerHTML = '';

    for(var i=0;i<popdata.length;i++) {
        graphdata.push(popdata[i][year]);
        if (popdata[i][year] > maxsize) {
            maxsize = popdata[i][year];
        }
    }
}
```

But the core portion that plots the statistical data is changed. Note how the icon is created. If you specify an existing icon when creating a new icon object, the new icon inherits all of the settings of the original. Those values can then be adjusted to create the new icon you want. You need to do this for each statistical value so that an icon of a different size is created for each data point.

Note Any icon parameter can be changed. If you want to use different icons for different elements and all the icons have the same size, you can just adjust the icon URL. In some cases, even the shadow can remain consistent.

To achieve this in the application, the icon is copied and then the height and width of the icon and its shadow are adjusted by multiplying the original value by a multiple of the percentage that has been calculated. The +1 at the end ensures that all the icons are at least the size of the original markers:

```
for(var i=0;i<graphdata.length;i++) {
    var volume =  (parseFloat(parseFloat(graphdata[i])/maxsize)*2)+1;
    var thisIcon = new GIcon(baseIcon);
```

```
        thisIcon.iconSize = new GSize(thisIcon.iconSize.width*volume,
                                  thisIcon.iconSize.height*volume);
        thisIcon.shadowSize = new GSize(thisIcon.shadowSize.width*volume,
                                    thisIcon.shadowSize.height*volume);
        thisIcon.iconAnchor = new GPoint((thisIcon.iconAnchor.x*volume),
                                    thisIcon.iconAnchor.y*volume);
        addmarker(points[i].x,points[i].y,titles[i] + ': ' + ⤸
popdata[i][year],thisIcon);
    }
}
```

The final map, showing the custom icons highlighting the population in 1994, is shown in Figure 10-13. A close up of an icon and its shadow is shown in Figure 10-14. Of course, the dramatic contrast of shade and color can be better seen on the web site (`http://maps.mcslp.com`).

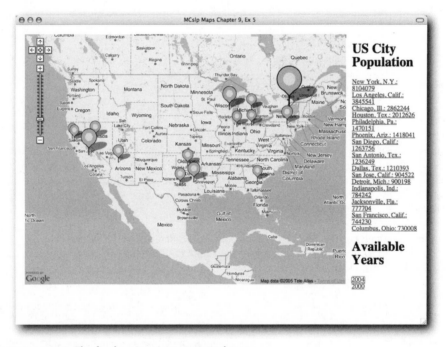

FIGURE 10-13: The final custom icon statistical map.

Note

The basic example is available at `http://maps.mcslp.com/examples/ch10-01.html`.

FIGURE 10-14: A close up of the icon and shadow.

Wrapping Up

In this chapter you have seen some examples of how statistical information can be displayed on the map. Lots of options are available, and which one you choose depends largely on the type of information you want to display and how best that information can be represented.

You could use simple pushpins to highlight the spread of different elements, or, as shown in this chapter, use polylines to show values for specific points. With some interesting adaptations, polylines can be used to simulate other elements. For complete control, though, the custom icon provides the best solution for laying out information.

With all these different options in mind, it is worth remembering that plenty of other solutions are available for adding further detail to the information. In the examples, you updated the text, but you could just as easily extend the content of the `InfoWindow` on a marker to hold more data, or you could build a separate panel into the application to give more detail. The Google Maps interface is a way of connecting statistical information to a map, but it is not the only method available. The Google Map can be part of a larger application and display that highlights the data in a geographical way, with other solutions available for providing more detail and information.

Building a Community Site

Community sites show information about a community and the facilities that it offers. The intention is to provide a resource that might form part of a newspaper, tourist information center, or other site where the local information is useful to both the community and visitors.

You can do this in a variety of ways through the Google Maps interface, but effectively relaying the information in a map means making some changes to the way information is overlaid on the map, how those overlays are controlled, and how the information is sourced and recorded on the map.

In this chapter, techniques from Chapters 9 and 10 are combined to provide a more extensive overview of the facilities. The chapter describes how the information is sourced, how the data is recovered from the database, and how to build a flexible interface to the information within a Google Map. In short, you will create your own example of a mash-up.

Displaying Highlighted Points

Displaying simple markers has been described in a number of previous chapters, but the markers displayed have always related to a specific type of information. From a simple representation standpoint, this makes the significance of the markers onscreen obvious.

For example, the final application in Chapter 9 displayed restaurants available in different cities, according to the information stored in a database. The application enabled the user to select a town or city and then display a list of markers showing the various restaurants. You can see a sample of the application in Figure 11-1.

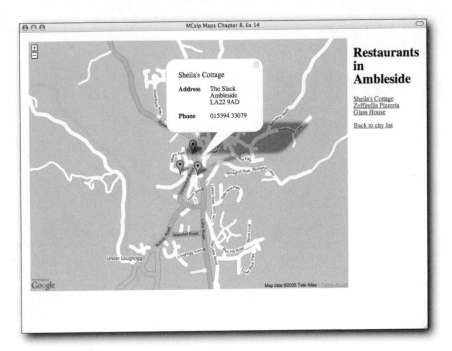

Figure 11-1: Restaurants in Ambleside.

The problem with the display is that the user only knows the markers represent restaurants because the text description tells them so. If you want to show the locations of different types of information, this can quickly become confusing. The output needs to be updated, first by supporting more types of businesses or items highlighted on the map, and then you need a way of highlighting the different types. For the latter, the custom icon techniques in the previous chapter are used.

Adding More Data to the Output

In Chapter 9, only restaurants were included in the output, and the information for each restaurant was hand-coded into the database that was used to extract the information. To get the large volume of information that would need to be inserted into a community database, you need a more automated solution.

To achieve this, you can use a modified version of the Google Maps script that was covered in Chapter 6 and is shown in the following code. The script works on the same basic premise, but searches for a list of entities, extracts the information returned by the Google Local service, and then obtains the latitude and longitude for each item by looking up the postal code, town, and country fragment extracted from the output. The assembled information can be inserted directly into the database that is used to generate the map.

The information generated by Google Local is not easy to dissect, but you can see the information for a single restaurant in this raw HTML fragment:

```
a href="/maps?q=restaurant,+grantham&amp;output=html&amp;hl=en&amp;
latlng=52915423,-640277,10098272919349949403">
The Market Cross Fish Bar &amp; Restaurant</a>
<br><nobr>01476 563782</nobr></td>
<td valign=top class=lad><font size=-1>9 Market Place</font>
<br><font size=-1>Grantham, NG31 6LJ, United Kingdom</font>
<br><font size=-1 class=fl>0.2 mi SW</font><font size=-1>
```

The latitude and longitude in this output is not useful when dealing with multiple restaurants because it refers to the middle point of all the results, not the single result shown here. The rest of the information is easy to identify—you can spot the title, telephone number, and address information. The second fragment of address information includes the town, postal code, and country; this can be used, with another request, to find the precise latitude and longitude for each item.

Storing and Creating the Data

To store the information, you create a database according to the following SQL statement. Here, a single table is being created that includes a unique ID, the latitude, longitude, entity type, title, telephone number, and address information:

```
create table ch11 (entityid int auto_increment not null primary key,
                    lat float,
                    lng float,
                    type varchar(80),
                    title varchar(80),
                    tel varchar(80),
                    adda varchar(80),
                    addb varchar(80))
```

Each record in the database contains all of the information extracted, along with the entity type (restaurant, bank, and so on).

The script that extracts all of the information from the Google Local search and inserts it into the database is as follows:

```
#!/usr/bin/perl

use strict;
use LWP::UserAgent;
use URI::Escape;
use Data::Dumper;
```

```perl
use DBI;

my $dbh = DBI->connect( 'dbi:mysql:database=mapsbookex;host=db.maps.mcslp.com',
                        'mapsbookex',
                        'examples',
                        );

if (!defined($dbh))
{
    die "Couldn't open connection to database\n";
}

my $ua = LWP::UserAgent->new(
    agent => "Mozilla/5.0 (X11; U; Linux i686; en-US; rv:1.0.2) ⤶
Gecko/20021120 Netscape/7.01",
                              );

my $response = $ua->get('http://maps.google.com/maps?q=' .
                uri_escape(sprintf('%s, %s',$ARGV[0],$ARGV[1])));

my $var = $response->{_content};

my @matches = ($var =~ m/<a href="\/maps(.*?)\ \;\-\ \;/g);

my $finds = [];

foreach my $entity (@matches)
{
    my ($lat,$lng,$title,$tel,$adda,$addb) = ($entity =~ ⤶
m/latlng=(.*?),(.*?),.*?>(.*?)<.*<nobr>(.*?)<\/nobr>.*<font
 size=-1>(.*?)<\/font.*-1>(.*?)<\/font>/);

    ($lat,$lng) = getlatlng($addb);

    $dbh->do(sprintf('insert into ch11 values(0,%s,%s,%s,%s,%s,%s,%s)',
                    $dbh->quote($lat),
                    $dbh->quote($lng),
                    $dbh->quote($ARGV[0]),
                    $dbh->quote($title),
                    $dbh->quote($tel),
                    $dbh->quote($adda),
                    $dbh->quote($addb),
            ));
}

sub getlatlng
{
    my ($text) = @_;

    my $response = $ua->get ⤶
```

```
                      ('http://maps.google.com/maps?q=' . uri_escape($text));

            my $var = $response->{_content};

            my ($lat,$lng) = ( $var =~ m/GLatLng\(([-\d.]+).*?([-\d.]+)\)/ms );

            return ($lat,$lng);
        }
```

The data is extracted from the HTML through a regular expression, and then the request is repeated to find the real latitude/longitude.

With this script, you can populate the database with different business types by specifying the type and town/city on the command line. For example, you could update the list of restaurants in Grantham using the following:

```
$ ch11inserter.pl restaurant Grantham
```

You could update the list of banks using this:

```
$ ch11inserter.pl banks Grantham
```

The list of what could be inserted into the database using this technique is virtually limitless.

Backend Database Interface

To extract the information from the database (that was populated using the script in the earlier section), another CGI script, similar to the one in Chapter 9, generates the information in suitable XML format when requested by the Google Maps applications. The basic script is identical, only the SQL required to extract the information and the XML format of the data that is returned are different:

```perl
#!/usr/bin/perl

use DBI;
use strict;
use CGI qw/:standard/;

print header(-type => 'text/xml');

my $dbh = DBI->connect( 'dbi:mysql:database=mapsbookex;host=db.maps.mcslp.com',
                        'mapsbookex',
                        'examples',
                      );

if (!defined($dbh))
{
    die "Couldn't open connection to database\n";
}

if (param('m') eq 'entitylist')
{
```

```
    entitylist();
}
elsif(param('m') eq 'getmarkers')
{
    getmarkers(param('entity'));
}
```

The `entitylist()` function returns a list of unique entity types (restaurants, banks, and so on) that were populated when the database was populated. For that, the SQL statement uses DISTINCT to get a list of unique types and then formats XML for the Google Maps application to extract:

```
sub entitylist
{
    my $sth = $dbh->prepare('select distinct(type) from ch11');
    $sth->execute();

    print "<types>";
    while (my $row = $sth->fetchrow_hashref())
    {
        printf('<type typename="%s"/>',ucfirst($row->{type}));
    }
    print "</types>";
}
```

The `getmarkers()` function is just a minor alteration from the script in Chapter 9.

```
sub getmarkers
{
    my ($entity) = @_;

    print("<markers>\n");

    my $sth = $dbh->prepare(sprintf('select * from ch11 where type = %s',
                                     $dbh->quote($entity)));
    $sth->execute();

    while (my $row = $sth->fetchrow_hashref())
    {
        printf('<marker lat="%f" lng="%f" title="%s"> ⏎
<infowindow><title>%s</title><address>%s</address><city>%s</city> ⏎
<phone>%s</phone></infowindow></marker>',
                $row->{lat},
                $row->{lng},
                $row->{title},
                $row->{title},
                $row->{adda},
                $row->{addb},
                $row->{tel},
                );

    }
```

```
    $sth->finish();

    print("</markers>\n");
}
```

Before the details of the Google Maps application are covered, the different icons that are used to highlight the different entities are described in the following section.

Using Custom Icons to Highlight Different Attractions

Using the same marker for all of the different types of information on the map is obviously less than optimal. Users will be unable to identify what the different points on the map refer to without clicking them for more information. To avoid this, different icons can be used to highlight different entities. The icons used in the application were sourced from the Open Clipart project and include different icons for pharmacies, banks, restaurants, sports shops, and travel agents. The icons used are shown in Table 11-1.

Table 11-1   Custom Icons

Icon	Name
	Pharmacies icon
	Banks icon
	Restaurant icon
	Sports shops icon
	Travel agent icon

The background of each icon is transparent to help the icons' visibility, particularly when they are placed close together or even on top of one another. Each icon is also the same size — 32x32 pixels. Finally, the shadow normally attached to an icon is not added, to further improve the visibility of stacked icons. You can see the effect in a sample of the map application showing many different types in Figure 11-2; even though the map is quite busy with information, you can still clearly see the different icon types on the map.

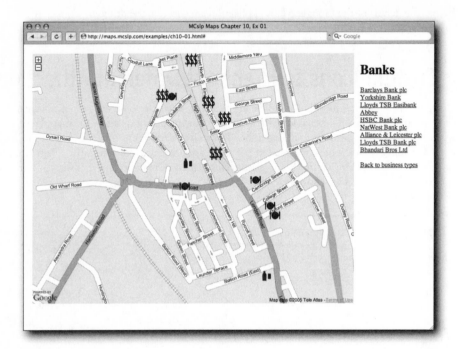

FIGURE 11-2: Busy, but clear, map information.

To match the icon with the entity type, you give each icon a name that is the lowercase version of the entity type that was given when the data was inserted into the database table. That way, when entities of a particular type are loaded from the database, the correct icon can be selected by name.

You can generate the icon within the Google Maps application with a simple icon-building sequence. Reference points are made for the bottom-left corner as the anchor point, and info panels are offset from the top-right corner of each icon:

```
var baseIcon = new GIcon();
baseIcon.iconSize = new GSize(32,32);
baseIcon.iconAnchor = new GPoint(0,32);
baseIcon.infoWindowAnchor = new GPoint(32,0);
baseIcon.image = "http://maps.mcslp.com/examples/" + ⏎
types[index].toLowerCase() + ".png";
```

The references used here for the offsets are probably a little generous, but the spacing helps the clarity on what could be a busy map.

Filtering Data through Layers of Information

The basic structure of the application is the same as in Chapter 9, except that the user selects entities, not towns, as the first step. Each time the user selects an entity from the list, the markers, using the appropriate icons, are populated on the page. Multiple entity types can be displayed on the map at the same time.

 Note You might want to read Chapter 9 if you have not already done so before continuing with the rest of this section because many of the basic principles are the same.

The effect is to provide multiple layers of information that the user can select or hide as required.

To achieve this, when entities are loaded they are created locally as objects within JavaScript. It is the objects, rather than the markers and points, that are added to a global array. That means that the markers on the map are identifiable by more than their marker object. Using this method, you can display the map with different types (using different icons), remove markers of different types, and perform other types of manipulation, because the marker information overlaid on the map is derived from an object that defines all the information required.

HTML Preamble

Once again, the HTML preamble is familiar:

```
<!DOCTYPE html PUBLIC "-//W3C//DTD XHTML 1.0 Strict//EN"
"http://www.w3.org/TR/xhtml1/DTD/xhtml1-strict.dtd">
<html xmlns="http://www.w3.org/1999/xhtml">
<head>
<meta http-equiv="content-type" content="text/html; charset=UTF-8"/>

<title>MCslp Maps Chapter 11, Ex 01</title>
<script src="http://maps.google.com/maps?file=api&v=1&key=XXX"
    type="text/javascript">
</script>

<script type="text/javascript">
```

Global Objects

Much less information needs to be stored in global variables, because the bulk of the marker information is stored as objects within a single array:

```
var map;
var index = 0;
var markindex = 0;
var types = [];
var markers = [];
var infopanel;
var message;
```

There are really only two critical global variables, the array of marker objects and the array of entity types. The other globals relate to the main Google Map, and the `infopanel` and `message` objects relate to the HTML DOM in the body of the page.

Entity Object

The `entitymarker` object is used to hold information about an individual marker that will be added to the map. For convenience, the object includes the latitude, longitude, title, type, marker, and XML to be used in an info window:

```
function entitymarker(lat,lng,title,type,marker,info) {
    this.lat = lat;
    this.lng = lng;
    this.title = title;
    this.type = type;
    this.marker = marker;
    this.info = info;
}
```

All of the information is recorded as attributes to the original object. In Chapter 9 arrays and indexes were used to store and recover the information; here, the information is instead written into a suitable object. You see some examples of where the object is used later in this chapter.

Initial Function

When the application is first loaded, the map is initialized, the global objects are initialized, and the map is zoomed to a map of the U.K.:

```
function onLoad() {
    if (GBrowserIsCompatible()) {
    infopanel = document.getElementById("infopanel");
    message = document.getElementById("message");
    map = new GMap(document.getElementById("map"));
    map.centerAndZoom(new GPoint(-2.944336,53.644638), 10);
    map.addControl(new GSmallZoomControl());
    showentitylist();
    }
}
```

The final stage is to load the list of entity types by calling the `showentitylist()` function.

Loading a List of Types

The `showentitylist()` function loads the XML from the backend CGI script. It also builds a list of types that the user can click to load the markers for a given entity. An identical link is provided to hide existing markers:

```
function showentitylist() {
    index = 0;
    types = [];
    message.innerHTML = 'Select a business type';
    infopanel.innerHTML = '';
    var request = GXmlHttp.create();
    request.open('GET','/examples/ch11-03.cgi?m=entitylist', true);
    request.onreadystatechange = function() {
    if (request.readyState == 4) {
        var xmlsource = request.responseXML;
        var typelist = xmlsource.documentElement.getElementsByTagName("type");
        for (var i=0;i < typelist.length;i++) {
          types.push(typelist[i].getAttribute("typename"));
          infopanel.innerHTML = infopanel.innerHTML +
            '<a href="#" onClick="loadentity(' +
            i +
            ');">' +
            typelist[i].getAttribute("typename") +
            '</a>  | ' +
            '<a href="#" onClick="clearmarkers(' +
            "'" + typelist[i].getAttribute("typename") + "'" +
            ');">Hide ' +
            typelist[i].getAttribute("typename") +
                    '</a><br/>';
        }
      }
    }
    request.send(null);
}
```

The process is the by now familiar case of getting a list of individual matching XML tags and extracting the attribute information to build the links.

Moving the Map

The `movemap()` function centers the map (using the latitude and longitude in the entity objects) on a marker when its name is clicked from the loaded list of markers:

```
function movemap(index) {
  map.recenterOrPanToLatLng(new GPoint(markers[index].lng,
                                       markers[index].lat));
  markers[index].marker.openInfoWindowXslt ⤸
  (markers[index].info,"/examples/ch08-12.xsl");
}
```

The function also triggers the info panel to open. The XML for the marker is loaded from the XML placed into the attribute for the marker object. This is a change from Chapter 9, where the XML was loaded using a unique index reference from a global array.

Removing Existing Markers

To remove existing markers from the map, you step through the list of marker objects, removing each marker overlay. You can do this by using the marker reference stored as an attribute in the marker object:

```
function clearmarkers(type) {
    var keeplist = [];
    for (var i=0;i<markers.length;i++) {
        if (markers[i].type == type) {
            map.removeOverlay(markers[i].marker);
        } else {
            keeplist.push(markers[i]);
        }
    }
    markers = [];
    for (var i=0;i<keeplist.length;i++) {
        markers.push(keeplist[i]);
    }
}
```

Markers also need to be removed from the array of markers displayed on the map. There are many ways to achieve this, but the most efficient and reliable that I have found is to push each marker that is not being deleted onto a new array. Then empty the original array and repopulate it with the markers that have not been deleted.

Adding Markers

Adding a marker involves creating the `point` and `marker` objects and accepting the icon information and type to populate an appropriate entity object. The marker is then created, and the listener for opening the info window to each marker is added:

```
function addmarker(x,y,title,info,icon,type) {

    var point = new GPoint(parseFloat(x),parseFloat(y));
    var marker = new GMarker(point,icon);
    GEvent.addListener(marker,
            'click',
            function() {
    marker.openInfoWindowXslt(info,"/examples/ch08-12.xsl");
    }
            );
    map.addOverlay(marker);
    markers.push(new entitymarker(y,x,title,type,marker,info));
    infopanel.innerHTML = infopanel.innerHTML +
```

```
        '<a href="#" onClick="movemap(' + index + ',' + index + ');">' +
        title +
        '</a><br/>';
    markindex++;
}
```

The entity is then created and added to the array of entities that were added to the map. Then a list of entities is shown in the information panel.

Loading Markers for a Type

Loading an entity parses the XML generated from the database, generates the markers, and recenters and zooms the map:

```
function loadentity(index) {
```

First, the entity type is determined, and the HTML message panel is populated to show the entity name:

```
    message.innerHTML = types[index];
    var entitytype = types[index];
```

The icon for the entity type is generated. Entity types from the database are generally in title case, so `toLowerCase()` is used on the type name to create a lowercase version of the image URL that is used to build the icon:

```
    var baseIcon = new GIcon();
    baseIcon.iconSize = new GSize(32,32);
    baseIcon.iconAnchor = new GPoint(0,32);
    baseIcon.infoWindowAnchor = new GPoint(32,0);
    baseIcon.image = "http://maps.mcslp.com/examples/" + ⊃
types[index].toLowerCase() + ".png";
```

Now the XML is parsed to extract the relevant information. The basic XML format is the same as before. In a nutshell, the markers are extracted by getting an array of all the XML tags of type `marker` and then extracting the attributes. Info window contents are extracted as XML using the same technique, and both pieces of data are used with the `addmarker()` function:

```
    infopanel.innerHTML = '';
    var points = [];
    var request = GXmlHttp.create();
    request.open('GET','/examples/ch11-03.cgi?m= ⊃
getmarkers&entity='+types[index], true);
    request.onreadystatechange = function() {
    if (request.readyState == 4) {
        var xmlsource = request.responseXML;
        var markerlist = ⊃
xmlsource.documentElement.getElementsByTagName("marker");
        var infowindow = ⊃
xmlsource.documentElement.getElementsByTagName("infowindow");
```

Now, for each marker the `addmarker()` function is called to create the marker with the custom icon:

```
for (var i=0;i < markerlist.length;i++) {
    addmarker(parseFloat(markerlist[i].getAttribute("lng")),
        parseFloat(markerlist[i].getAttribute("lat")),
        markerlist[i].getAttribute("title"),
        infowindow[i],
        baseIcon,
        entitytype);
}
```

Once all the markers have been created, the map is recentered. However, the application no longer builds an array of points to be used:

```
        recenterandzoom(markers);
        infopanel.innerHTML = infopanel.innerHTML +
            '<br/>' +
            '<a href="#" onClick="showentitylist()"> ↩
Back to business types</a><br/>';
    }
    }
    request.send(null);
}
```

Instead, you supply the array of markers that have been added, and a small modification is made to the `recenterandzoom()` function to use the new object array for the source information.

Recentering the Map

To recenter the map, you need to extract the data from the marker objects. To do this, you make a small change to the function to extract the data straight from the objects, rather than from the array of points from a global variable used in previous examples. The remainder of the function is the same, though:

```
function recenterandzoom(markers) {
    var latpoints = [];
    var lngpoints = [];

    for(var i=0;i<markers.length;i++) {
    latpoints.push(markers[i].lat);
    lngpoints.push(markers[i].lng);
    }

    latpoints.sort(function(x,y) { return x-y; });
    lngpoints.sort(function(x,y) { return x-y; });
    var newlat = latpoints[0] + ((latpoints[latpoints.length-1] - ↩
latpoints[0])/2);
```

```
        var newlng = lngpoints[0] + ((lngpoints[lngpoints.length-1] - ⤸
lngpoints[0])/2);

        var newpoint = new GPoint(parseFloat(newlng),parseFloat(newlat));

        var idealspan = new GSize(parseFloat(Math.abs(lngpoints ⤸
[lngpoints.length-1]-lngpoints[0])),
                    parseFloat(Math.abs(latpoints ⤸
[latpoints.length-1]-latpoints[0]))));

        map.zoomTo(1);
        var idealzoom = 1;

        for(var i=1;i<16;i++) {
        var currentsize = map.getSpanLatLng();
            if ((currentsize.width < idealspan.width) ||
            (currentsize.height < idealspan.height)) {
                map.zoomTo(i);
                idealzoom = i;
            } else {
                break;
            }
        }

        map.centerAndZoom(newpoint,idealzoom);
}
```

One of the benefits of the using the global array of all the objects on the map is that the map is recentered according to all of the entities displayed, not just the most recently added entities to the map.

Closing HTML

The closing HTML provides the structure for the page, incorporating the same map-on-the-right, info-panel-on-the-left structure used before:

```
//]]>
</script>
</head>
<body onload="onLoad()">
<table cellspacing="15" cellpadding="0" border="0">
<tr valign="top">
<td><div id="map" style="width: 800px; height: 600px"></div></td>
<td><h1><div id="message"></div></h1><div id="infopanel"></div></td>
</tr>
</table>
</body>
</html>
```

Final Application

The final application provides a simple method for adding entities to the map for display. The application starts off with a list of entity types, shown in Figure 11-3.

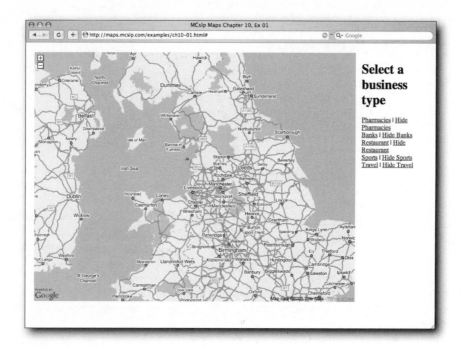

FIGURE 11-3: Initial application.

Note   You can view the application featured in this chapter at http://maps.mcslp.com/examples/ch11-01.html.

When you add an entity type to the map (for example, restaurants), you get a zoomed and focused overlay (see Figure 11-4).

Adding more entities adds to the data, as shown in Figure 11-5.

Finally, you can hide a shown entity for clarity (see Figure 11-6).

And of course, info panels are available for all the points on the map (see Figure 11-7).

To extend the information shown on the map, you only have to run ch11insert.pl with the appropriate entity type and location information and provide a suitable icon to display the data.

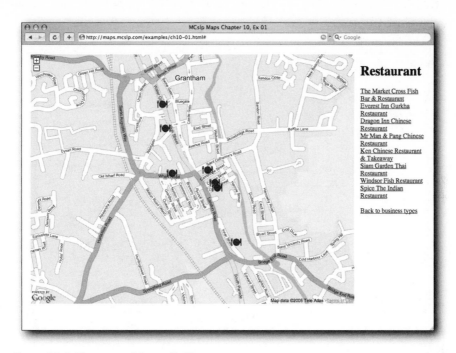

FIGURE 11-4: The zoomed-in application.

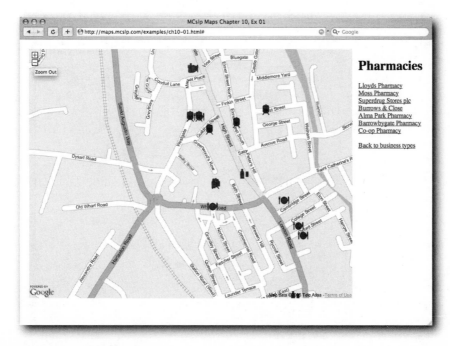

FIGURE 11-5: Adding more icons.

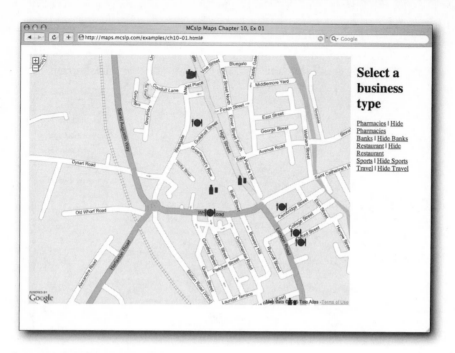

FIGURE 11-6: Hiding existing icons.

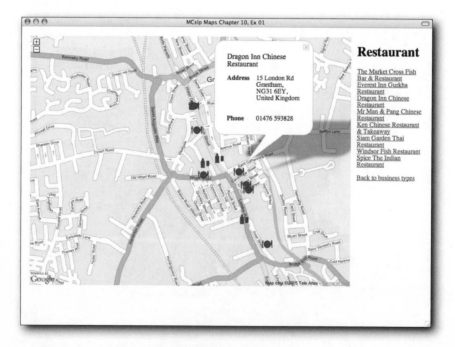

FIGURE 11-7: Info panels are still available.

Wrapping Up

Providing different layers of information is an effective way to stack your map with as much data as possible, but you must have a strategy for portraying the information on your map that will make the data as visible as possible. In this chapter, different icons were used to display the different types of information, but there are other methods for displaying that information, such as using overlays, numbered icons, or third-party extensions.

The application in this chapter also demonstrated the importance of objects for storing information about markers on the map. By building some intelligence into the markers and objects, manipulating and displaying the information onscreen becomes much easier.

The next chapter expands on the icon-based flexibility shown here by using a different method for overlaying information on the map that is more practical when you want the marker to be more flexible and explicit than a simple, predetermined icon.

The Realtors and Archaeologists Toolkit

in this chapter

☑ Use alternative
   marker technology

☑ Embed photos and
   icons as highlights

☑ Overlay images and
   drawings

☑ Identify locations
   from clicks

Sometimes the maps you create are less about information, statistics, or features that are on the map and more about the features that are not on the map. A good example of this is maps for the typical Realtor or property developer. Their needs are not necessarily centered on what elements are already on a map but instead on what can be achieved within a particular space, such as planning a new building, redevelopment, or other project. In this respect, the focus of the map they are using is how their property integrates with other elements in the area. Archaeologists' interest lies at the other end of the scale. They are not interested in what might happen, but what has happened in the past and comparing that to the current lay of the land.

Both change the way you interact with Google Maps. Instead of overlaying routes, markers, and other elements, you need to embed or overlay information on the map on a larger and much more visual scale. For example, with a Realtor you might overlay the plans for a new set of buildings for an existing plot. For an archaeologist, you might want to provide an image of a discovered object or an overlay of the dig on top of a map or satellite images to provide a context for the specifics of the dig.

This chapter examines solutions for both these situations, and in the process looks at alternative ways of representing information and different ways of interacting with the Google Maps application.

Alternative Markers

Previous chapters used custom markers to represent different pieces of information on a Google Map. You've even looked at generating your own custom icons using different images. One of the issues with the Google Maps marker system is that the markers themselves are not very flexible.

Although you can introduce any image as a marker, generating that image is not something that can easily be handled on the fly. Adding text to a marker is only possible by providing an info window that pops up when you click the marker, and there is very little control over the opacity and appearance of the icon that is displayed.

The TLabel Extension

The answer to the problem is the TLabel v1 extension, written by Thomas C. Mangan and available through his Google Maps web site (http://gmaps.tommangan.us/tlabel .html). TLabel enables you to create a simple point on a map based on text or an image. It is like creating a unique marker or info window, but without the hassle of creating the custom icon first.

The result is best demonstrated with a simple text example, something which is not possible with the standard Google Maps API. Figure 12-1 shows a basic TLabel object overlaid on top of a Google Map.

FIGURE 12-1: The basic TLabel object.

You can see from the figure that the label is just that — a simple piece of text placed on top of the map. The text in the label is completely dynamic; this is not an icon that I have previously generated. The contents, layout, and opacity of the object are all controllable when the TLabel object is generated.

Basic TLabel Creation

To use TLabel, copy the TLabel javascript file from the web site mentioned in the preceding section. This ensures that the JavaScript for the label is always available in your applications. You can then import the JavaScript using a line like the following:

```
<script src="tlabel.10.js" type="text/javascript"></script>
```

To create a new TLabel, you just create a new object based on the TLabel class defined in the preceding JavaScript file:

```
var tlabel = new TLabel();
```

Labels can be added and removed from the map using extensions to the Google Maps object. For example, to add a TLabel to your Google Map, use the following:

```
map.addTLabel(tlabel);
```

And to remove a previously added label, use this:

```
map.removeTLabel(tlabel);
```

Finally, the TLabel class exposes two methods that control the location (setPosition()) and the opacity (setOpacity()) of the label on the map. Some examples of how to use these are shown later in this chapter.

Anchor Points and Other Properties

The properties of the TLabel object control how it appears. The critical elements are the anchorPoint and anchorLatLng properties, which specify the relative location on the label that will be pinned to the specified location.

Table 12-1 lists the properties supported by the TLabel object.

Table 12-1   TLabel Properties

Property	Required	Description
id	Yes	The ID of the label. It is exposed through the standard DOM interface, so you can edit and control the content style by modifying the value of the DOM element directly, rather than updating the property value of the TLabel object.
anchorLatLng	Yes	The GPoint object that refers to the latitude/longitude where the label will be anchored. This works in tandem with the anchorPoint property to determine which point of the label is attached to the lat/long on the map.

Continued

Table 12-1 *(continued)*

Property	Required	Description
anchorPoint	No	The point on the label that will be used as the reference point for pinning the label to the map. Possible values are `topLeft`, `topCenter`, `topRight`, `midRight`, `bottomRight`, `bottomCenter`, `bottomLeft`, `midLeft`, or `center`. The default value is `topLeft`, meaning the top-left corner of the label will be pinned to the lat/long on the map.
markerOffset	No	The offset (using a `GSize` object) of the label in relation to a `GMarker` object, if you are using a `GMarker` and `TLabel` object together.
content	Yes	The XHTML code that will be displayed within the label.
percentOpacity	No	The starting opacity for the label, using a number from 0 (completely transparent) to 100 (completely opaque). You can separately set this value using the `setOpacity()` method to the `TLabel` object.

For example, you can create a simple `TLabel` using the following code:

```
var label = new TLabel();
label.id = 'label';
label.anchorLatLng = lastpoint;
label.anchorPoint = 'topRight';
label.content = '<div>Content</div>';
label.percentOpacity = 50;
```

It is generally a good idea to be specific about the style of the text (using standard XHTML markup) that you use in the `content` property, particularly with respect to the background color (which sets the color of the label) and the size of the font, which affects the appearance of the label, especially when combined with an arrow pointer.

Adding an Arrow Pointer

By default, a `TLabel` is just a bare box with XHTML contents. You will probably want to add an arrow that links the lat/lng point that you are using to the label itself. To do this, you need to create the arrow and then use the XHTML to incorporate the image and offset the image from the rest of the text as a background image. Figure 12-2 demonstrates this process in more detail.

From Figure 12-2 you can see that the anchor point remains as the point for the entire label (according to the apex of the arrow). An offset then specifies the location of the arrow in relation to the content of the rest of the label. You achieve this in XHTML by specifying the padding around the text label and using the arrow as the background image.

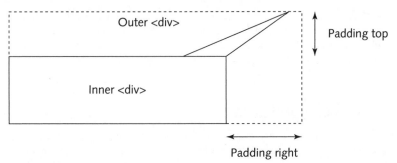

FIGURE 12-2: Adding an arrow to the label.

An outer XHTML block defines the entire label, and the inner XHTML block defines the text portion of the label. The label demonstrated in Figure 12-1 can be created using the following XHTML:

```
<div style="padding: 16px 24px 0px 0px; background: url(topright.png) ⤶
no-repeat top right;">
<div style="background-color: #ff0000; padding: 2px; font-size: 0.7em;">
<nobr>Inner text</nobr>
</div>
</div>
```

The padding defines the offset size of the arrow being used, which is also used as the background image, appended to the top right of the displayed fragment. The effect is to offset the arrow away from the actual label.

The only issue with this process is that you must separately define and create a suitable arrow according to the anchor point you want to use for your label. In the preceding example, the arrow is on the top right; separate arrows (and appropriate XHTML) would be required if you wanted an anchor point on the bottom left, top middle, and so on.

There is one final trick with the TLabel extension — using it for embedding an arbitrary image.

Embedding Pictures as Labels

You can adapt the TLabel object so that it shows an image, rather than text. Simply change the XHTML so that the embedded component is an image, rather than some text. It really is as simple as that.

However, the effect is more dramatic. An embedded image in a `TLabel` works in the same way as a text label, even using the same arrow structure. The effect is a simpler and cleaner way of highlighting items on a map without going to the trouble of using the full `GIcon` object or having to worry about developing an icon that has practical points for anchoring the image to the map.

Returning to the original goals outlined at the beginning of this chapter, using a photo or image in this way can be a useful way of highlighting an object. For example, you can use a picture of the object found at a location and accentuate it by embedding some text. Both text and images can be used in an archaeological application for highlighting different elements on a map.

Building a TLabel Application

The sample application provides a very simple way for the user to highlight different items on the map from an archaeological perspective. The interface is simple and straightforward — the user clicks the map and then clicks a link to add an appropriate object, creating a `TLabel` in the process. A number of different `TLabels` are available, including some basic user-generated text labels and an image type that projects an image of a vase over a particular location.

The whole system works through an event handler that records the position when the user clicks the map. When the user then chooses to create a point, the recorded map point is used as the basis for the anchor point.

In addition, you record all the points placed onto the map so that you can later hide and show individual object groups. This will enable the user to control the interaction between different objects placed onto the map.

The preamble is the same as usual:

```
<!DOCTYPE html PUBLIC "-//W3C//DTD XHTML 1.0 Strict//EN"
"http://www.w3.org/TR/xhtml1/DTD/xhtml1-strict.dtd">
<html xmlns="http://www.w3.org/1999/xhtml">
<head>
<meta http-equiv="content-type" content="text/html; charset=UTF-8"/>

<title>MCslp Maps Chapter 12, Ex 1</title>
<script src="http://maps.google.com/maps?file=api&v=1&key=XXX"
      type="text/javascript">
</script>
<script src="tlabel.10.js" type="text/javascript"></script>
<script type="text/javascript">
```

For global variables, you need arrays to record the `TLabels` placed onto the map, the location of the last clicked point, and the panels used to store and display information:

```
var map;
var index = 0;
var selpanel;
```

```
var mapcontrols;
var lastpoint;
var objectfinds = [];
var trenchs = [];
var ruins = [];
```

Setting Up the Map

For the location you'll use a bare field outside Oklahoma City. It happens to be clear and a uniform size, although of course the map could be located anywhere. The mapping information is irrelevant; you want to be able to compare the lay of the land with the archaeological finds. The Google Satellite photos can actually show quite a lot of information. For example, some buried elements are only visible from the sky and then only because the coloration of the land changes or minor variations in height change the appearance of the land when photographed. As far as I know, the field being used here has no archaeological features, although you can see patterns on the ground, probably the result of small hills and/or the effects of farming.

Unfortunately, there is not yet enough of the U.K. viewable at high enough quality to examine some of the sites I know well where the information is visible, so you'll work with the fake farmland dig using this field.

To start, you zoom right in to the field, switch the display type for the map using setMapType(), and then create the event listener that will record map clicks. Each time the map is clicked, the function is called, supplying the object overlay and the point where the user clicked. It is the latter item that needs to be recorded, and this is placed into the global variable:

```
function onLoad() {
    if (GBrowserIsCompatible()) {
        selpanel = document.getElementById("selections");
        mapcontrols = document.getElementById("mapcontrols");
        map = new GMap(document.getElementById("map"));
        map.setMapType(G_SATELLITE_TYPE);
        map.centerAndZoom(new GPoint(-97.58790493011475, 35.28039711620333), 1);
        map.addControl(new GLargeMapControl());
        GEvent.addListener(map, 'click', function(overlay,point) {
            lastpoint = point;
        });
    }
}
```

Adding a Label

The main function is addpoint(), which accepts a single argument, the type of point to be added to the map. The type is referenced in the link that the user clicks to generate the TLabel object. The different types adjust two elements: the background color of the label that is created and, in the case of the vase, the inclusion of the vase image in place of the text description.

The function gets the reference to the text box that will be used to populate the label and sets a default color for the label. The function also makes sure that the user has actually clicked the map by checking the value of the global `lastpoint` variable:

```
function addpoint(pointtype) {
    if (lastpoint) {
        entityname = document.getElementById("entityname");
        color = '#f2efe9';
```

Next, the label object is created by setting the common `TLabel` properties for all the different types of entities. The index reference used here is important, so a simple incrementing value is used:

```
var label = new TLabel();
label.id = 'label' + index++;
label.anchorLatLng = lastpoint;
label.anchorPoint = 'topRight';
label.content = content;
label.percentOpacity = 50;
```

For each entity type, the color is configured using a local variable, and the object is pushed onto the array for each object type. These arrays will be used when the user hides or shows object groups on the map. Although the definition of the object is not complete at the time it is pushed onto the array (the label content has not been set), the object ID is enough to identify the object when showing/hiding the labels.

```
if (pointtype == 'object') {
    objectfinds.push(label);
    color = '#f20000';
}

if (pointtype == 'trench') {
    trenchs.push(label);
    color = '#f2ef00';
}

if (pointtype == 'ruin') {
    ruins.push(label);
    color = '#f2efe9';
}
```

If the object being created is a vase, the label content is populated with the appropriate HTML containing the reference to the image of the vase, rather than the text of the input box:

```
if (pointtype == 'vase') {
    objectfinds.push(label);
    color = '#f20000';

    label.content = '<div style="padding: 16px 24px 0px 0px; ⤶
background: url(topright.png) no-repeat top right;"> ⤶
```

```
<div style="background-color: #f2efe9; padding: 2px;">
<img src="woodvase.png" alt="" style="border: none;"></\div></div>';
        }
```

If the entity isn't a vase, the content of the input box is checked and the content is then populated. If the input box is empty, a warning is raised and no label is created.

```
    else {
        if (entityname.value.length == 0) {
            alert('You must give this point a name');
            return;
        }

        var content = '<div style="padding: 16px 24px 0px 0px;
background: url(topright.png) no-repeat top right;"><div style=
"background-color: ' + color + '; padding: 2px; font-size: 0.7em;">
<div style="color: #0000ff; font-weight: bold">' + pointtype +
'</div><nobr>' + entityname.value + '</nobr></div></div>';
        label.content = content;
    }
```

Finally, the label is added to the map:

```
        map.addTLabel(label);
    }
```

An alert is raised if the map has not been clicked and a point has not been created:

```
    else {
        alert("No point has been set");
    }
}
```

Showing and Hiding Points

To show and hide the points, links on the main page call the showpoints() and hidepoints() functions, which accept the name of an array and iterate through the objects, showing or hiding them as appropriate:

```
function showpoints(pointtype) {
    for(var i=0;i<pointtype.length;i++) {
        map.addTLabel(pointtype[i]);
    }
}

function hidepoints(pointtype) {
    for(var i=0;i<pointtype.length;i++) {
        map.removeTLabel(pointtype[i]);
    }
}
```

The HTML Interface

Finally, here is the HTML that contains the map, links, and input box for controlling and overlaying information and entities on the map. The layout is similar to previous examples; the map is on the left and the control interface is on the right:

```
</script>
</head>
<body onload="onLoad()">
<table cellspacing="15" cellpadding="0" border="0">
<tr valign="top">
<td><div id="map" style="width: 800px; height: 600px"></div></td>
<td><h1>Overlay Selection</h1><div id="selections"></div>
<form action="#"><b>Entity title</b>: ⤶
<input type="text" size="20" id="entityname"></form><br/>
<a href="#" onClick="addpoint('vase')">Add Vase</a> |  ⤶
<a href="#" onClick="hidepoints(objectfinds)">Hide Vase</a> ⤶
 | <a href="#" onClick="showpoints(objectfinds)">Show Vases</a><br/>
<a href="#" onClick="addpoint('object')">Add Object</a> |  ⤶
<a href="#" onClick="hidepoints(objectfinds)">Hide Objects</a> ⤶
 | <a href="#" onClick="showpoints(objectfinds)">Show Objects</a><br/>
<a href="#" onClick="addpoint('trench')">Add Trench</a> ⤶
 | <a href="#" onClick="hidepoints(trenchs)"> ⤶
Hide Trenchs</a> | <a href="#" onClick="showpoints(trenchs)"> ⤶
Show Trenchs</a><br/>
<a href="#" onClick="addpoint('ruin')">Add Ruin</a> |  ⤶
<a href="#" onClick="hidepoints(ruins)">Hide Ruins</a> |  ⤶
<a href="#" onClick="showpoints(ruins)">Show Ruins</a><br/>
</td>
<td><h1>Map Control</h1><div id="mapcontrols"></div></td>
</tr>
</table>
</body>
</html>
```

The Application in Use

The application starts out with a blank map, waiting for the user to click a point and create a suitable label, as shown in Figure 12-3.

Clicking a point and then clicking the Add Vase link creates a vase label on the map. Two have been generated in Figure 12-4.

Other elements can be added to the map accordingly. Figure 12-5 shows a variety of different entities added to the map.

You can see that the labels are created and even overlap, but the opacity, set at 50 percent, helps to make the elements on the map more readable. This is one of the reasons why the system also includes the facility to hide groups of objects, as shown in Figure 12-6, where the vases have been hidden from the map.

FIGURE 12-3: The initial interface.

FIGURE 12-4: Vases highlighted on the map.

FIGURE **12-5**: Adding multiple entities.

FIGURE **12-6**: Hidden entities.

Obviously the information created here is not stored and retained, but there is no reason why the same principles shown in other chapters couldn't be used to either generate the labels or store the user-created labels in the system for later use. The key is in the generation and interaction between the user, the map, and the `TLabel` extension.

Overlaying Images and Drawings

In the preceding part of this chapter, the `TLabel` extension was used to allow text or image-based labels to be placed onto a Google Map. The `TPhoto` extension enables you to overlay a photo on top of a Google Map, either to fully replace the information shown on the map or to augment the detail in some way.

For example, you could overlay an infrared photograph on top of the map to show particular highlights, or perhaps use an overlay to artificially create the existence of a particular structure, building, or object onto the map.

The former case is a good example where a localized area photo, perhaps from an archaeological survey, could be used to enhance the information displayed on the map. Imagine if the dig highlighted in the previous section had an aerial infrared (or perhaps underground ultra-sonic) survey that could be overlaid precisely onto a live map of the region.

In this section the same basic method is used to overlay a very simple map of a new office complex onto the same field used in the previous section. The idea is to give a live impression of the office buildings, their location, and potential relationships with other objects on the map.

The TPhoto Extension

The `TPhoto` extension is from the same developer as `TLabel`, but unlike `TLabel` it is designed as a method for overlaying an image (usually a large one) on top of a Google Map, rather than acting as a label for a particular point on the map.

As such, unlike `TLabel`, the reference point for an image to be overlaid on top of the map is based on either matching a pixel of the image with a specific latitude/longitude or matching the top left and bottom right of the image to specific latitudes/longitudes. In the case of the former method, anchoring a single point gives you control over the zoom level of the overlaid image. In the case of the latter method, the anchoring of top left and bottom right of the image determines the zoom level (the image will be located between those points and zoomed accordingly). For the office plan overlay example, the latter method is used.

As with `TLabel`, you should download the JavaScript that creates the `TLabel` (from `http://gmaps.tommangan.us/TPhoto.html`) and place the script on your own server to ensure that it is always available. After the script has been imported into your Google Maps page, you can configure the image to be overlaid using the following code fragment:

```
photo = new TPhoto();
photo.id = '[id]';
photo.src = '[src]';
photo.percentOpacity = [percent];
```

```
photo.anchorTopLeft = new GPoint(lng,lat);
photo.anchorBottomRight = new GPoint(lng,lat);
map.addTPhoto(photo);
```

The `id` property should be used and enabled in the same way as `TLabel`. The opacity controls the visibility of the image when it is overlaid, and the anchors for the top-left and bottom-right extremities of the image should be self-explanatory.

Using TPhoto Overlays

A simple overlay has been generated that maps out some simple office structures, shown in Figure 12-7.

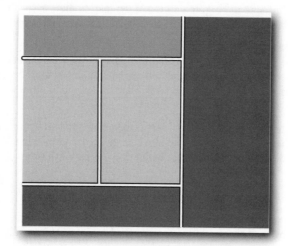

FIGURE 12-7: Office plan overlay.

To overlay the image, it is a simple case of initializing the map, creating a `TPhoto` object, and adding it to the map. The preamble is familiar, this time importing the `TPhoto` JavaScript extension during the process:

```
<!DOCTYPE html PUBLIC "-//W3C//DTD XHTML 1.0 Strict//EN"
"http://www.w3.org/TR/xhtml1/DTD/xhtml1-strict.dtd">
<html xmlns="http://www.w3.org/1999/xhtml">
<head>
<meta http-equiv="content-type" content="text/html; charset=UTF-8"/>

<title>MCslp Maps Chapter 12, Ex 2</title>
<script src="http://maps.google.com/maps?file=api&v=1&key=XXX"
    type="text/javascript">
```

```
</script>
<script src="tphoto.16.js" type="text/javascript"></script>
<script type="text/javascript">

var map;
var index = 0;
var message;
var mapcontrols;
var lastpoint;
var photo;
var opacity = 50;
var mapobjects = [];
```

The initialization function for the page also covers familiar ground. Initially the map is set to show satellite images, and the map is centered on the same field outside Oklahoma City. A larger map control is added to the map to enable the user to move around:

```
function onLoad() {
    if (GBrowserIsCompatible()) {
        message = document.getElementById("message");
        mapcontrols = document.getElementById("mapcontrols");
        map = new GMap(document.getElementById("map"));
        map.setMapType(G_SATELLITE_TYPE);
        map.centerAndZoom(new GPoint(-97.58790493011475, 35.28039711620333), 1);
        map.addControl(new GLargeMapControl());
```

The basic overlay can then be constructed and added to the map. An earlier script was used to determine the top left and bottom right of the field so that the overlay could be added to the map:

```
        photo = new TPhoto();
        photo.id = 'overlay';
        photo.src = 'ch12-overlay.png';
        photo.percentOpacity = 50;
        photo.anchorTopLeft = new GPoint(-97.59286165237427, 35.28367266426725);
        photo.anchorBottomRight = new GPoint(-97.58256196975708, ⟲
35.27654336061367);
        map.addTPhoto(photo);
    }
}
```

To help view the overlay and the map in relation to the live elements on the map (roads, other buildings, rivers, hills, and other natural structures), a control is added to change the opacity of the overlay. The opacity value is stored locally (rather than querying the object), and it is updated higher or lower (according to the supplied value). Attempts to modify the opacity value beyond the available limits are ignored.

```
function changeopacity(changevalue) {
    var newopacity = opacity + changevalue;

    if (newopacity < 0) {
```

```
        return;
    }
    if (newopacity > 100) {
        return;
    }
    photo.setOpacity(newopacity);
    opacity = newopacity;
}
```

Finally, the HTML for the application interface provides a very simple way of changing the map type and the opacity of the overlay:

```
</script>
</head>
<body onload="onLoad()">
<table cellspacing="15" cellpadding="0" border="0">
<tr valign="top">
<td><div id="map" style="width: 800px; height: 600px"></div></td>
<td><h1>New Office Grand Plan</h1><div id="message">
Click Map for Info</div><br/>
<h1>Overlay Control</h1><a href="#" onClick="changeopacity(-10);">
Reduce overlay</a> | <a href="#" onClick="changeopacity(10);"
>Increase overlay</a><br/>
<a href="#" onClick="map.setMapType(G_MAP_TYPE)">Show Map</a> | 
<a href="#" onClick="map.setMapType(G_SATELLITE_TYPE)">Show Satellite</a>
 | <a href="#" onClick="map.setMapType(G_HYBRID_TYPE)">
Show Hybrid</a></td>
</tr>
</table>
</body>
</html>
```

The initial application is shown in Figure 12-8.

The TPhoto extension handles the positioning and zooming of the overlay onto the map. Because the overlay is linked to specific latitude/longitude points, zooming out or moving the map will move the overlay accordingly. You can see the effects in Figure 12-9.

The overlay is also visible over any map type. For clarity, map type buttons have not been added to the map itself. Instead a suite of external buttons controls the interface. Figure 12-10 shows the map and overlay, this time on the basic map instead of the satellite images.

There are some problems with this map from the perspective of information. There are allocated blocks on the map, but there is no information on what they are. TLabels of GMarkers could be used to highlight the different areas. Instead, a solution that involves the map providing you with information and parsing it, rather than the other way around, offers a little more flexibility.

FIGURE 12-8: The initial overlay example.

FIGURE 12-9: The overlay is locked.

FIGURE **12-10: Reducing the overlay visibility.**

Identifying Elements from Click Locations

Adding information to a map extends and enhances the data that the map can provide. However, the map itself can help to provide information or trigger the display of information. For example, when clicking on a map you might want to determine what is located in that area without necessarily highlighting that information with a marker or overlay. This can be achieved in many ways, but the most effective way is to create a new object type. Each object will contain the confines of different areas on the map, a simple description of the area, and a method that checks a supplied point against the object to determine if the click was within the defined area.

The map application in the previous section can then be updated. First, the different areas on the map are registered using the new object. A number of events are also added to the map so that a click on the map will trigger a check of the registered objects, and movements and changes to the map will trigger modifications to the overlay.

Creating a Unique Map Object

The first step is to create a new object class to hold the top-left and bottom-right areas on the map for a given location. The information will be stored in properties for the object. Objects within JavaScript use the special `this` value to reference and define entities of the object.

Storing the properties is therefore a simple case of assigning the function's supplied arguments to the properties of the new object. Just in case the information provided is not in the obvious top-left/bottom-right order, the input values are checked and the properties are set accordingly:

```
function MapObject (topleftx,toplefty,botrightx,botrighty,text) {
    if (topleftx < botrightx) {
        this.minX = topleftx;
        this.maxX = botrightx;
    } else {
        this.minX = botrightx;
        this.maxX = topleftx;
    }

    if (toplefty < botrighty) {
        this.minY = toplefty;
        this.maxY = botrighty;
    } else {
        this.minY = botrighty;
        this.maxY = toplefty;
    }
    this.description = text;
```

To check a given point against the outline area for an object, you need a method to check a given latitude/longitude against the registered bounds for the object. To define a method for an object in JavaScript, you must first create a reference to the function as a property of the object and then define the function itself.

The function definition is simple. It checks whether the arguments supplied to the method are within the minimum and maximum values supplied when the object was created:

```
    this.inbounds = inbounds;
    function inbounds(x,y) {
        if (((x > this.minX) && (x < this.maxX)) &&
            ((y > this.minY) && (y < this.maxY))) {
            message.innerHTML = this.description;
        }
    }
}
```

Now the areas just have to be defined within your application.

Registering the Objects on the Map

Each area object is placed into an array, and the following code defines the bounds and description for each of the areas based on the overlay created in the previous section:

```
mapobjects.push(new MapObject(-97.58590936660767, 35.27654336061367,
                              -97.58260488510132, 35.28360260045482,
                              'Car Park'));

mapobjects.push(new MapObject(-97.58904218673706, 35.282008632343754,
```

```
                          -97.58638143539429, 35.278137436300966,
                          'Sales Office'));

mapobjects.push(new MapObject(-97.59279727935791, 35.283585084492245,
                          -97.58638143539429, 35.282376473923584,
                          'Packaging/Delivery Office'));

mapobjects.push(new MapObject(-97.59277582168579, 35.282008632343754,
                          -97.59017944335938, 35.278137436300966,
                          'Admin Office'));

mapobjects.push(new MapObject(-97.59277582168579, 35.27776957546562,
                          -97.5864028930664, 35.27657839558136,
                          'IT/Support Services'));
```

Now the map just has to trigger a check of each of these objects when the map is clicked.

Identifying the Click Location

By modifying the click event that was used in the previous example, a click on the map can trigger checking the list of registered areas. This is achieved by iterating over the array of objects and then calling the `inbounds()` method on each object. The following fragment should be placed into the `onLoad()` function to be initialized with the rest of the application:

```
GEvent.addListener(map, 'click', function(overlay,point) {
    message.innerHTML = 'Empty';
    for(var i=0;i<mapobjects.length;i++) {
        mapobjects[i].inbounds(point.x,point.y);
    }
});
```

If it matches, the information will be placed into the information area of the application.

Resetting the Map Location

To prevent the user from getting distracted by other nearby entities on the map, a timeout can be added to the window that automatically resets the map's center point location after a given interval. The method is actually a function of the JavaScript, not Google Maps, but it can be used to trigger a Google Maps event, for example a reload of map data. The interval is specified in milliseconds, and a value of 60000 milliseconds (or 60 seconds) is used in the following example.

This is actually a two-stage process. First, a function that recenters the map and resets the timeout (so that it is continually active) must be defined:

```
function recenter() {
    map.centerAndZoom(new GPoint(-97.58790493011475, 35.28039711620333), 1);
    window.setTimeout('recenter()',60000);
}
```

Then you set the initial timeout, either by calling this function within onLoad() or by calling the setTimeout() method on the window object within onLoad(); the effect is the same:

```
window.setTimeout('recenter()',60000);
```

Resetting the Object Opacity

One final element of convenience is to ensure that the overlay is visible when the user changes between map types. For example, when changing from satellite to map, it can be useful to get reacquainted with the position of the new office block on the map. To achieve this, another listener is added to the map. This one is triggered each time the map type is changed, and it explicitly resets the opacity of the overlay image:

```
GEvent.addListener(map, 'maptypechanged', function() {
    photo.setOpacity(50);
    opacity = 50;
});
```

Final Overlay Application

The final map application can be seen in Figure 12-11, showing the initial overlay highlighted on the satellite image of the field, just as shown earlier in the chapter.

FIGURE 12-11: Overlay image.

If the user clicks in a specific area within the map, the information panel updates with the title of the area, as defined when you created the area object (see Figure 12-12).

FIGURE 12-12: Getting area detail.

A basic description is shown here, but it could just as easily incorporate more detailed information on the office space, even a photo of the artist's mock-up. Adding extra information to the process is comparatively easy.

Wrapping Up

The first map example demonstrates some very simple methods of overlaying information that makes the highlighted points more visible and useful through the use of the TLabel extension. The extension improves the quality of the information on the map without relying on the two-stage interface that is available with the standard Google Map GMarker object. The label works exactly as its name suggests. The simple label is more flexible and probably more useful in areas where you want to dynamically highlight points to the user.

The second map (and the later extension) shows that a Google Map can provide more than just mapping data. By using an overlay, you can extend the information provided far beyond the built-in data in the map. In the extension, the overlay was also used as a basis for determining additional information. The same technique could have been played to an underground survey, technical schema, or other data so that it was possible to match information you know with the live map data that Google provides. With the right overlays and some basic mathematics, it is possible to build a multi-layer view of a site, perhaps showing different floors, underground levels, and even services such as electricity cables, water pipes, and sewage conduits.

As you can see in both examples, you can use the live Google Map data with other information to give that information context. To an archaeologist, this means providing reference data that relates the lay of the land as you know it now with historical information about the location of objects, finds, buildings, and other elements.

For the Realtor, providing contextual information about a future development enables you to check whether a site is suitable, whether it's going to have the right services and connections, and whether the plan for the site matches the plan in the client's head. It wouldn't be hard to extend the information given, perhaps with photographs of potential views in different locations, and you could even use the `TLabel` extension to show the photos on the map.

I Need to Get To...

O ne of the most common roles that a map has to play is as a guide from one place to another. Think about the last time you used a map. Were you trying to find the location of something or to plan a route from one location to another? Perhaps you were planning a walking trip, a city tour, or just a way to avoid the latest bout of highway mainte-nance on your route to work. These are simply examples. The point is that people use maps to find and locate a route or distance between points.

This chapter examines an application that provides an interface for record-ing, saving, and loading routes from a database. The user will be able to cre-ate a new route, manually create the route's sequence and point layout, and save and name the route. The application can also obtain a list of the exist-ing routes and their starting points and load an existing route. For an addi-tional level of functionality, the application also allows the user to edit and modify the route details, making a truly dynamic map route application.

The application is divided into two parts: the front end (the HTML and the Google Maps interface) and the backend (the CGI script that provides and stores information for the front-end application in a database). Each of these parts is covered individually.

Front-End Interface

As usual, the front end of the application is a combination of some wrapper HTML and the JavaScript that provides the interface to the Google Maps API and provides the connectivity between the front-end application and the backend CGI that provides the interface to the database that stores information.

Note The application is large and is described here in individual sec-tions according to the role or function that is being described. The individual code fragments can be re-assembled into a final application, or you can download the application from the book's web site (http://maps.mcslp.com).

HTML Wrapper

The HTML for the application obviously provides the visual interface to the main components of the application, including the encapsulation of the main Google Maps window:

```
<!DOCTYPE html PUBLIC "-//W3C//DTD XHTML 1.0 Strict//EN"
"http://www.w3.org/TR/xhtml1/DTD/xhtml1-strict.dtd">
<html xmlns="http://www.w3.org/1999/xhtml">
<head>
<meta http-equiv="content-type" content="text/html; charset=UTF-8"/>
<title>MCslp Maps Chapter 13, Ex 1</title>
<script src="http://maps.google.com/maps?file=api&v=1&key=XXX"
    type="text/javascript">
</script>

<script type="text/javascript">
...
</script>
</head>
<body onload="onLoad()">

<div id="map" style="width: 800px; height: 600px"></div>
<table width="100%" cellspacing="5" cellpading="0" border="0">
<tr valign="top">
<td width="33%"><h3>Controls</h3>
<a href="#" onClick="newroute()">New route</a><br/>
<a href="#" onClick="startRoute()">Start recording route</a><br/>
<a href="#" onClick="endRoute()">Stop recording route</a><br/>
<a href="#" onClick="clearLastPoint()">Clear last point</a><br/>
<a href="#" onClick="clearRoute()">Clear current route</a><br/>
<a href="#" onClick="showroutelist()">List saved routes</a><br/>
<a href="#" onClick="delroute()">Delete current route</a></td>

<td width="33%"><h3><div id="message">Messages</div></h3>
<div id="infopanel"></div></td>
<td width="33%"><h3>Route information</h3>
<input type="hidden" id="routeid" value="0" size="10">
<b>Name</b><br/> <input type=text id="routetitle" size="40"/><br/>
<b>Description</b><br/> <textarea id="routedesc" rows=10 ⤶
cols=40></textarea><br/>
<a href="#" onClick="saveroute()">Save route</a></td>
</tr>
</table>
</body>
</html>
```

The HTML is used to create a four-panel layout. The main panel at the top is the one used to hold the Google Map. The table at the bottom holds three columns of equal width. The first holds the links that control the application, a space for a message, and the current route recording status. The middle panel is a generic information window, used to hold items such as the list of existing routes. The last panel holds a simple form used to hold route details for use when saving and editing routes.

You can see a sample of the layout in Figure 13-1, showing the application in its initial state.

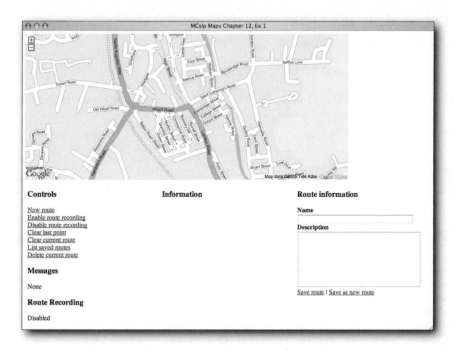

FIGURE 13-1: Simple route recording application layout.

Note You can try out this application at the web site using the URL `http://maps.mcslp.com/examples/ch13-01.html`.

The HTML also highlights the main operations supported by the application:

- Creating a new route.
- Enabling route recording.
- Disabling route recording.
- Clearing the last point.
- Clearing the current route.
- Obtaining a list of the current routes.
- Deleting the current route from the database.
- Saving a route into the database.
- Saving an existing route as a new route into the database.

By association there are also the following operations:

- Loading a saved route.

- Editing a saved route (by re-saving an existing route).

The information panel is used to list different routes and other data, the message window helps instruct the user on using the system, and the recording status area displays the current state of the recording mechanism.

Global Variables

A number of global variables are required to hold the information for the application. Many of these variables are used to hold references to the HTML elements used to show messages and other information during the execution of the application. Check the following code, which includes annotations for each of the variables:

```
var map;               // the main map object
var points = [];       // the list of active points in the current route
var route;             // the GPolyline of the current route
var routelistener;     // the listener object for updating the current route
var rrecording;        // the HTML reference for current recording mode
var routeidfield;      // the HTML reference of the ID in the form
var routetitle;        // the HTML reference of the title in the form
var routedescription;  // the HTML reference of the description in the form
var message;           // the document reference of the message panel
var infopanel;         // the document reference of the info panel
var icontags = 'ABCDEFGHIJKLMNOPQRSTUVWXYZ';
```

The last item (which is not commented) is a simple string of the alphabet that you'll use to select the right icon for a marker when displaying a list of the available routes.

With these in place the rest of the application that uses these elements can be built.

Enabling the Route Recording Process

The main component of the application is the ability to record a route, which is accomplished using the `startRoute()` function. The process has several stages. First, a listener must be added to the map so that each time the user clicks the map, you record the location of the click and push it onto an array of points. As a visual aid for the user, a marker is placed on the map for the first click, and then the line is drawn for each point pair to show the route they are recording onto the map.

Note, however, that the array of points is not emptied. This enables the user to start and stop the recording process without affecting the list of existing points. This enables the user to load an existing route and extend or modify it, changing the application from a basic route recording system into a more useful route editing system.

Here is the code for the `startRoute()` function:

```
function startRoute() {
  routelistener = GEvent.addListener(map, 'click', function(overlay,point) {
    if (route) {
      map.removeOverlay(route);
    }
    if (points.length == 1) {
      addmarker(point,'Start Point');
    }
    points.push(point);
    if (points.length > 1) {
      route = new GPolyline(points);
      map.addOverlay(route);
    }
  });
  rrecording.innerHTML = 'Enabled';
}
```

The core of the function is the addition to the map of an event listener to record clicks. The listener is an inline function. The function has to handle a number of different states, any of which may be true at the time the event listener function is called, hence the use of individual `if` statements, rather than an `if/else` structure. The function tracks and handles the states in the following ways:

- If there is already a route overlay (stored in the `route` variable referring to the active `GPolyline`) in place on the map (meaning that a route has been defined), it deletes the route overlay. (It will be re-created when the new point is added.)

- If this is the first point, it also adds a marker to indicate the start of the route. There is no reason to record this marker because it will never need to be referenced directly.

- If there is more than one point, it creates a polyline overlay to show the route on the map. This is recorded in the `route` variable so that it can easily be removed if necessary.

Embedded in this process is the addition of the point (passed to the listener when the user clicks the map) into the array of points for the current route. All of these operations take place as part of the route listener.

The final part of the wrapper function that initiates the recording process is to update the indicator showing the current status of the recording process.

Disabling the Route Recording Process

The most straightforward method of disabling the recording process is simply to remove the listener that was added to the map. That stops the function triggered by the listener from being executed:

```
function endRoute() {
  GEvent.removeListener(routelistener);
  rrecording.innerHTML = 'Disabled';
}
```

Nothing else changes aside from the status message. By not zeroing the list of points or changing any other details, the application returns the route and retains the route display and, because the enable process doesn't modify anything either, the recording process can be restarted.

Clearing the Last Point

So that users can edit an existing route (or a new route that they are recoding), the application includes the ability to remove the last point added to a route. This is achieved by popping the last point off of the array (which removes the point from the array). Then the existing overlay is removed, the GPolyline object is re-created, and the overlay is added back:

```
function clearLastPoint() {
    if (points.length > 0) {
        points.pop();
    }
    if (points.length == 0) {
        map.clearOverlays();
        return;
    }
    map.removeOverlay(route);
    route = new GPolyline(points);
    map.addOverlay(route);
}
```

The application only pops a point off the array if the array has at least one item. If all of the points in the array are removed from the display, the starting marker object is also removed.

Clearing the Current Route

If the user wants to clear the current route but not delete the route from the list of saved routes, a convenient function is provided that clears all the overlays (including the starting marker and any GPolyline overlays) and then empties the array of existing points:

```
function clearRoute() {
  map.clearOverlays();
  points = [];
}
```

Note that nothing else has changed. The application could still be in recording mode, and the process would continue as normal.

Initializing a New Route

Different from clearing the route, creating a new route zeros not only the list of points, but also all the other variables, before enabling the recording of the route by calling startRoute():

```
function newRoute() {
  points = [];
  routeidfield.value = 0;
  routetitle.value = '';
```

```
   routedescription.value = '';
   infopanel.innerHTML = '';
   message.innerHTML = 'Recording a new route';
   map.clearOverlays();
   startRoute();
}
```

The route ID variable is set to zero, because this triggers the creation of a new route when the route is saved to the backend CGI interface.

Deleting a Route

Deleting a route means removing the route not only from the current view within the browser, but also from the database itself (if the route was one loaded from the database):

```
function delRoute() {
  if (routeidfield.value != 0) {
    routeidtext = '&routeid=' + escape(routeidfield.value);
    var request = GXmlHttp.create();
    request.open('GET','/examples/ch13-backend.cgi?m=delroute' ⤵
+ routeidtext,true);
    request.onreadystatechange = function() {
      if (request.readyState == 4) {
        var xmlsource = request.responseXML;

        var msg = xmlsource.documentElement.getElementsByTagName("message");
        if (msg.length > 0) {
          message.innerHTML = msg[0].getAttribute('text');
        }
        else
        {
          message.innerHTML = 'Error sending request';
        }
      }
    }
  }
  request.send(null);
  map.clearOverlays();
  routeidfield.value = 0;
  routetitle.value = '';
  routedescription.value = '';
  infopanel.innerHTML = '';
}
```

It is easy to identify a route that has previously been saved (as opposed to one currently being recorded): A saved route has a non-zero route ID.

To actually delete the route, the application has to compose a request to the CGI backend that connects to the database. The request consists of the command delroute and the route ID number. The return value from the process should be a message, encoded in XML, that indicates that the deletion was completed successfully. If the message could not be extracted properly (which probably means the return value was not XML), it reports there was an error sending the request to the backend.

To finish off the process, you also zero all of the variables used for storing information about the route (including the form fields) and then clear the overlays for the map, effectively putting the application into the same position as when the application was first started.

Saving a Route

To save a route, the JavaScript must compose a suitable request string to the backend, consisting of the title, the description, and a list of points. To ensure that the sequence of the points is retained, the array element number of the points is also included in the list of points, so that for each point there is a sequence, latitude, and longitude.

So that the application can save new routes, re-save new routes, and save an existing route as a new route (perhaps with different points and description details), the saveRoute() function checks the value of the route ID field (which is hidden) and the value of the supplied argument (oldnew). The former enables the function to distinguish between saving new and existing routes. If the route ID is zero, a new route is saved (because a zero value for the route ID triggers a new sequence ID in the database). A non-zero value updates the existing route.

So that an existing route can be saved as a new route, the value of the oldnew argument is used. If the route to be saved is a new route, a zero is supplied when the route is saved, and this indicates to the backend (and the database) that a new route is being recorded. For convenience, the value of the field/value pair that would be supplied as part of the request string is set to a blank string, and only populated if the user specifically wants to create a new route:

```
function saveRoute(oldnew) {
  pointstring = "";
  for(i=0;i<points.length;i++) {
    pointstring = pointstring + i + ':' + points[i].x + ':' + points[i].y + ',';
  }
  var request = GXmlHttp.create();
  var routeidtext = '';
  if ((routeidfield.value != 0) &&
      (oldnew == 1)) {
    routeidtext = '&routeid=' + escape(routeidfield.value);
  }
```

The request string is necessarily large; it has to incorporate the title, the description, the list of route points and, if necessary, the route ID information:

```
request.open('GET','/examples/ch13-backend.cgi?m=saveroute&title=' +
             escape(routetitle.value) + routeidtext +
             '&desc=' + escape(routedescription.value) +
             '&points=' + escape(pointstring), true);
request.onreadystatechange = function() {
   if (request.readyState == 4) {
```

Once the request has been sent, the script must determine the status of the submission. The response should be an XML document containing a message stating success and the ID of the new route. If this information has been successfully extracted, it means the request was successful, and the route is now loaded by supplying a suitable route ID and message to the loadRoute() function. A failure to parse the returned XML indicates a failure, so a warning message is produced instead:

```
        var xmlsource = request.responseXML;
        var msg = xmlsource.documentElement.getElementsByTagName("message");
        if (msg.length > 0) {
          if (msg[0].getAttribute('routeid') > 0) {
            loadRoute(msg[0].getAttribute('routeid'),
                    msg[0].getAttribute('text'));
          }
        }
        else
        {
          message.innerHTML = 'Error sending request';
        }
      }
    }
    request.send(null);
}
```

The loading of the just saved route serves as a good indication that the route has been saved
and also means that the route is displayed just as it would be if the route were loaded from the
list of available routes.

Loading a List of Routes

The user can obtain a list of the available routes by clicking the link, which in turn runs the
showRouteList() function. With some minor modifications, this is basically an adaptation
of the XML parser used in Chapter 9 to show a list of registered points on the map.

The backend CGI script sends back a list of route titles, the route ID, and the latitude and longitude of the start point for each route. The following code shows the creation of a marker for
each route start point.

The first stage is to empty all of the variables of any information and empty the map, because
the function is building a new inline display:

```
function showRouteList() {
  map.clearOverlays();
  points = [];
  message.innerHTML = 'Select a route';
  infopanel.innerHTML = '';
  routetitle.value = '';
  routedescription.value = '';
```

Next, create an icon template that will be used to create custom icons (with a unique character
for identification). The icon will be one of the standard Google Maps icons, using a standard
shadow, so the same basic structure can be used as with other icon samples. The full details of
the base icon, including the image size, shadow size, and the anchor points have been specified
according to the Google Map standards:

```
  var baseIcon = new GIcon();
  baseIcon.shadow = "http://www.google.com/mapfiles/shadow50.png";
  baseIcon.iconSize = new GSize(20,34);
  baseIcon.shadowSize = new GSize(37,34);
  baseIcon.iconAnchor = new GPoint(9,34);
  baseIcon.infoWindowAnchor = new GPoint(9,2);
  baseIcon.infoWindowAnchor = new GPoint(18,25);
```

Next, the function sends a suitable request through to the backend database interface. The script only has to ask for the list of routes. There is no additional information to be supplied. The response will be an XML document, looking similar to this:

```
<routes>
<route routeid="3" title="A1 to Station (North)" lat="-0.652313" lng="52.9164"/>
<route routeid="13" title="Barrowby to Nottingham" ⤵
lat="-0.685959" lng="52.9197"/>
<route routeid="14" title="Courthouse to Shell Garage" ⤵
lat="-0.645833" lng="52.9094"/>
<route routeid="12" title="Home to Asda" lat="-0.683942" lng="52.9164"/>
<route routeid="15" title="Home to Sainsburys" lat="-0.683942" lng="52.9164"/>
<route routeid="11" title="One on Wharf to St Wulframs" lat="-0.639954"
lng="52.9094"/>
</routes>
```

Note that the XML is already in alphabetical order. It is easy to do this when submitting the query to the database and it saves having to perform any kind of ordering within the JavaScript.

When the information is extracted, the script needs to build a list of markers to highlight the starting point of each route (the embedded latitude and longitude), provide each marker with a custom icon, and build a textual list of available routes:

```
var request = GXmlHttp.create();
request.open('GET','/examples/ch13-backend.cgi?m=listroutes', true);
request.onreadystatechange = function() {
  if (request.readyState == 4) {
    var xmlsource = request.responseXML;
    var routelist = xmlsource.documentElement.getElementsByTagName("route");
    for (var i=0;i < routelist.length;i++) {
```

First the icon for the marker is determined. Because there is a count of the parsed items available, the current count is used to extract a single character from the icontags. This letter is combined with a standard icon URL to produce the URL of one of the standard Google Maps markers for use on the map. The information is placed into a new variable because it is used on both the map and the textual list:

```
var iconloc =  'http://www.google.com/mapfiles/marker' +
               icontags.charAt(i) + '.png';
```

Next, the information panel, which contains a textual list of the routes, is composed. The list consists of the lettered icon, the name of the route, and a link to the local loadRoute() function with the unique route ID number (as generated by the database). Clicking this link loads the route into the application and shows the route, start point, and other information.

```
infopanel.innerHTML = infopanel.innerHTML +
  '<img src="' + iconloc + '" border="0">' +
  '<a href="#" onClick="loadRoute(' +
  routelist[i].getAttribute("routeid") +
  ');">' + routelist[i].getAttribute("title") +
  '</a><br/>';
```

A new point is created and pushed onto an array of points. The array is to recenter the map so that all of the available routes are highlighted and displayed on a single map:

```
var point = new GPoint(parseFloat(routelist[i].getAttribute("lat")),
                       parseFloat(routelist[i].getAttribute("lng")));
points.push(point);
```

The unique icon for this point is generated by calling `GIcon()`. By supplying the basic icon generated at the start of the function, the new icon inherits all of the base icon properties. The only property to add is the location of the unique icon for this marker:

```
var thisIcon = new GIcon(baseIcon);
thisIcon.image = iconloc
```

The `addmarker()` function is called to create a point and display a marker object on the map. The function call includes the point reference and the HTML that is placed into the info window for the marker, plus, of course, the icon:

```
addmarker(point,
          '<a href="#" onClick="loadRoute(' +
          routelist[i].getAttribute("routeid") +
          ');">' + routelist[i].getAttribute("title") +
          '</a>',
          thisIcon);
}
```

Finally, the map is recentered and zoomed based on the list of points (and markers) being displayed on the map:

```
    recenterandzoom(points);
  }
}
request.send(null);
}
```

You can see a sample of the list of available routes and the map showing the highlighted routes in Figure 13-2.

The most important element of this function is really the collection of the point references and how this is used in combination with the `recenterandzoom()` function that is shown later. The effect is to give an automatic (and correctly formatted) overview of all the available points.

Loading a Single Route

Loading a single route is much like loading a single marker from a list. Submitting the request to the backend generates a simple XML file consisting of the basic route information (ID, title, and description), then a series of point tags containing the latitude and longitude of each point, and finally a calculated distance of the given route. Following is a sample of the XML (trimmed for brevity):

```
<route>
<routeinfo routeid="13" title="Barrowby to Nottingham" description=""/>
<point lat="-0.685959" lng="52.919700"/>
<point lat="-0.685959" lng="52.919700"/>
<point lat="-0.713425" lng="52.929600"/>
...
```

```
<point lat="-1.139830" lng="52.947000"/>
<point lat="-1.139830" lng="52.947000"/>
<distance km="51.67" miles="32.10"/>
</route>
```

When parsing the XML, each of the elements of the information is extracted and placed into the corresponding structure within the application. For example, the title of the route is placed into the title field on the web form. The reason for this is that by adding the information to the form (rather than displaying it separately), the title can be updated and modified and re-saved into the database.

Because of this simplicity, the bulk of the code is actually about extracting the relevant information from the XML and populating the interface, rather than anything more exciting.

To begin with, any existing route, overlay, and other information is cleared:

```
function loadRoute(routeid,msgtext) {
  map.clearOverlays();
  index = 0;
  points = [];
  routes = [];
  message.innerHTML = 'Loading route';
  infopanel.innerHTML = '';
```

Then the request is sent to the database interface. Note that the route ID is specified because the link that enabled the user to select the route was embedded within the route ID extracted from the list of available routes:

```
  var request = GXmlHttp.create();
  request.open('GET','/examples/ch13-backend.cgi?m=getroute&routeid=' ⤶
+ routeid, true);
  request.onreadystatechange = function() {
    if (request.readyState == 4) {
      var xmlsource = request.responseXML;
```

Before trying to parse the expected XML, the function tries to parse a standard XML message instead. If the XML document returned includes a message string, it probably indicates an error, which should be reported and the rest of the process should be terminated.

```
      var msg = xmlsource.documentElement.getElementsByTagName("message");
      if (msg.length > 0) {
        message.innerHTML = msg[0].getAttribute('text');
        return;
      }
```

If there wasn't a message in the XML, it's probably a genuine response, so the user is told that the route has been correctly loaded. The function also accepts an alternative message, which is used when a route has been saved into the system to show that the route has been saved (rather than simply loaded from the database). If a custom message isn't provided, use a standard one instead.

```
      if (msgtext) {
        message.innerHTML = msgtext;
      }
      else {
        message.innerHTML = 'Route Loaded';
      }
```

FIGURE 13-2: Showing a list of available routes and starting points.

Then the individual elements from the data are extracted. First, the base route information is extracted. Although you extract all of the potential route elements, only one should be returned at a time, so the information from the first element is used first:

```
var routeinfo = ⊃
xmlsource.documentElement.getElementsByTagName("routeinfo");

    routeidfield.value = routeinfo[0].getAttribute('routeid');
    routetitle.value = routeinfo[0].getAttribute('title');
    routedescription.value = routeinfo[0].getAttribute('description');
```

Then the distance information is extracted, which includes the distance in both kilometers and miles:

```
var distanceinfo = ⊃
xmlsource.documentElement.getElementsByTagName("distance");

    infopanel.innerHTML = 'Distance: ' + distanceinfo[0].getAttribute('km') +
' km, ' +
    distanceinfo[0].getAttribute('miles') + ' miles';
```

After this the list of points is obtained, pushing each point onto an array. Because the points are supplied in the correct sequence from the database backend, there is no requirement to sort or order the points that are extracted. The order they are parsed from the document is the correct order for them to be generated onto the map.

```
var routepoints = xmlsource.documentElement.getElementsByTagName("point");
for (var i=0;i < routepoints.length;i++) {
  var point = new GPoint(parseFloat(routepoints[i].getAttribute("lat")),
                         parseFloat(routepoints[i].getAttribute("lng")));
  points.push(point);
}
```

Once there is an array of points, a `GPolyline` object can be created and added as an overlay to the map. For convenience, start and end markers are also added to the map:

```
    route = new GPolyline(points);
    map.addOverlay(route);
    addmarker(points[0],'Start here');
    addmarker(points[points.length-1],'Finish here');
    recenterandzoom(points);
    }
  }
  request.send(null);
}
```

As when generating a list of routes, the map is also recentered. The difference is that the map will now be recentered and zoomed according to all of the points in the route, rather than all the start points of the available routes.

Adding Markers

A simple function adds a marker at a given point and includes the supplied info window text. The function also accepts an icon so that custom icons can be used for the marker. Conveniently, if the icon is undefined, Google Maps will use the standard icon. The function doesn't even need to take into account a missing icon reference.

```
function addmarker(point,message,icon)
{
    var marker = new GMarker(point,icon);
      GEvent.addListener(marker,
                         'click',
                         function() {
        marker.openInfoWindowHtml('<b>' + message + '</b>');
      }
                        );
      map.addOverlay(marker);
}
```

The application is almost finished.

Initializing the Application

With all the other functions in place, the final stage is to initialize all of the different variables, and particularly the document elements, that are required for the application to operate:

```
function onLoad() {
  if (GBrowserIsCompatible()) {
    infopanel = document.getElementById("infopanel");
```

```
    message = document.getElementById("message");
    rrecording = document.getElementById("rrecording");
    routeidfield = document.getElementById("routeid");
    routetitle = document.getElementById("routetitle");
    routedescription = document.getElementById("routedesc");
    routeidfield.value = 0;
    routetitle.value = '';
    routedescription.value = '';
    map = new GMap(document.getElementById("map"));
    map.addControl(new GSmallZoomControl());
    map.centerAndZoom(new GPoint(-0.64,52.909444), 2);
  }
}
```

With the variables initialized, you create the map object, add a simple zoom control, and then zoom to a suitable area on the map according to the application.

Recentering and Zooming the Map

The recenterandzoom() function is the same as that shown in previous chapters, starting with Chapter 10. The function accepts an array of points, calculates the center point and span of those points, and both centers and zooms the Google Map until all of the supplied points are displayed on the map.

You can see that in this application the process works just as well on points used to generate markers as it does to generate routes.

Backend Database Interface

The server side of the route recording system must respond to a number of requests from the Google Maps application. There are four basic operations to be supported:

- Listing existing routes
- Saving a route
- Deleting a route
- Getting a route

Response is obviously through XML, but in addition to the standard responses for a given operation, there is also a requirement to send back error messages in the event of some sort of failure of the backend process.

In addition to the four main functions, a fifth function returns a standardized message (and, optionally, a number of attributes) and is primarily used when a function needs to return an error message. Using a single function in this way makes it easier for the format of the message to be standardized regardless of the function generating the error.

Database Structure

The application stores routes, and for each route there are two distinct sets of information. The first is the basic information about the route (the name and description). A route ID will be added so that you have a unique identifier for the route.

That route table (called `ch13_routesimple` for the purposes of this example) will be linked by the unique route ID to another table that contains the list of points. The table consists of the route ID, the latitude and longitude of each point, and a unique sequence ID.

Basic Wrapper

The core of the CGI backend is the wrapper. The wrapper includes the interface to the database. It also controls how communication between the JavaScript components and the backend work to exchange information, such as route submissions, requests for lists of routes, and individual route information.

For that there is a simple wrapper, as in previous examples, that initiates the connection to the database and then extracts requests through the CGI interface and makes calls to the right function to perform the desired option. The code for this follows:

```perl
#!/usr/bin/perl

use DBI;
use Math::Trig;
use strict;
use CGI qw/:standard/;

print header(-type => 'text/xml');

my $dbh = DBI->connect( 'dbi:mysql:database=mapsbookex;host=db.maps.mcslp.com',
                        'mapsbookex',
                        'examples',
                        );

if (!defined($dbh))
{
    die "Couldn't open connection to database\n";
}

if (param('m') eq 'saveroute')
{
    saveroute();
}
if (param('m') eq 'delroute')
{
    delroute(param('routeid'));
}
elsif(param('m') eq 'listroutes')
{
    listroutes();
}
```

```
elsif(param('m') eq 'getroute')
{
    getroute(param('routeid'));
}
```

This section is just a simple dispatcher; the code for individual request types is in the additional functions.

Message Response

For each operation there should be an XML response to the Google application, even if it is a basic message to indicate completion. The same system can also be used to return errors. Depending on the application, the fact that the message is an error doesn't even have to be highlighted.

```
sub xmlmessage
{
  my ($message,$attrib) = @_;

  printf('<msg><message text="%s" %s/></msg>',
      $message,
      join(' ',map {sprintf('%s="%s"',$_,$attrib->{$_}) } keys %{$attrib}));
}
```

For convenience, the function accepts a second argument; a reference to a hash that contains an additional list of attributes to return to the caller. This is used, for example, when saving a route so that the mapping application knows the ID of the route. In this example application, the JavaScript component uses the extracted ID to immediately load the route as if it had been selected by the user, which in turn triggers both the start and end markers and the route calculation.

Listing Existing Routes

All it takes to ask for a list of the existing routes is a suitable SQL query. When returning the list, four pieces of information will be returned:

- Route ID (used to select a route to load)
- Route title
- Latitude of the first point in the route
- Longitude of the first point in the route

This requires a small join that looks for the first point from the database (identified from the sequence ID). That point data is used by the application to show a marker at the start of each route in the database.

The resulting list of rows is then returned as XML, using attributes to identify the individual elements. Remember that you must embed the list of valid entries into an enclosing XML tag, because of the way in which you extract that information from within the Google Maps XML parser:

```
sub listroutes
{
    my $sth = $dbh->prepare('select ch13_routesimple.routeid,title,lat,lng ' .
                            'from ch13_routesimple,ch13_routepoints where ' .
                            'ch13_routesimple.routeid = ' .
                            'ch13_routepoints.routeid and seqid = 1 order ⮑
by title');
    $sth->execute();

    print "<routes>";
    while (my $row = $sth->fetchrow_hashref())
    {
        printf('<route routeid="%s" title="%s" lat="%s" lng="%s"/>',
               $row->{routeid},
               $row->{title},
               $row->{lat},
               $row->{lng}
               );
    }
    print "</routes>";
}
```

The function is probably the simplest and most straightforward of the functions in the backend application because it is a simple database query and XML formatting task. Incidentally, if the query finds no routes, it effectively returns an empty tag pair, displaying no routes in the application. By effectively returning an empty list, the need to return an error message is negated; instead a valid XML document is returned that contains no information.

Saving a Route

When saving a route, the backend needs to account for saving a new route (a route with an existing ID of zero), which requires an insert into the database of the base route information, and saving an existing route, which requires an update statement for the base route information. For both situations, the rows for the actual route points need to be inserted. Rather than updating the route points (which would be overly complicated because the application would need to record the existing points and how they had changed), the existing points are simply deleted and the new points are created in their place.

The information is supplied to the backend as standard CGI field/value pairs. The only complexity is the extraction of the individual points, which are separated first by commas for the individual points and then by colons for the sequence number, longitude, and latitude in each point:

```
sub saveroute
{
  my $title = param('title');
  my $description = param('desc');
  my $points = param('points');
```

```perl
   my @pointlist = split(/,/,$points);
   my $routeid;

   if (defined(param('routeid')) && param('routeid') != 0)
   {
     $routeid = param('routeid');

     $dbh->do(sprintf('update ch13_routesimple set title=%s, ' .
             'description=%s where routeid=%s',
             $dbh->quote($title),
             $dbh->quote($description),
             $routeid));
     $dbh->do(sprintf('delete from ch13_routepoints where routeid=%s',
             $routeid));
   }
   else
   {
     $dbh->do(sprintf('insert into ch13_routesimple values(0,%s,%s)',
             $dbh->quote($title),
             $dbh->quote($description)));
     $routeid = $dbh->{mysql_insertid};
   }

   foreach my $point (@pointlist)
   {
     my ($seqid,$x,$y) = split(/:/,$point);
     $dbh->do(sprintf('insert into ch13_routepoints values(%s,%s,%s,%s)',
             $dbh->quote($routeid),
             $dbh->quote($x),
             $dbh->quote($y),
             $dbh->quote($seqid)));
   }
   xmlmessage('Route added',{routeid => $routeid});
}
```

Once the route has been added or updated in the database, the function returns a simple message and the route ID of the route that was added or updated.

Deleting an Existing Route

To delete an existing route you need only execute the delete statement for the supplied route ID on each table:

```perl
sub delroute
{
  my ($routeid) = @_;

  $dbh->do(sprintf('delete from ch13_routesimple where routeid=%s',
          $routeid));
  $dbh->do(sprintf('delete from ch13_routepoints where routeid=%s',
          $routeid));

  xmlmessage('Route deleted');
}
```

Again, a simple message is returned to indicate the completion of the operation.

Obtaining a Single Route

To get a single route is a two-stage process. First, the base route information needs to be extracted. Then the route points need to be extracted from the database in the correct order for them to be represented on the map. The sequence is important. A sequence ID is added to each route point when the route is saved; otherwise the individual points would skip around the map, instead of following the proscribed route.

The function also has to take into account what might happen if the route had been deleted after the list was generated, but before the chosen route had been requested. This error event is handled by returning a suitable error message through the `xmlmessage()` function back to the JavaScript component of the application:

```
sub getroute
{
  my ($reqrouteid) = @_;

  my $routedata =
    $dbh->selectrow_hashref('select routeid,title,description ' .
                            'from ch13_routesimple where routeid = ' .
                            $dbh->quote($reqrouteid));

  if ($routedata->{routeid} != $reqrouteid)
  {
    xmlmessage('Error: route not found');
    return();
  }

  printf('<route><routeinfo routeid="%s" title="%s" description="%s"/>',
         $routedata->{routeid},
         $routedata->{title},
         $routedata->{description});
```

With the basic route information in place you can proceed to return a list of points. Remember that the points must be extracted in the right sequence, so a suitable `order by` clause is added to the SQL statement:

```
my $sth =
  $dbh->prepare(sprintf('select lat,lng from ch13_routepoints ' .
                        'where routeid = %s order by seqid',
                        $dbh->quote($routedata->{routeid})));
$sth->execute();
```

As the script works through the individual points of the table, it will also calculate the distance between two points. To do this, the current set of points is recorded; once at least two points are known (the recorded set and the current set) the calculation can take place. Thus if you have a route with three points, A, B, and C, you can calculate the total distance by adding the distance between A and B and B and C together. The process is examined in more detail in the next section, "Calculating Distance."

In addition to calculating the total distance, the XML for each point also needs to be generated. As with other elements, the information is embedded into attributes for a suitable named
XML tag:

```
my $distance = 0;
my $seq = 0;
my ($lastx,$lasty) = (undef,undef);

while (my $row = $sth->fetchrow_hashref())
{
  $seq++;
  printf('<point lat="%f" lng="%f"/>',
         $row->{lat},
         $row->{lng},
         );
  if ($seq >= 2)
  {
    $distance += latlngdistance($lastx,
                                $lasty,
                                $row->{lat},
                                $row->{lng});
  }
  ($lastx,$lasty) = ($row->{lat},$row->{lng});
}
$sth->finish();
```

The final part of the process is to return the final distance, and for convenience both metric
and imperial measures are provided:

```
printf('<distance km="%.2f" miles="%.2f"/>',
       $distance,
       ($distance/1.609344));
print("</route>\n");
}
```

The actual calculation of the distance is complicated and takes place in a separate function.

Calculating Distance

When returning a given route it is nice to be able to supply a distance from the start point to
the destination point. There is no easy way to determine this information; Google does not
supply a convenient method.

The only way to determine the information is to take the points given and calculate the distance. This is itself difficult because latitude and longitude are measures of degrees on the surface of the earth. To calculate the distance between points, what you actually have to calculate
is the distance between two points on a sphere (effectively the portion of the circumference on
the surface of the earth).

Describing, in detail, the exact method required is beyond the scope of this book, but the equa-
tion is called the Haversine formula. To determine the distance between two points, you calculate the arc on the surface of the earth, using the radius of the earth (in kilometers) as a base
reference. You may want to visit the Movable Type Scripts web site (http://www.movable-
type.co.uk/scripts/LatLong.html).

Note that even with this formula, the exact distance may be different because the earth is not a perfect sphere (it is slightly "flat" and therefore wider at the equator than at the poles), but the difference for most small routes is so small that it is not noticeable.

Rather than performing the calculation within JavaScript on the host, the information is determined by the backend script as it returns the route point information. The function accepts four arguments, the long/lat pairs for the start and end points. This is called for each pair during the point extraction loop in the getroute() function. By adding each point pair distance together, the distance for the entire route can be calculated:

```perl
sub latlngdistance
{
  my ($xdeg1,$ydeg1,$xdeg2,$ydeg2) = @_;

  my ($x1,$y1,$x2,$y2) = (deg2rad($xdeg1),
            deg2rad($ydeg1),
            deg2rad($xdeg2),
            deg2rad($ydeg2));

  my $radius = 6371;
  my $latdistance = $x2 - $x1;
  my $lngdistance = $y2 - $y1;

  my $a = sin($latdistance/2) * sin($latdistance/2) +
    cos($x1) * cos($x2) * sin($lngdistance/2) * sin($lngdistance/2);
  my $c = 2 * atan2(sqrt($a), sqrt(1-$a));
  my $d = $radius * $c;

  return $d;
}
```

The same process could have been carried out within the browser, which would have also enabled the application to show a live distance calculation as the route was being calculated, but this information is easier and more straightforward to calculate within the backend function and also takes some load off of the browser.

Using the Application

The best way to get to know the application in use is, of course, to try it out. The basics of the system (saving a route, listing available routes, and then loading a single route) can easily be shown, at least in terms of how they look.

First, Figure 13-3 shows the application in its initial state, showing the map (centered, for a change, on Grantham).

Click New Route to enable routing and select the first point for your route. Click further points until you have a route displayed onscreen, as shown here in Figure 13-4. Note that the route title and a description have also been given here.

In Figure 13-5 you can see the final route when saved, here showing its final distance and the start and end markers.

Figure 13-6 shows the list of available routes, including the one just created.

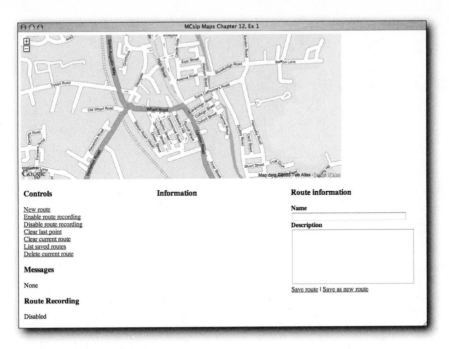

FIGURE 13-3: Initial application state.

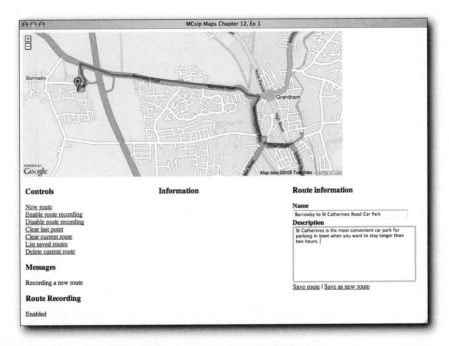

FIGURE 13-4: A recorded route ready for saving to the database.

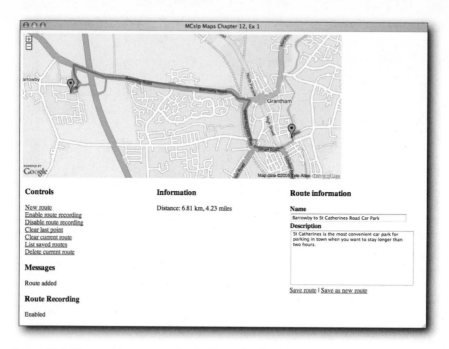

FIGURE **13-5:** The saved route, now loaded from the database.

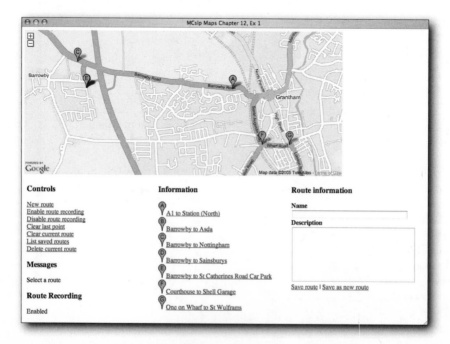

FIGURE **13-6:** The list of available routes.

Figure 13-7 shows an alternative route loaded into the application.

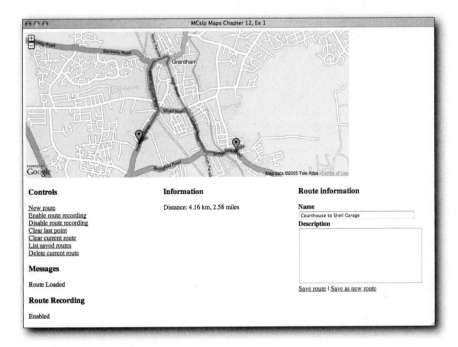

Figure 13-7: Another route already in the database.

Finally, Figure 13-8 shows the original route loaded and partly modified, and Figure 13-9 shows the modified route when saved (with an alternative description and title) into the system.

Obviously there are some elements that cannot easily be shown. For example, demonstrating deleting routes is difficult, but I encourage you to try different routes on the live map at the web site.

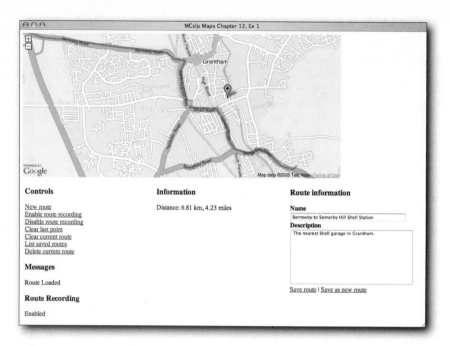

FIGURE 13-8: Modifying the existing route.

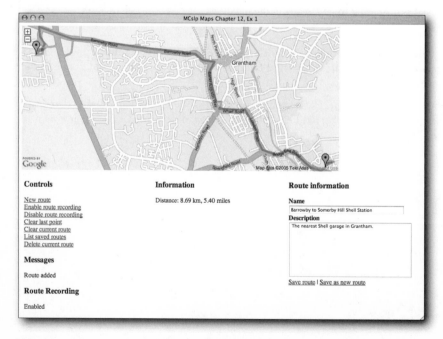

FIGURE 13-9: A modified route saved into the database.

Wrapping Up

As in many other examples, the application relies on two distinct components: the front-end interface and the backend database connection and XML generator. Although there is some additional intelligence in this solution, the bulk of the code is still relying on the basic process of adding data to the database and requesting XML versions of the information already stored. What is important is just how complex an application you can produce using that basic process.

The techniques shown in this chapter can be adapted for a wide range of different uses. For example, the application could be adapted to work as a method for directing clients and customers to your home or office from key intersections. The application could also be used as a method to promote different walking routes in your city or town, highlighting different areas. With a small amount of expansion (by adding key points to the database as well as the route points that make up the route sequence), you could turn the system into a way of highlighting important landmarks on an unguided tour of a city.

The current application also stores only a basic amount of information about each route. It would be a fairly trivial process to add other features, such as photos, additional markers, or other information. All of the functionality and potential has been demonstrated in this chapter and in earlier chapters about how to add this information.

Merging with Flickr Photos

Flickr has become something of a phenomenon. At its heart, Flickr is a service for uploading and sharing your photos, but one of the key elements of Flickr is that photos can be shared with the public, specific friends, or just kept secret.

The other aspect of Flickr photos is that individual photos can be "tagged": given a special keyword that can be used for searching and organizing your photos. Because photos are shared among users, you can search for photos with the same keywords as your own or simply browse Flickr photos for the content you are looking for.

The tagging system can also be adapted so that you can tag your photos with information about the latitude and longitude where the photo was taken. By using this information and a Google Map, you can build a view of Flickr photos according to their location. This chapter covers the basics of the Flickr API, which lets you extract Flickr photos and information and combine that with a Google Map.

Flickr and the Flickr API

There are three key elements to using Flickr and the Flickr API with Google Maps. The first is that you must upload your photos to Flickr, which requires a Flickr account. You also need a Flickr API key to access the Flickr database, whether that is for your own photos or other people's.

The third key element is the use of tags to identify the content of the photos. Tags are freeform and can be any valid text string. You have can have multiple tags, and the tags become a method for searching and locating photos (as well as using other well-known constructs such as albums). Tags on Flickr photos can be used to extract photos with geographical tags and then plot the locations of the photos onto a Google Map.

The Flickr API

The Flickr API provides access to Flickr photos. A variety of different search and access methods exist to get the information stored in the Flickr database according to the information you are looking for.

The API has three methods of access:

- **REST:** This is the method used in earlier examples in this book, and by parts of the Google Maps API, to submit requests. The request and any options or arguments are supplied as part of the URL. The return value is an XML document with the information you were looking for.

- **XML-RPC:** This is one of the web services interfaces. Information is returned as an object (according to your request environment).

- **SOAP:** This is the other web service interface. Information is returned as an object.

The REST interface is the easiest to use from within JavaScript and a browser. The techniques REST uses to parse and extract the XML returned are just the same as those that have been demonstrated in earlier examples.

Whichever method you use, the array of available functions and operations remains constant.

Getting a Flickr API Key

To use the API you must have a unique API key. There are fewer restrictions on the Flickr API key and its use compared to the Google Maps API key, but the Flickr system also only provides access to publicly uploaded photos, rather than the copyrighted material used in Google Maps and satellite images.

To obtain a key, you need to create an account with Flickr (where you will also need to upload your photos). Once you have your account, go to the Flickr Services API page (`http://www.flickr.com/services/api/`) to request your key.

The key you are given provides access to all of the Flickr photos. It also provides special information for your own photos that might not generally available to the public.

Adding Geographic Data to Your Flickr Photos

Adding geographic data to a photo within Flickr is a simple case of adding suitable tags to the photo. There are many ways in which you can do this, including an automatic system using the GreaseMonkey script environment within the Firefox browser. However, because the basic process of writing the tag to the Flickr photo is the same, it is safe to concentrate on the basic tag structure.

Three tags are used to record geographical information:

- `geotagged`: This simply indicates that the photo is tagged with geographical information. Generally the existence of the tag is designed to make searching for `geotagged` photos easier.

- `geo:lat=XXX`: This is the latitude of where the photo was taken.

- `geo:lon=XXX`: This is the longitude of where the photo was taken.

For the latitude/longitude values, you should supply a floating-point value, just as with any other value used within Google Maps.

How you obtain the latitude/longitude of your photo is entirely up to you. Some users are beginning to record photo locations with a simple GPS receiver when the photo is taken. Others just use Google Maps to locate the position where the photo was taken. If you are uploading a number of photos that were taken at similar locations, you can tag photos in groups or during upload to specify the geotagged information in bulk.

Adding Flickr Photos to a Google Map

Adding Flickr photos to a Google Map based on their geographical tags is a two-phase process. First, you need to search for the photos that you want to overlay on the map. The search process will return the photo ID information (as demonstrated earlier). However, to obtain the tags, and therefore the embedded geographical information, the info for each photo must be individually obtained to determine where the photo should be placed on the map.

Before that, though, you need to get around a security issue built into most browsers.

A Flickr Proxy

Most browsers do not allow you to send XML HTTP requests like those used in Google Maps applications to domains other than the source of the HTML file they are being loaded from. There are ways to get around this issue on certain browsers, but none that are compatible across a range of different browsers without writing complex JavaScript to change the security preferences. Even where it is possible, users will normally have to accept some security message that may also reduce the security of their browser.

The easiest way to get around the issue is to provide a proxy service that passes on the request from the Google Maps application through the server used to host the HTML and then on to the destination service (in this case Flickr). The data can then be echoed back verbatim to the script as if it had directly accessed the remote service.

A sample proxy service, here written in Perl, is as follows.

```
use strict;
use CGI qw/:standard/;
use LWP::UserAgent;

my $ua = LWP::UserAgent->new(env_proxy => 1,
                             keep_alive => 1,
                             timeout => 30,
                             agent => "Mozilla/5.0 (X11; U; Linux i686; ⤶
en-US; rv:1.0.2) Gecko/20021120 Netscape/7.\
01",
                            );
```

```
print header(-type => 'text/xml');

my @query;

foreach my $param (param())
{
    push @query,sprintf('%s=%s',$param,param($param));
}

my $query = 'http://www.flickr.com/services/rest/?' . join('&',@query);

my $response = $ua->get($query);

print $response->{_content};
```

Now you can build a URL just as if you were directly building one for the Flickr service and access the information returned by Flickr without hitting the browser security issue that prevents you from doing this directly.

Searching Flickr for Photos

You can search for Flickr photos using a variety of criteria with the `flickr.photos.search` method. You can request photos based on the following search criteria:

- User ID
- Tags (you can also specify whether to search for photos matching any tags or to search for all of them)
- Text search (based on title, description, or tag)
- Upload date
- Taken date
- License

You can also specify the sort order of the returned list of photos, the number of photos to be returned in a page (up to 500), and which page of the search requested to return photos. For example, if you request 100 photos per page from page 3, photos start at number 301 in the returned results.

Sending a Search Request

You can submit a search for a specific user's photos (I'll use my photos as an example) and look for photos with specific tags. When you send the request with the REST interface, XML for the photo information is returned. You can see a sample of the returned data in the following code:

```
<rsp stat="ok">
<photos page="1" pages="1" perpage="100" total="79">
<photo id="24910903" owner="54256647@N00" secret="ad24b49370" server="23" ⤵
title="IMG_0776" ispublic="1" isfriend="0" isfamily="0"/>
<photo id="24910888" owner="54256647@N00" secret="1b92a07883" server="23" ⤵
title="IMG_0777" ispublic="1" isfriend="0" isfamily="0"/>
```

```
<photo id="24910877" owner="54256647@N00" secret="8c15a21389" server="23"
title="STA_0724" ispublic="1" isfriend="0" isfamily="0"/>
...
<photo id="24865509" owner="54256647@N00" secret="53e7584368" server="23"
title="IMG_0713" ispublic="1" isfriend="0" isfamily="0"/>
<photo id="24865497" owner="54256647@N00" secret="4c6f065c3d" server="23"
title="IMG_0729" ispublic="1" isfriend="0" isfamily="0"/>
<photo id="24865488" owner="54256647@N00" secret="155fc590f0" server="23"
title="IMG_0709" ispublic="1" isfriend="0" isfamily="0"/>
</photos>
</rsp>
```

The `photo id` is the unique identifier for each photo. The `owner` is the username of the user that owns the photos. The `secret` and `server` values are provided to enable you to display an image in a web page. You don't need the `secret` and `server` values to provide a link to the Flickr page for the image. However, you do need this information if you want to display only the image in a web page. You also need this information when you want to select alternative sizes or formats for an image.

In these applications, the photos are being retrieved as part of a Google Map. As you know, photos that have geographical information have a specific tag. To retrieve photos suitable for display on the map, you need to search for photos with the tag `geotagged`.

Using the REST interface, you can search for `geotagged` photos using this URL:

```
http://maps.mcslp.com//examples/ch14-02flickrproxy.pl?method=
flickr.photos.search&api_key=XXX&user_id=54256647@N00&tags=geotagged
```

This returns the following XML:

```
<rsp stat="ok">
<photos page="1" pages="1" perpage="100" total="2">
<photo id="24910903" owner="54256647@N00" secret="ad24b49370" server="23"
title="IMG_0776" ispublic="1" isfriend="0" isfamily="0"/>
<photo id="24910877" owner="54256647@N00" secret="8c15a21389" server="23"
title="STA_0724" ispublic="1" isfriend="0" isfamily="0"/>
</photos>
</rsp>
```

You can parse this information within JavaScript and your Google Map page using the built-in DOM parser.

Parsing the Response in JavaScript

To parse the data you need to create a generic `XMLHttpRequest()` object to download the XML and parse the contents. Following is the code for this:

```
function loadPhotos() {
    photoids = [];
    geopoints = [];
    map.clearOverlays();

    var request = new XMLHttpRequest();

    request.open('GET',
```

```
                              '/examples/ch14-02flickrproxy.pl?method= ↩
flickr.photos.search&api_key=' +
                    'XXX' + '&user_id=54256647@N00' +
                    '&tags=toronto,geotagged&tag_mode=all',true);
    request.onreadystatechange = function() {
        if (request.readyState == 4) {
            var xmlsource = request.responseXML;

            var photos = ↩
xmlsource.documentElement.getElementsByTagName("photo");
            for(i=0;i<photos.length;i++) {
                var img = document.createElement('img');
                photoids.push(photos[i].getAttribute('id'));
            }
            getphotoinfo(0);
        }
    }
    request.send(null);
}
```

Only the ID of the photo is required. You have found the photos you are looking for. To determine the geographical information, you have to get the specific information for each photo to extract the `geotags` and plot the photo location on the map. Unfortunately, this requires sending one request per photo and then parsing another XML file for each photo to extract the data required.

That operation of getting individual photo data is handled by the `getphotoinfo()` function. Because you are sending multiple asynchronous HTTP transfers, you create a chain of requests, starting with the first photo ID. Each `getphotoinfo()` call then calls the function again for the next photo and so on. I've found this to be more reliable than calling `getphotoinfo()` within a `for` loop.

Getting Individual Photo Data

The Flickr database stores a lot of information about each photo. The basic data returned about a photo includes the photo ID and other data used for loading and locating the photo, the photo dates, the tag information, and the URL of the photo's page within the Flickr site.

You need to separately extract this information for each photo. From that, you can get the geographic data and then create a marker on the map where the photo was taken. You'll also use an XSL Transformation to convert the returned XML into an info window that displays the basic photo data and a thumbnail of the photo without your map.

Getting Specific Photo Data

When you request the information for a single photo, you get a comparatively large XML document returned that contains a wealth of information. The bulk of this will be converted by an XSL Transformation into the `InfoWindow` for each marker, but the tag information will be used to determine the location of where the photo was taken.

Again, using the REST interface, a URL requests the XML document containing the information about the photo:

```
http://maps.mcslp.com//examples/ch14-02flickrproxy.pl?method=
flickr.photos.getInfo&api_key=XXX&photo_id=24910903
```

The preceding returns a hefty XML document:

```
<rsp stat="ok">
<photo id="24910903" secret="ad24b49370" server="23"
dateuploaded="1121009689" isfavorite="0" license="0" rotation="0"
originalformat="jpg">
<owner nsid="54256647@N00" username="mcslp" realname="Martin Brown"
location=""/>
<title>IMG_0776</title>
<description/>
<visibility ispublic="1" isfriend="0" isfamily="0"/>
<dates posted="1121009689" taken="2005-07-10 16:34:49"
takengranularity="0" lastupdate="1140791972"/>
<editability cancomment="0" canaddmeta="0"/>
<comments>0</comments>
<notes>
</notes>
<tags>
<tag id="700506-24910903-449" author="54256647@N00" raw="toronto">toronto</tag>
<tag id="700506-24910903-2563662" author="54256647@N00"
raw="geo:lon=-79.38724994659424">geolon7938724994659424</tag>
<tag id="700506-24910903-1700" author="54256647@N00"
raw="geotagged">geotagged</tag>
<tag id="700506-24910903-2563668" author="54256647@N00"
raw="geo:lat=43.64178982199113">geolat4364178982199113</tag>
</tags>
<urls>
<url type="photopage">http://www.flickr.com/photos/mcslp/24910903/</url>
</urls>
</photo>
</rsp>
```

There are two portions of this document that you are particularly interested in. The first is the main photo information (within the `<photo>` tag) about the `secret` and `server`. You need this information to enable you to embed a thumbnail of the photo within your info window.

The second is the `<tags>` portion, because that is where the geotagging information is stored. Note the use of the `raw` attribute to a `<tag>`; this contains the real data required. The `<tag>` value is a "flattened" version, used internally by Flickr, and is also the version you would use when searching for a specific tag.

The bulk of the XML generated by Flickr in this process is going to be parsed by an XSL Transformation.

Building an XSL Layout

The XSL takes the XML format, extracts the photo title, description, and taken date. It also builds a URL for the embedded thumbnail:

```
<?xml version="1.0" encoding="UTF-8"?>
<xsl:stylesheet xmlns:xsl="http://www.w3.org/1999/XSL/Transform" version="1.0">
    <xsl:template match="/">
        <xsl:apply-templates select="rsp" />
    </xsl:template>
    <xsl:template match="photo">

        <table width="230" cellspacing="15">
            <tr>
                <td style="font-size:10pt;font-weight:bold;text-align:Left;">
                    Title
                </td>
                <td style="font-size:10pt;text-align:Left;" colspan="2">
                    <xsl:value-of select="title" />
                </td>
            </tr>
            <tr>
                <td style="font-size:10pt;font-weight:bold;text-align:Left;">
                    Description
                </td>
                <td style="font-size:10pt;text-align:Left;" colspan="2">
                    <xsl:value-of select="description" />
                </td>
            </tr>
            <tr>
                <td style="font-size:10pt;font-weight:bold;text-align:Left;">
                    Taken
                </td>
                <td style="font-size:10pt;text-align:Left;" colspan="2">
                    <xsl:value-of select="dates/@taken" />
                </td>
            </tr>
            <tr valign="top">
                <td style="font-size:10pt;font-weight:bold;text-align:Left;">
                    Image
                </td>
                <td style="font-size:10pt;text-align:Left;">
                    <a>
                        <xsl:attribute name="href">
                            <xsl:value-of select="urls/url" />
                        </xsl:attribute>
                    <img>
                        <xsl:attribute name="src">http://static.flickr.com/ ⤶
<xsl:value-of select="@server" />/<xsl:value-of select="@id" />_ ⤶
<xsl:value-of select="@secret" />_s.jpg</xsl:attribute>
```

```
                        </img>
                            </a>
                    </td>
                </tr>
            </table>

        </xsl:template>
    </xsl:stylesheet>
```

It is probably difficult to determine from the preceding XSL, but to select a specific size and format of image from the Flickr server, you have to construct a URL based on the photo ID, server ID, secret key, and required format. For example, to pull out a tiny thumbnail, in the shape and size of a 75x75 pixel square, you use the following image URL:

```
http://static.flickr.com/{server-id}/{id}_{secret}_s.jpg
```

The s at the end of the URL specifies the 75x75 pixel square. Other available sizes include a 100-pixel thumbnail (letter t), a small image (240 pixels on the longest side, letter m), a large image (1024 pixels on the longest side, letter b), and a medium image (no letter).

Parsing Photo Data

To pick out the information required, the XML original must be parsed for the data you need. From the perspective of the Google Maps application, only the tag data actually needs to be extracted. The rest of the XML processing takes place as part of the XSL Transformation. Extracting the tag data is made a little more complex by the textual nature of the latitude or longitude being embedded into the tag string.

The process starts with a simple request and the extraction of a list of tags from the response XML:

```
function getphotoinfo(index)
{
    var request = new XMLHttpRequest();

    request.open('GET',
                '/examples/ch14-02flickrproxy.pl?method= ↵
flickr.photos.getInfo&api_key=' +
                'XXX' + '&photo_id=' + photoids[index], true);

    request.onreadystatechange =  function() {
        if (request.readyState == 4) {
            var xmlsource = request.responseXML;
            var tags = xmlsource.documentElement.getElementsByTagName("tag");
```

The tags are then individually processed to identify the information. Each tag must be checked to see if it contains the data required:

```
            for(i=0;i<tags.length;i++) {
                var lat;
                var lng;
```

Using JavaScript you can determine the location of a string within a string using the `indexOf()` method on the `string` object. Because you are looking for a prefix of `geo:lon`, the return value should be zero. If it is, you split the string on the = character, the right hand of which should be a floating-point value for the longitude. The same process can be repeated for the latitude.

```
if (tags[i].getAttribute('raw').indexOf('geo:lon') == 0) {
    var elems = tags[i].getAttribute('raw').split('=');
    lng = elems[1];
}
if (tags[i].getAttribute('raw').indexOf('geo:lat') == 0) {
    var elems = tags[i].getAttribute('raw').split('=');
    lat = elems[1];
}
```

If you have both the latitude and longitude, you can then create a point and a marker. You can point to the XSL Transformation and the original XML returned by the HTTP request to generate a suitable info window:

```
if (lat && lng) {
    var point = new GPoint(parseFloat(lng),parseFloat(lat));
    var marker = new GMarker(point);
    map.addOverlay(marker);
    GEvent.addListener(marker,
                        'click',
                        function() {
            marker.openInfoWindowXslt ⏎
(xmlsource,"/examples/ch14-02.xsl");
                        }
                        );
    geopoints.push(point);
}
}
```

Finally, you request the photo from the list of available photos for the same process. If this was the last request in the list, then recenter and zoom (using the function used in previous examples) to re-align the map on the selected photos:

```
index++;
if (index < photoids.length) {
    getphotoinfo(index);
} else {
    recenterandzoom(geopoints);
}
}
}

request.send(null);
}
```

You can see the basic result and the information window generated when the user clicks a marker in Figures 14-1 and 14-2, respectively.

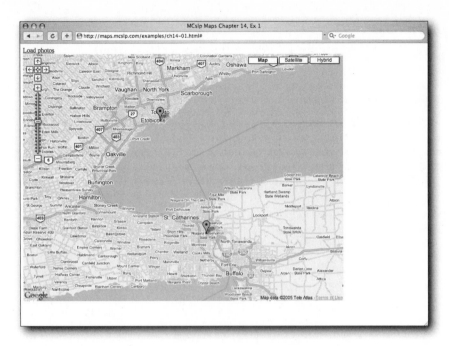

FIGURE 14-1: The basic map display showing locations of photos.

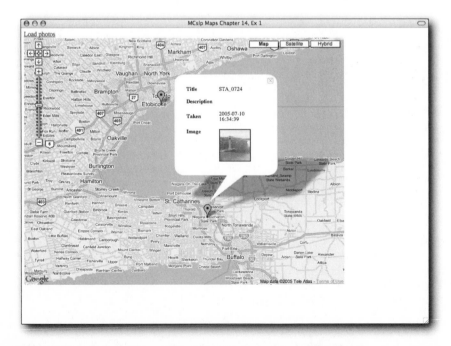

FIGURE 14-2: An information window showing photo data and thumbnail.

Wrapping Up

The Flickr web site does an excellent job of storing your photos and other images in a share-able format. The API gives you a convenient method of getting the photos back out. Using Google Maps to provide a geographical representation of that information is an excellent way to make your photos accessible in an alternative way.

The methods used in this chapter for extracting the photos are basic, but the system could be altered to allow you to search and show information from different users or for a variety of additional tags. Care would need to be taken to ensure that multiple markers were not created on the same latitude/longitude, but you could also combine those images into an album-like display by comparing the values as the photos are processed.

Google Earth Hacks

Introducing
Google Earth

All of the preceding chapters focused on the Google Maps API. The Google Maps system provides a browser-based interface to the data in the Google database, both in terms of the map and the satellite photos. The API provides the ultimate in flexibility for building and incorporating Google Maps data into web-based applications. That flexibility, however, comes at the potential price of limiting the environment and interface.

Even with the flexibility of the JavaScript language and the ability to create and organize content in ways that suit the application, you can add additional layers of data to the map information already demonstrated. In particular, the web-based Google Maps interface is incapable of providing the interaction and display of three-dimensional data. The limitations extend not only to the base data, but also to the information that you can overlay on the map.

Google Earth, on the other hand, has no restrictions on the interface and how the user interacts with the Google Earth data. Google Earth is a desktop application available for Windows and Mac OS X that enables you to browse Google Earth images in a more dynamic environment. Using Google Earth you move about the earth in 3D, moving and manipulating the Google Earth data in real time. This provides additional information that would be difficult to represent within the Google Maps interface, such as "tilting" the earth so that you can see the relative height of different areas of land.

This chapter looks at ways in which you can use Google Earth and how to create some basic data to be used within the application to extend the information and functionality of the application.

Google Earth Overview

The most critical difference between Google Maps and Google Earth is the environment. Google Earth is a standalone application that is available for a limited number of platforms. It is designed as an earth browser for showing satellite images of the earth's surface in an interactive, 3D environment. The satellite images and the backup data (such as local businesses) in Google Earth are the same as those in Google Maps in satellite mode. The difference is in the way in which the information can be viewed and manipulated.

Obtaining the Application

Google Earth can be downloaded from the Google Earth homepage (http://earth
.google.com). There are three versions of the Google Earth application:

- **Google Earth** is free for personal use and incorporates satellite images that cover the entire surface of the earth. The free client also provides access to all of the different Google Local–supported databases, including those that provide information about locations, local businesses, and route finding. Google Earth also incorporates the technology for generating and representing information based on the Keyhole Markup Language (KML). This is the version that is described throughout the rest of this chapter.

- **Google Earth Plus** is an optional (and low-cost) upgrade to the free client that extends the functionality of Google Earth to include interfaces to GPS devices, higher resolution for printed images (higher than onscreen), extended annotation and drawing tools, and a data importer that will read files in CSV format. Google Earth Plus is supported only on Windows (at the time of writing).

- **Google Earth Pro** is a professional product and is therefore significantly more expensive than the Google Earth Plus upgrade. It incorporates much faster download times and data streaming, extended layers and overlay support, and improvements to the annotation system that enable you to develop much more detailed overlays directly within the Google Earth application. Google Earth Pro is supported only on Windows (at the time of writing). Google Earth Pro also supports a number of extension modules, including those for making movies (by "flying" through the Google Earth data), a high-resolution printing module, and data modules providing traffic and shopping data.

For all three applications, Google Earth is merely the desktop interface to the data on the Google Earth servers. You must first download the client that enables you to view and interact with the data. Then you can connect to the Internet to obtain and download the images that are displayed onscreen.

Note There is a fourth Google Earth application, Google Earth Enterprise, which is designed to provide Google Earth features in combination with heavily customized information within an enterprise environment. Google Earth Enterprise is technically a range of applications that work together to provide Google Earth data, combined with your own enterprise information, such as statistical and customer data. For more information see the Google Earth Enterprise web site at http://earth.google.com/earth_enterprise.html.

Google Earth Features

The Google Earth application provides an interface to the Google satellite imagery, and because it is not limited by the interface available through a web browser and JavaScript, there is a lot more flexibility and interactivity in the Google Earth application. Some of the key differences are detailed shortly. First, examine Figure 15-1, which shows the basic interface of the Google Earth application.

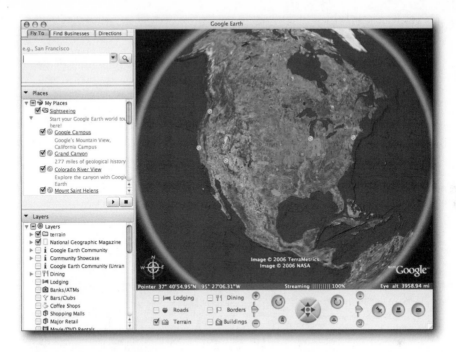

FIGURE 15-1: The basic interface.

The interface is divided into three panels. The panel on the left provides the data points, overlays, and search interface that enable you to add data and move around the map using town, city, and other information point references. The panel at the bottom of the application window provides an interface for moving and working around the earth. The larger, main panel is the window to the Google Earth satellite imagery.

Core Functionality

The fundamental difference between Google Maps and Google Earth is the way in which the satellite imagery can be viewed and manipulated. The satellite images are the same as Google Maps, but the way in which the data is displayed differs in that it is slightly more fluid than the Google Maps interface.

For example, the default start position is high above the United States. With Google Earth, you can tell exactly how high. The information immediately beneath the Google Earth image provides, from left to right:

- The longitude/latitude of the current center point of the map (called the Pointer).

- The elevation (height above sea level) of that point.

- The status of the information satellite images that are streamed to the application.

- The altitude of the current view; that is, the height (above sea level) from which you see information.

You can see, from Figure 15-1, just how high up you would have to be to see the same information. If you double-click one of the points on the left, say, the Google Campus, you will "fly" to the Google Campus, with the satellite imagery flowing past, until the map centers on the Google Campus. This is almost impossible to represent within a book, but Figures 15-2 through 15-4 show some interstitial images from the starting point in Figure 15-1 to give you some idea.

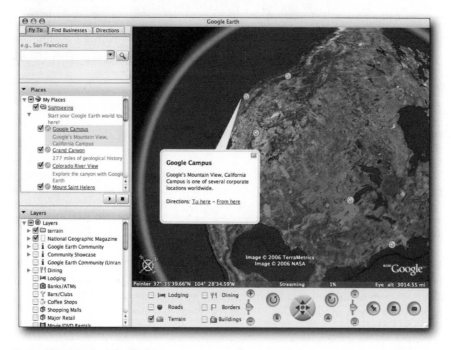

FIGURE **15-2: Starting the flight.**

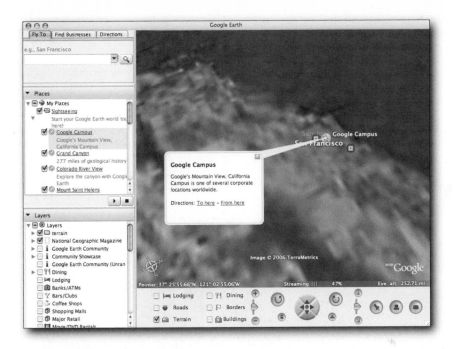

FIGURE 15-3: Almost there.

FIGURE 15-4: The Google Campus.

At no time are areas of the map missing while Google Earth loads the satellite image data. Instead Google Earth streams the necessary information from Google's servers to gradually load the image data as you zoom in through different levels.

This sequence is automatic and much more visual than even the panning option provided within the Google Maps interface. To manually move around the map, a number of options are available:

- **Click and drag:** The same basic method as available within Google Maps. Click anywhere on the map, drag the map in the direction you want, and then release the mouse. You will move to the new location.

- **Cursor keys:** The standard cursor keys on your keyboard move the map in the direction you choose.

- **Joystick:** There is a built in "joystick" in the center of the control panel on the map. Clicking the different arrows on the joystick moves the map.

- **Click and move:** If you click the mouse and move the map quickly and then release, the map will begin to scroll in the direction you moved the mouse. To stop the scrolling, click the red button in the middle of the joystick or click once on the map with the mouse.

By default, your map will always be oriented to face north. You can rotate the map using the two buttons to the top left and right of the joystick, which rotate the map counterclockwise and clockwise. You can always tell the current orientation by using the built-in compass shown in the bottom left of the map panel. You can reset it using the "N" button on the bottom left.

Finally, you can zoom in and out of the map using the slider on the left, or, if your mouse has a scroll wheel, using the scroll wheel to zoom out (roll forward) and in (roll back).

Simple Overlays

Numerous built-in overlays are provided with the application. To see them in action, move to Seattle by typing Seattle into the search box and clicking the search button. You should get a window like the one shown in Figure 15-5.

From the Layers panel on the left, select "Crime Stats" and then zoom out slightly and you'll see the crime statistics for 2000 for a number of counties across the Seattle region, as shown in Figure 15-6.

FIGURE 15-5: Seattle.

FIGURE 15-6: Crime statistics in Seattle.

Each icon is an example of a data point, the equivalent of the `GMarker` object used in the Google Maps to highlight a single point on the map.

Points of Interest

In addition to locating the key points on the map, you can also overlay and move to key points of interest on the map. The Google headquarters was an example of this, and a huge number of other examples exist throughout the Google Maps application. There is no point in listing those examples here; they are far too numerous and constantly updating. Much of the content is U.S.-centric at the moment, but more data is being added all the time.

You can add as many of these overlays to the map as you like. There is no limit, although the application will slow down as you add more and more points and overlays to the map. The data and overlay information can be extensive and interesting. For example, Figure 15-7 shows the airports and train stations in Seattle.

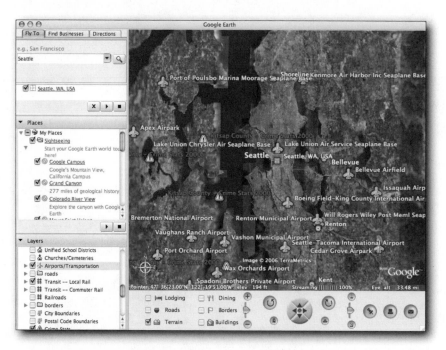

FIGURE 15-7: Adding airport and train station data.

Routes and Paths

Searches for information and locations work just the same as they do within Google Maps. You can move directly to an address and also find routes between two different points. If all you want to see is an overlay of the roads, select the "roads" overlay from the Layers panel. This provides a view similar to the Hybrid view in Google Maps, where roads are overlaid directly on top of the satellite imagery. You can see this more clearly in Figure 15-8, where the roads overlay has been added to the southern tip of Manhattan Island.

FIGURE 15-8: Roads in Google Earth.

Just as with Google Local, you can determine a route's two points by searching for the first point and using the pop-up panel to select the destination. Figure 15-9 shows a route between Ambleside and Whitehaven in the Lake District in the U.K.

So far the routing shows nothing different from what you might expect within Google Maps. There is, however, a slightly different view of the route available within Google Earth.

Terrain and Altitude

Google Earth includes altitude information for the whole of the earth. This means that you can get a fairly accurate idea of the altitude of a particular point within Google Earth. Google has, however, gone one stage further and provided the ability to display this information interactively on the map. If you select the Terrain checkbox in the bottom left of the control panel, the view of the map adjusts slightly, but probably imperceptibly.

But, change the attitude (or tilt) of your view, and the difference becomes obvious. To adjust the tilt, use the slider on the right of the joystick in the control panel. Moving the slider down tilts the map so that the top of the view rotates horizontally, moving your perspective closer to the ground. Moving the slider up rotates the map up.

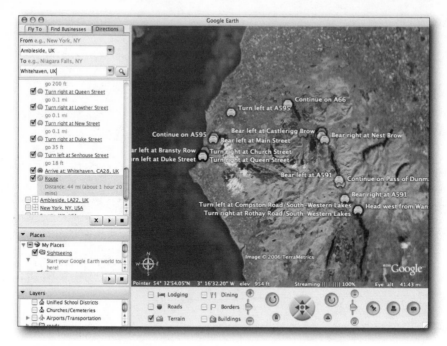

FIGURE 15-9: Ambleside to Whitehaven in Google Earth.

The result is dramatic. You can see the altitude of the different areas of the map and the route, and Google Earth now shows the route winding through some of the lower-lying mountains in the Lake District (see Figure 15-10).

For another dramatic representation, try going to Sorrento. I visited Sorrento for a conference and was immediately struck by the nearby mountains, which seemed to dominate the skyline more than Vesuvius, a much more well-known entity on the beautiful coastline of Naples. The mountains to the right of Sorrento (as you look northeast) came as a complete surprise by the time I arrived at the hotel. What I should have done, of course, is quickly check Google Earth to see the lay of the land, as shown in Figure 15-11, which shows the mountains immediately to the right and behind the hotel. Vesuvius cannot be seen in this shot, but is immediately to the left of the view shown here.

FIGURE 15-10: Ambleside to Whitehaven with altitude.

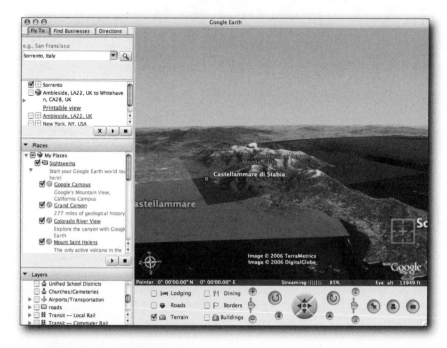

FIGURE 15-11: Sorrento and mountains.

Buildings

The geological aspects of Google Earth are of course important, but man has had a significant impact on how different locations around the world appear because of the buildings and structures that he has created. For completeness, Google Earth includes some man-made structures in the Google Earth map. If you visit Seattle and click the Buildings checkbox, Google Earth displays the various buildings in Seattle on the map (see Figure 15-12).

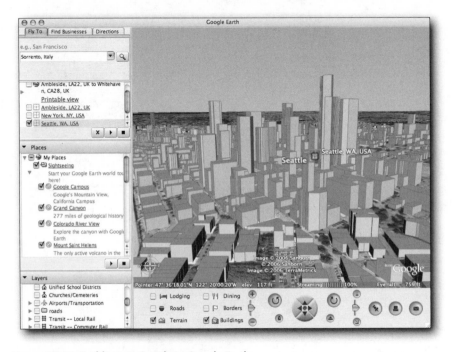

FIGURE 15-12: Buildings in Seattle in Google Earth.

The result shows one of the effects we experienced: the apparent lack of very tall skyscrapers, which helps give the wonderful impression of space and open-air feel that we discovered in Seattle compared to New York.

Extending Google Earth Information

Earlier in this chapter, you saw the information that can be built and overlaid within Google Earth. Google Earth obviously comes with its own massive library of data, information points, and highlights that can be overlaid on the map. All of this information is provided through a series of data files that are in the Keyhole Markup Language (KML) standard. KML is a specialized type of XML that enables you to build and organize points, routes, and other information.

The format of the data is not very difficult to understand or generate. Many of the principles that have been used through the rest of the book, such as specifying the latitude and longitude of a point and adding icons and other data, should be familiar. Unlike Google Maps, where the applications that build and overlay this information on the map had to be encoded, the extension method within Google Earth is provided entirely within the structure and format of the KML files.

This section looks at some of the basics of the KML system.

Exporting Your Tags

The easiest way to generate and share points, routes, and other data within Google Earth is to save the points you find and put them into your My Places folder (or another folder you create). You can then save the folder contents into a KML or KMZ file (a Zipped version of a KML file) that you can then share with other people by simply distributing the file. You can see the result of the KML file generated during the earlier examples here:

```
<?xml version="1.0" encoding="UTF-8"?>
<kml xmlns="http://earth.google.com/kml/2.0">
<Document>
  <name>My Places.kml</name>
  <Folder>
    <name>My Places</name>
    <open>1</open>
    <Placemark>
      <name>Seattle, WA, USA</name>
      <address>Seattle, WA, USA</address>
      <styleUrl>root://styleMaps#default+nicon=0x304+hicon=0x314</styleUrl>
      <Point>
        <coordinates>-122.330833,47.606389,0</coordinates>
      </Point>
    </Placemark>
    <Placemark>
      <name>New York, NY, USA</name>
      <visibility>0</visibility>
      <address>New York, NY, USA</address>
      <styleUrl>root://styleMaps#default+nicon=0x304+hicon=0x314</styleUrl>
      <Point>
        <coordinates>-74.006389,40.714167,0</coordinates>
      </Point>
    </Placemark>
    <Placemark>
      <name>Ambleside, LA22, UK</name>
      <visibility>0</visibility>
      <address>Ambleside, LA22, UK</address>
      <styleUrl>root://styleMaps#default+nicon=0x304+hicon=0x314</styleUrl>
      <Point>
        <coordinates>-2.9623,54.428376,0</coordinates>
      </Point>
    </Placemark>
```

```
      <Placemark>
        <name>Ben Nevis, UK</name>
        <visibility>0</visibility>
        <address>Ben Nevis, UK</address>
        <styleUrl>root://styleMaps#default+nicon=0x304+hicon=0x314</styleUrl>
        <Point>
          <coordinates>-5.003529,56.796859,0</coordinates>
        </Point>
      </Placemark>
      <Placemark>
        <name>sorrento</name>
        <open>1</open>
        <View>
          <longitude>14.366667</longitude>
          <latitude>40.616665</latitude>
          <range>31855</range>
          <tilt>0</tilt>
          <heading>0</heading>
        </View>
        <styleUrl>root://styleMaps#default+nicon=0x304+hicon=0x314</styleUrl>
        <Point>
          <coordinates>14.366667,40.616665,0</coordinates>
        </Point>
      </Placemark>
      <Placemark>
        <name>Seattle, WA, USA</name>
        <open>1</open>
        <address>Seattle, WA, USA</address>
        <styleUrl>root://styleMaps#default+nicon=0x304+hicon=0x314</styleUrl>
        <Point>
          <coordinates>-122.330833,47.606389,0</coordinates>
        </Point>
      </Placemark>
    </Folder>
  </Document>
</kml>
```

The structure and content of the file is, as you can see, very simple and doesn't differ in many respects from some of the XML documents that you used in examples earlier in this book.

Basic KML Principles

The KML standard is huge. Google's own documentation on KML is almost 120 pages, and the contents are not going to be reproduced here. Instead, look at the highlights and key points, starting with the basic format of a KML file. The basis of the KML file structure is as follows:

- The main KML XML root tag.

- The Document tag defines the content of the document (and contains global document information and a number of folders).

- The Folder tag defines the contents of a single folder, with each folder containing the details of one or more placemarks, routes, or other structures.

Within a folder, you add placemarks, and these are composed of further elements and definitions that describe the placemark and its components.

Placemarks

The placemark is the primary method of highlighting information within a Google Earth KML document. A placemark is a single entity within the Google Earth application and can refer to a single point, a line, a route, a polygon, or any combination of these. For example, a placemark could be your house, or it could be a re-creation of the stones at Stonehenge. Both are single entities but are composed of one and many points and coordinates, respectively.

The points that you define as part of a placemark can consist not just of the latitude and longitude, but also the altitude and even the relationship between the ground and your point on the map. You can also add a custom icon to the placemark (just as with a GMarker in Google Maps).

Finally, you can control the appearance of the placemark, from the display text and information panel to the name, style, and color of the label. You can also set the camera "view," that is, the location, altitude, direction, and tilt of the map when the user selects the placemark.

Geometry

Google Earth provides the ability to draw single points, lines, and polygons onto the map. All geometry types consist of the coordinates (latitude, longitude), altitude, enabling points, lines, and polygons to appear either on the ground or in the air. Coordinates are specified using the coordinates tag, specifying the longitude, latitude, and altitude in that order. Hence, you can find Sorrento using the KML:

```
<coordinates>14.366667,40.616665,0</coordinates>
```

All coordinates can be given a color, and polygons can be transparent (only their lines are drawn) or solid (enabling you to construct buildings and other elements).

All points, lines, and polygons can be extruded; their location can be linked to another location. For example, you can tether a coordinate to the ground even though it is displayed in the air.

For absolute flexibility you can group points, lines, and polygons into a collection, which in turn can be used to describe single elements. For example, when constructing a building, you could group the polygons that make up the building into a collection.

Overlays

Images can be overlaid on the map. Two types are available: a ground overlay and a screen overlay. Ground overlays ping the image to specific areas on the ground of the map. Screen overlays enable you to "float" information in the Google Earth display.

The overlay image can be a JPG, PNG, GIF, or TIFF. You can either make the image available over the Internet (or other network) or embed the image into a KMZ file along with the KML file that uses it.

Wrapping Up

The Google Earth application provides a different environment for viewing the Google satellite images in a method that also adds additional layers of information, such as terrain and 3D buildings. The information displayed is the same as Google Maps, but the methods that are available to extend the Google Earth application are different and rely on an XML-based format called KML.

KML is limited to providing additional data points for overlaying on top of the Google Earth data. There is little of the interactivity provided within Google Maps and the browser, but the Google Earth application provides a richer environment for displaying some types of data. Now that you know the basics of Google Earth and what the KML format is capable of, you can examine some samples of overlays that use the data generated in the previous Google Maps examples, but using the KML format in Google Earth.

Generating Google Earth Feeds

With Google Maps, the JavaScript language and Google Maps object environment were required to build the marker and then overlay the marker onto the Google Map. Google Earth provides a much simpler method for adding points of interest to the map. With Google Earth, the Google Earth application does all of the overlay legwork. All you need to do is create a suitable KML file that provides the bare structure and coordinates of the point you want to highlight.

Because there is no programming involved, the structure and content of the KML file is critical. This chapter describes the basics of the KML file format required for a basic point, along with some extensions and examples of dynamism that can be added to the system.

Showing Points

The basic KML point is the `<Placemark>` tag. There were some examples of this in the previous chapter, but the structure is quite straightforward. Only two components are required for a `<Placemark>` tag: the name and the point (containing coordinates for latitude/longitude) to which the point refers. You can also add further information, such as the `<address>` tag, icons, and further descriptive data to the `<Placemark>` tag according to your needs.

For example, here's a small `<Placemark>` tag defining the location of the Yorkshire Bank in Grantham:

```
<Placemark>
    <name>Yorkshire Bank</name>
    <address>10 High St,Grantham, NG31 6PU, United
Kingdom</address>
    <Point>
        <coordinates>-0.642539,52.913,0</coordinates>
    </Point>
</Placemark>
```

The `<coordinates>` tag specifies the longitude, latitude, and altitude of the point, in that order, separated by a comma.

Generating KML from Existing Data

To demonstrate how easy it is to create a KML document with appropriate information, you can adapt the data that was generated for the database in Chapter 11 (local Grantham businesses) and instead generate a KML document.

To generate the information, you follow the same basic method as in Chapter 11 to generate the XML that was previously parsed by JavaScript. Unlike the Google Maps example, where the XML was loaded on a business type-by-type basis, you can dump the entire database and organize the information automatically by type by using the Google Earth folder system. The Google Earth application can handle the filtering and selection process.

The KML document defines one set of data and therefore has only one folder in it. To further subdivide information you have to add subfolders. The result is a KML file structure that looks like this:

- Grantham Business Folder
    - Banks
    - Pharmacies
    - Restaurant
    - Sports
    - Travel

The Perl script for generating the file is as follows:

```perl
#!/usr/bin/perl

use DBI;
use strict;

my $dbh = DBI->connect( 'dbi:mysql:database=mapsbookex;host=db.maps.mcslp.com',
                        'mapsbookex',
                        'examples',
                        );
```

You start with the opening structure. The <open> tag defines that the folder is open and the contents should be displayed when the file is first opened within Google Earth:

```
print<<EOF;
<?xml version="1.0" encoding="UTF-8"?>
<kml xmlns="http://earth.google.com/kml/2.0">
<Folder>
<name>Grantham features</name>
<open>1</open>
EOF
```

The SQL statement picks all available options but orders the information by type so that the individual folders can be created:

```
my $sth = $dbh->prepare(sprintf('select * from ch10 order by type'));

$sth->execute();
```

To generate the individual <Placemark> tags, you only have to generate a suitable XML structure. The $currenttype variable is used to identify first the current type so that you can determine whether to create a new folder. The $count variable is used to identify the count to determine whether the closing tag needs to be created (for the first change of type, it doesn't). Note that for the subfolders, you don't open the contents; this doesn't affect whether the enclosed points are displayed, only whether the list of points in the folder is displayed:

```
my ($currenttype,$count) = ('',0);

while (my $row = $sth->fetchrow_hashref())
{
    if ($currenttype ne $row->{type})
    {
        if ($count > 0)
        {
            print "</Folder>";
        }
        printf("<Folder>\n<name>%s</name>\n<open>0</open>\n",$row->{type});
        $currenttype = $row->{type};
    }

    $count++;
```

Each individual placemark is composed of the name, coordinates, and address of each entity in the database:

```
    printf("<Placemark>\n<name>%s</name>\n<address>%s,%s</address> ↲
\n <Point>\n<coordinates>%s,%s,0</coordinates> ↲
\n</\Point></Placemark>\n",
            $row->{title},
            $row->{adda},
            $row->{addb},
            $row->{lng},
            $row->{lat},
            );

}
$sth->finish();
```

Finally, you close the last entity type folder, the global KML folder, and finally the KML document itself:

```
print("</Folder></Folder>\n</kml>\n");
```

Using the information that is in the final version of the database created in Chapter 11, the preceding script generates the following KML. The quantity of KML included here is shown to provide an overview of the overall structure, as well as the individual points. Even so, the document has been shortened for inclusion in the book.

Note The code for this chapter (and all chapters of the book) is available on the web site that accompanies the book, `http://maps.mcslp.com`.

```
<?xml version="1.0" encoding="UTF-8"?>
<kml xmlns="http://earth.google.com/kml/2.0">
    <Folder>
        <name>Grantham features</name>
        <open>1</open>
        <Folder>
            <name>banks</name>
            <open>0</open>
            <Placemark>
                <name>Yorkshire Bank</name>
                <address>10 High St,Grantham, NG31 6PU, United Kingdom</address>
                <Point>
                    <coordinates>-0.642539,52.913,0</coordinates>
                </Point>
            </Placemark>
            <Placemark>
                <name>Abbey</name>
                <address>1 St. Peters Hill,Grantham, NG31 6QB, United ⏎
Kingdom</address>
                <Point>
                    <coordinates>-0.64075,52.9112,0</coordinates>
                </Point>
            </Placemark>
            <Placemark>
                <name>HSBC Bank plc</name>
                <address>88 Westgate,Grantham, NG31 6LF, United ⏎
Kingdom</address>
                <Point>
                    <coordinates>-0.644091,52.9119,0</coordinates>
                </Point>
            </Placemark>
            <Placemark>
                <name>Lloyds TSB Bank plc</name>
                <address>42 St. Peters Hill,Grantham, NG31 6QF, United ⏎
Kingdom</address>
                <Point>
                    <coordinates>-0.641202,52.9101,0</coordinates>
                </Point>
            </Placemark>
            <Placemark>
                <name>Alliance &amp; Leicester plc</name>
                <address>34 St. Peters Hill,Grantham, NG31 6QF, United ⏎
Kingdom</address>
                <Point>
                    <coordinates>-0.641202,52.9101,0</coordinates>
```

```
                        </Point>
                    </Placemark>
...
                    <Placemark>
                        <name>Travel Quest</name>
                        <address>8-9 Westgate,Grantham, NG31 6LT, United ⤶
Kingdom</address>
                        <Point>
                            <coordinates>-0.643614,52.9119,0</coordinates>
                        </Point>
                    </Placemark>
                    <Placemark>
                        <name>Voyager</name>
                        <address>99 Westgate,Grantham, NG31 6LE, United ⤶
Kingdom</address>
                        <Point>
                            <coordinates>-0.644091,52.9119,0</coordinates>
                        </Point>
                    </Placemark>
                    <Placemark>
                        <name>Quality Travel</name>
                        <address>50 East St,Grantham, NG31 6QJ, United Kingdom</address>
                        <Point>
                            <coordinates>-0.640053,52.9121,0</coordinates>
                        </Point>
                    </Placemark>
                    <Placemark>
                        <name>Global Flights</name>
                        <address>99 Westgate,Grantham, NG31 6LE, United ⤶
Kingdom</address>
                        <Point>
                            <coordinates>-0.644091,52.9119,0</coordinates>
                        </Point>
                    </Placemark>
                </Folder>
        </Folder>
</kml>
```

If you save the file (for example, using redirection) and then open the file within Google Earth (by selecting File ➜ Open), you get a window similar to the one shown in Figure 16-1.

You can see that Google Earth has zoomed to a point that shows all the loaded <Placemark> tags. You can also see, in the panel on the left, that the folders you created within the KML are displayed. Unlike Google Maps, where individual business types had to be enabled and disabled through a JavaScript function you created, Google Earth now handles the selection process for you. Figure 16-2 shows just banks and restaurants displayed on the map.

Of course, generating a static file and distributing it is not particularly efficient, especially if the data changes frequently.

FIGURE 16-1: Opening the Chapter 11 KML information.

FIGURE 16-2: Selecting folders for display.

Generating KML Dynamically

The static KML file generation shown in the previous section is less than ideal when the data changes regularly. For static elements, such as documenting the location of mountains or seas, the information displayed is unlikely to change. For business details, the information is likely to change at least monthly.

With some applications, you might want to update the information even more frequently than that. For the moment, you'll just handle the dynamic generation of information and how that can be loaded into the Google Earth application.

Changing the Script

To generate the information dynamically, a similar change to that used when moving from the static XML to dynamic XML system used in Chapters 9 and 10 for Google Maps applications is required. The change comes down to a single line: The correct HTTP header and content type must be output by the script.

Google Earth supports two file types: KML and KMZ. The former, the uncompressed version, requires the following content type:

```
application/vnd.google-earth.kml+xml xml
```

For KMZ files use the following content type:

```
application/vnd.google-earth.kmz kmz
```

The script will be generating KML, so the change is very straightforward. The entire script is included here for reference to show that there are no differences between this and the static generation version:

```perl
#!/usr/bin/perl

use DBI;
use strict;
use CGI qw/:standard/;

print header(-type => 'application/vnd.google-earth.kml+xml xml');

my $dbh = DBI->connect( 'dbi:mysql:database=mapsbookex;host=db.maps.mcslp.com',
                        'mapsbookex',
                        'examples',
                        );

print<<EOF;
<?xml version="1.0" encoding="UTF-8"?>
<kml xmlns="http://earth.google.com/kml/2.0">
<Folder>
<name>Grantham features</name>
<open>1</open>
EOF
```

```
my $sth = $dbh->prepare(sprintf('select * from ch10 order by type'));

$sth->execute();

my ($currenttype,$count) = ('',0);

while (my $row = $sth->fetchrow_hashref())
{
    if ($currenttype ne $row->{type})
    {
        if ($count > 0)
        {
            print "</Folder>";
        }
        printf("<Folder>\n<name>%s</name>\n<open>0</open>\n",ucfirst($row-> ⤶
{type}));
        $currenttype = $row->{type};
    }

    $count++;

    printf("<Placemark>\n<name>%s</name>\n<address>%s,%s</address>\n<Point> ⤶
\n<coordinates>%s,%s,0</coordinates>\n</Point></Placemark>\n",
            $row->{title},
            $row->{adda},
            $row->{addb},
            $row->{lng},
            $row->{lat},
            );

}
$sth->finish();

print("</Folder></Folder>\n</kml>\n");
```

Although not demonstrated in this script, error handling with dynamic KML files is very strict, because Google Earth refuses to use the network link if the file is not valid. Therefore, all dynamic KML generators should always return an HTTP response of 200. To show an error, generate the appropriate KML, for example:

```
<?xml version="1.0" encoding="UTF-8"?>
<kml xmlns="http://earth.google.com/kml/2.0">
    <Folder>
        <name>Error loading file</name>
        <open>1</open>
    </Folder>
</kml>
```

Care should be taken to ensure you follow this approach.

Subscribing to a Network Resource

The CGI method shown in the previous section generates the necessary KML with the correct headers and structure. However, you need to load the file within Google Earth using a specific option so that that the KML is requested from the URL, rather than loaded from a file.

To add a network resource to your Google Earth application, you choose Network Link from the Add menu in Google Earth. You are presented with a window like the one shown in Figure 16-3.

FIGURE 16-3: Opening Network resources in Google Earth.

Give the Network Link a name. In the Location field, provide the URL of the CGI script that generates the KML. To use the previously detailed example script, use the URL http://maps.mcslp.com/examples/ch16-02.cgi.

You should get a Google Earth display like the one in Figure 16-4.

FIGURE 16-4: Viewing the dynamic Grantham entities.

Here you can see that the resulting folder structure is more or less identical to that produced using the static option. The difference is that the information is being loaded from KML that has been generated dynamically. Now the database can be updated and the Google Earth application can load the updates. The information is manually refreshed when you open the application, when you re-select the Network Link, or when you specifically request a refresh by right-clicking the Network Link and selecting Refresh.

Using the Auto-Update Function

The network source for KML can be further enhanced by enabling the auto-update function. Using this option, the network KML source is regularly reloaded at an interval that you can specify. To demonstrate this functionality in action, first change the Grantham network resource to automatically reload at specific intervals. Right-click the link generated in the previous option and select Edit. You should see the window in Figure 16-5.

Click the checkbox for Refresh Parameters and then set the parameters. You can specify that the refresh occurs at specified intervals or when the view changes (including setting a delay after the view has changed).

Within the book, it's difficult to demonstrate this in perfect action, but you can see some simple changes. First, see Figure 16-6, which shows Google Earth and the dynamic KML in its initial state. Refresh has been set for every five minutes.

FIGURE 16-5: Setting refresh options.

FIGURE 16-6: Dynamic KML.

Using the script in Chapter 11 that adds new entities to the database, Saddler's, Shoe Shops, and Stationers have been added to the database. Figure 16-7 shows the new changes after the automatic reload.

FIGURE 16-7: Automatic reload of KML data.

In this example, the data is unlikely to be reloaded and regenerated so regularly, but the refresh system can be used to help regenerate all sorts of information. For example, KML could be generated to show the current location of an aircraft or a team on an expedition. Each reload would update the position accordingly.

Creating a Self-Reloading KML File

Not only can this be controlled from within the Google Earth application, but you can set the refresh parameters from within a KML file. You cannot set it in the file that you generate, but you can instead generate a static KML file that refers to the dynamic KML file and includes the refresh parameters.

Following is a sample of the KML file, designed to refresh the dynamic example:

```
<?xml version="1.0" encoding="UTF-8"?>
<kml xmlns="http://earth.google.com/kml/2.0">
<Document>
<visiblity>1</visbility>
<NetworkLink>
    <name>ExtremeTech Google Maps: Grantham Entities</name>
    <Url>
        <href>http://maps.mcslp.com/examples/ch16-03.cgi</href>
        <refreshMode>onInterval</refreshMode>
        <refreshInterval>300</refreshInterval>
        <viewRefreshMode>onStop</viewRefreshMode>
        <viewRefreshTime>7</viewRefreshTime>
    </Url>
</NetworkLink>
</Document>
</kml>
```

Looking at the individual elements, you can pick out the main points. First, you define the name of the network link:

```
<name>ExtremeTech Google Maps: Grantham Entities</name>
```

Then you specify the URL, the refresh mode, the interval (specified in seconds), and the viewing format. Open the KML file in Google Earth, and the dynamic KML will automatically be loaded.

Adding Icons

You can stylize a `<Placemark>` tag with a custom icon by using the `Style` element. The `Style` element enables you to set custom styles for a `<Placemark>` tag. The `IconStyle` element defines the icon details. For example:

```
<Style>
    <IconStyle>
        <Icon>
            <href>http://maps.mcslp.com/examples/bank.png</href>
        </Icon>
    </IconStyle>
</Style>
```

The `<href>` element defines the location of the icon graphic. In this case, the location specified is the same as that used for the Bank icon example demonstrated in Chapter 11. You can use a single source file for the icon and extract the icon using the x/y reference of the left/bottom edge and the height and width of the icon (using the `<h>` and `<w>` tags).

For the final example, you'll use a simple icon, chosen using the type name to generate the icon, just as used in Chapter 11. The resulting script is shown as follows:

```perl
#!/usr/bin/perl

use DBI;
use strict;
use CGI qw/:standard/;

print header(-type => 'application/vnd.google-earth.kml+xml xml');

my $dbh = DBI->connect( 'dbi:mysql:database=mapsbookex;host=db.maps.mcslp.com',
                        'mapsbookex',
                        'examples',
                        );

print<<EOF;
<?xml version="1.0" encoding="UTF-8"?>
<kml xmlns="http://earth.google.com/kml/2.0">
<Folder>
<name>Grantham features</name>
<open>1</open>
EOF

my $sth = $dbh->prepare(sprintf('select * from ch10 order by type'));

$sth->execute();

my ($currenttype,$count) = ('',0);

while (my $row = $sth->fetchrow_hashref())
{
    if ($currenttype ne $row->{type})
    {
        if ($count > 0)
        {
            print "</Folder>";
        }
        printf("<Folder>\n<name>%s</name>\n<open>0</open>\n",ucfirst($row->
{type}));
        $currenttype = $row->{type};
    }

    $count++;

    printf("<Placemark>\n<name>%s</name>\n<address>%s,%s</address>\n",
           $row->{title},
           $row->{adda},
           $row->{addb},
           );
```

```
    printf("<Style><IconStyle><Icon><href>http://maps.mcslp.com/⤸
examples/%s.png</href><Icon></IconStyle></Style>",lc($row->{type}));

    printf("<Point>\n<extrude>1</extrude>\n<altitudeMode>relativeToGround ⤸
</altitudeMode>\n<coordinates>%s,%s,250</c\oordinates>\n</Point></Placemark>\n",
          $row->{lng},
          $row->{lat},
          );

    }
$sth->finish();

print("</Folder></Folder>\n</kml>\n");
```

The preceding script also introduces another concept. You extrude the point from the ground. This creates a line between the icon used to represent the entity and its actual location on the ground. To do this, when defining the `<Point>` tag of the KML you add the extrude option:

```
<extrude>1</extrude>
```

You then need to set the altitude of the point, first by defining the relationship between the actual point on the ground and the elevation at which you want to create the `<Placemark>` tag:

```
<altitudeMode>relativeToGround</altitudeMode>
```

The `relativeToGround` specification sets the system so that the height is relative to the height of the ground where the marker is created. So, if you specify the altitude of the point as 250m, but the elevation of the location is already 68m, then the marker would display at 318m above sea level.

Other options are `clampedToGround` (the altitude is ignored, this is the default mode) and `absolute`, where the altitude is exactly as specified (250m would display at 250m above sea level, even if the elevation of that point was more than that amount).

Figure 16-8 shows the resulting information in Google Earth. You can see how the markers appear to float above the map, but a line is clearly connected from the marker to the real latitude/longitude of the point.

Because the information is floating, rotating the map shows the icons constantly associated with the right location (see Figure 16-9).

Although the view is quite confusing here, users have the ability to include and exclude the different businesses they want to view because businesses are grouped into appropriate folders. The organization (providing the KML is generated appropriately) is automatic and is a lot easier to use than the system that had to be developed within Google Maps.

FIGURE 16-8: Using custom icons and extruding information.

FIGURE 16-9: Viewing icons with a tilted and rotated map.

Wrapping Up

Google Earth handles a lot of the application logic that requires JavaScript and programming in Google Maps. To create similar effects within Google Earth you need only generate the appropriate KML.

This chapter covered the basics of generating markers and points within KML. The basic point is easy to create. In most cases it requires only the latitude and longitude of the point. Markers can then be further customized by adding icons and you can even help to improve the visibility by extruding the icon above the map, making the marker more visible, particularly when the map is rotated or tilted.

You also saw how to refresh KML data. The refresh system allows KML to be automatically reloaded, and that provides an element of interactivity that enables sequences or time-based interaction to be overlaid on top of the Google Earth satellite data.

History and Planning with Google Earth

Location Photos

I was fortunate enough to go Pompeii during the writing of this book. Pompeii is a fascinating place, because almost the entire town (or at least that which has been uncovered) is intact — an amazing feat considering it is almost 2,000 years old and was buried under many feet of volcanic ash from the eruption of Mount Vesuvius in 87 A.D. As a Roman town it offers a unique insight into Roman life.

While there I took hundreds of photos, but though I can show and describe the contents of the photos, it is difficult to give a context in terms of the layout of the town to someone who has never been there.

Using Google Earth, the photos taken at Pompeii can be shown in the context of a satellite shot of the Pompeii site. The view can include the heading and even the photo itself to help the viewer make sense of both the satellite image and the photo.

Using a Photo for a Placemark

In Chapter 16, icons were used to highlight particular areas on the map that related to specific businesses. Using a photo as an alternative mark is one way of highlighting the places you visited while on vacation. It can also be used with any photo to give the photos some context. For example, Realtors could use photos of a property and a satellite image (or the view from the windows of different rooms) to show what the real estate looks like from different directions.

When using this method, be aware that the photos may overlap each other. Some careful placing — using altitude and extrusion — to highlight the points can help to make the individual items visible. Figure 17-1 shows an example using icons in this way, and Figure 17-2 shows the same information but with a slightly different camera angle, to show how the overlapping of the icons can obscure, rather than help, the display of information.

To achieve this display, a number of different techniques were used.

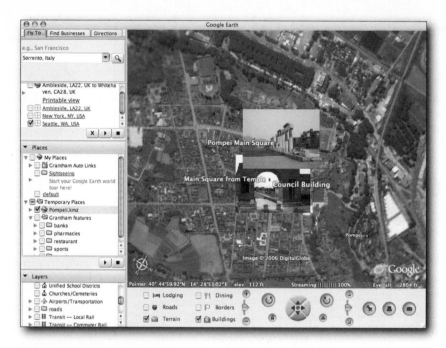

FIGURE 17-1: Using photos for icons.

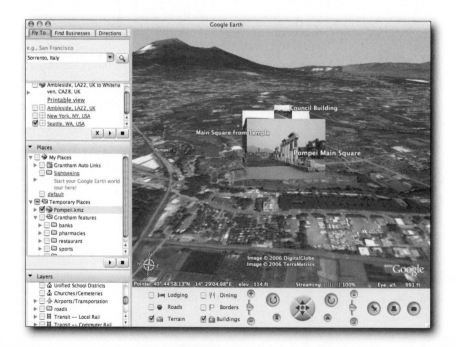

FIGURE 17-2: An alternative photo-based icon view.

Scaling the Icon

By default, Google Earth creates a relatively small icon based on the image that is provided, regardless of the size of the image. This is to prevent the image from dominating the map, when it is only really referring to a placemark.

To alter this behavior, styles must be defined that specify the format of the icon and the label used to highlight the placemark. The key element in the following code is the `Icon` reference, which refers to the image that will be used for an icon, and the `scale` entity, which scales the size of the icon in the placemark:

```
<Style id="basestylea">
        <IconStyle id="mainsquareicon">
                <scale>4</scale>
                <Icon>
                        <href>images/DSC01155.JPG</href>
                </Icon>
        </IconStyle>
</Style>
```

Figure 17-3 shows the difference between a non-scaled and a scaled icon.

FIGURE 17-3: A non-scaled (small) and scaled (large) icon.

Setting a View

When dealing with photographs, the direction in which the camera was pointing when the photograph was taken is a significant part of what makes the photo special. For example, a photo of the Bay of Naples, where Pompeii is located, can show a number of different elements. If the photo was taken from Naples facing the southeast, you'd be taking a photo of some mountains. To a visitor to the area, they are quite obviously the mountains to the east of Sorrento, but they could easily be confused for a picture of Vesuvius. By adding a heading and direction to a placemark, the direction of the camera lens is obvious.

To achieve this, a LookAt element must be included with each tag. When the user double-clicks a tag, the information in the LookAt tag is used to determine the camera (or eye) view point within Google Earth. There are six elements to the LookAt fragment:

- **Longitude:** The longitude of the point.
- **Latitude:** The latitude of the point.
- **Altitude of the point:** (Optional.) The altitude of the point.
- **Range:** The altitude of the camera or eye.
- **Tilt:** The angle of the camera.
- **Heading:** The compass heading of the camera.

Thus a view point equal to a bird's-eye view of the main square in Pompeii can be created using the following code:

```
<LookAt>
        <longitude>14.4850001287074</longitude>
        <latitude>40.74889804414286</latitude>
        <altitude>0</altitude>
        <range>254.0000000037327</range>
        <tilt>67.63540763119519</tilt>
        <heading>-17.02539065750064</heading>
</LookAt>
```

The LookAt element is placed immediately within the Placemark element:

```
<Placemark>
        <name>Council Building</name>
        <open>1</open>
        <LookAt>
...
        </LookAt>
</Placemark>
```

When the placemark is double-clicked, the camera moves to this location. When it is single clicked, nothing happens.

Adding Detail to a Placemark

The info window in Google Maps is an effective way of providing more detailed information for a placemark. Google Earth automatically creates these windows based on information within the `<description>` tag within a placemark. For example, the Pompeii town square placemark can be described using this:

```
<description>The Pompeii town square photo was taken here.</description>
```

The content in this section can be plain text, as shown here, but it can also be HTML. To embed HTML it must be escaped. There is a longer solution for this that requires escaping the HTML (particularly the angle brackets), like this:

```
<description>The main square of Pompeii, looking towards the ⊃
temple. &lt;img src="images/DSC01155.JPG"&gt;</description>
```

A simpler method is to use the XML data embedding format. For example, you could include the photo in the placemark window using the following:

```
<description><![CDATA[The main square of Pompeii, looking towards the ⊃
temple. <img src="images/DSC01155.JPG">]]></description>
```

Using this method, the points on the map could be returned to standard placemarks and the placemark window used to display the photo.

Final KML

Putting everything in the previous sections together, you can build a single KML file that describes a number of points, and the photos taken at those points, for the trip to Pompeii. Only three points are detailed here, but an unlimited number could theoretically be introduced:

```
<?xml version="1.0" encoding="UTF-8"?>
<kml xmlns="http://earth.google.com/kml/2.0">
<Document>
    <name>Pompeii.kmz</name>
    <Folder>
        <name>Pompeii</name>
        <open>1</open>
        <Placemark>
            <name>Council Building</name>
            <description><![CDATA[This is one of the council buildings off ⊃
the main square. <img src="images/DSC01196.JPG">]]></description>
            <open>1</open>
            <LookAt>
                <longitude>14.48469513913974</longitude>
                <latitude>40.75006838268123</latitude>
                <altitude>0</altitude>
                <range>498.0008872980769</range>
                <tilt>67.6354076394704</tilt>
                <heading>105.3299769917819</heading>
            </LookAt>
```

```
        <Point>
            <extrude>1</extrude>
            <altitudeMode>relativeToGround</altitudeMode>
            <coordinates>14.48469513930003,40.75006838317384,0</coordinates>
        </Point>
    </Placemark>
    <Placemark>
        <name>Main Square from Temple</name>
        <description><![CDATA[Looking back towards the main square, ↵
this time from the temple and looking through the arch from one of the ↵
streets leading off the square. <img src="images/DSC01216.JPG">]]></description>
        <LookAt>
            <longitude>14.48442827437565</longitude>
            <latitude>40.75001642868543</latitude>
            <altitude>0</altitude>
            <range>254.000032893549</range>
            <tilt>67.63460936190043</tilt>
            <heading>160.5058044783431</heading>
        </LookAt>
        <Point>
            <extrude>1</extrude>
            <altitudeMode>relativeToGround</altitudeMode>
            <coordinates>14.48442827406559,40.7500164285698,0</coordinates>
        </Point>
    </Placemark>
    <Placemark>
        <name>Pompeii Main Square</name>
        <description><![CDATA[The main square of Pompeii, looking ↵
towards the temple. <img src="images/DSC01155.JPG">]]></description>
        <open>1</open>
        <LookAt>
            <longitude>14.4850001287074</longitude>
            <latitude>40.74889804414286</latitude>
            <altitude>0</altitude>
            <range>254.0000000037327</range>
            <tilt>67.63540763119519</tilt>
            <heading>-17.02539065750064</heading>
        </LookAt>
        <Point>
            <extrude>1</extrude>
            <altitudeMode>relativeToGround</altitudeMode>
            <coordinates>14.4850001287074,40.74889804414284,0</coordinates>
        </Point>
    </Placemark>
    </Folder>
</Document>
</kml>
```

Figure 17-4 shows the main map, with Figures 17-5 and 17-6 showing two of the photos from the available points. Note that in each case the placemark has been double-clicked to move the map to the new viewpoint.

FIGURE 17-4: Basic placemark in Pompeii.

FIGURE 17-5: A council building in Pompeii.

FIGURE 17-6: Looking backwards toward the main square.

Generating the Information in Google Earth

Although it is tempting to produce all of the information completely manually (which is certainly possible for typical addresses and locations that can be determined using techniques shown earlier in this book), an easier alternative is to use the Google Earth application. To create a new point, choose File ➔ Add ➔ New Placemark.

All of the options, including the camera view, description, elevation, and extrusion information can be set entirely within the panel. Click the Advanced checkbox to set the additional options. You can see the various settings across three different panels: Style (Figure 17-7), Location (Figure 17-8), and View (Figure 17-9).

Once you have created the various placemarks that you want, you can save the placemarks into a separate file and even generate a suitable folder structure. If you have included graphics for icons into your placemarks, Google Earth will create a KMZ file rather than a KML file that incorporates the KML and images into a single Zip file.

The same method can be used with your own creations.

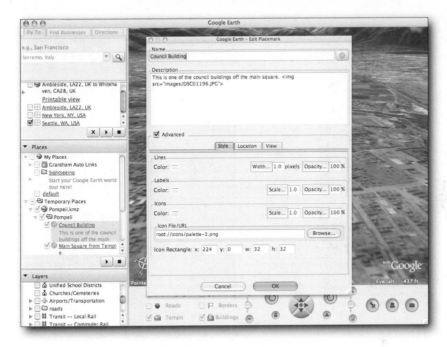

FIGURE 17-7: Setting a placemark Style.

FIGURE 17-8: Setting a placemark Location, altitude, and extrusion.

FIGURE 17-9: Setting the View for a placemark.

Generating a KMZ File

Generating a plain KML file is fine when either the information or the icons and other data are available freely on the Internet. However, there are times when you want to create a standalone file that incorporates the KML with the icons, images, and any other files that make your Google Earth file.

The format is quite straightforward. It is simply a Zip file that contains the KML and images. For clarity, you should use the following format:

- `doc.kml`: The main KML file.
- `images/`: A directory for icons and photos to be included in the file.

Within the KML, you can refer to files directly according to this structure. For example, a photo could be included in the description for a placemark using this:

```
<img src="images/DSC01155.JPG">
```

You can use any appropriate Zip-compatible software. From a Unix or Linux machine (including Mac OS X) with a command-line client, you could use the following, for example:

```
$ zip -r Pompeii.kmz doc.kml images/
```

Within Windows you can use WinZip to create a suitable file, but you need to rename the file to have the .kmz extension.

Revisiting the Realtor's Toolkit

In Chapter 12 examples of both archaeological- and realty-related tools in Google Maps were examined. Both followed similar principles, the overlay of information that is known about a location, either in the past or the potential in the future.

Within Google Earth the same principles can be used to display information, either in an identical manner or in a far more interesting alternative.

Using an Overlay

A simple overlay was used in Chapter 12 to suggest a potential office plan and layout. The display was simplistic, partially because of limitations in Google Maps, but also because with just a flat image to play with, there is very little that could be done to alter the view and representation of the office plan. With Google Earth you can follow the same principles to add an image overlay to the map.

Figure 17-10 shows the overlay in an almost identical situation to the one used in Chapter 12.

FIGURE 17-10: Display of a simple overlay.

Because this is Google Earth, the overlay is of course attached to the map. If the view is rotated or tilted, the overlay rotates and tilts with the map accordingly, as demonstrated in Figure 17-11.

FIGURE 17-11: Rotated map and overlay.

The KML generated in the preceding process shows how the image is overlaid. Unlike Google Maps, where the TPhoto extension was used, Google Earth supports the operation directly within the application using KML to define the structure:

```
<?xml version="1.0" encoding="UTF-8"?>
<kml xmlns="http://earth.google.com/kml/2.0">
<Document>
        <name>New Office Layout.kmz</name>
        <GroundOverlay>
                <name>New Office Layout</name>
                <color>77ffffff</color>
                <Icon>
                        <href>images/ch11-overlay.png</href>
                        <viewBoundScale>0.75</viewBoundScale>
                </Icon>
                <LatLonBox>
                        <north>35.2838663590014</north>
                        <south>35.27641626890076</south>
```

```
                    <east>-97.58248738034948</east>
                    <west>-97.59315654329896</west>
            </LatLonBox>
        </GroundOverlay>
</Document>
</kml>
```

The key element is how the location of the overlay is associated with the map. The `north`, `south`, `east`, and `west` elements set the borders of the image as it will be associated on the map. The other elements are as follows:

- `Icon`: Defines the overlay image.
- `viewBoundScale`: Specifies how much of the display real estate should be used to show the overlay.
- `Color`: Specifies the color and opacity of the overlay. The color is specified as four two-character hexadecimal values, between 0 and 255. The first value is the alpha (opacity) channel. The value specified in this case is 77 (hex), or 119 decimal, or about 47 percent.

Although the information displayed is useful, with a 3D environment it would be much better to give a proper 3D representation of the offices.

Creating a 3D Structure

To create a 3D structure, for example, the representation of an office, you combine latitude/longitude references with extrusion and altitude to generate a "solid" 3D object on the map.

The key is the `Polygon` element, a base structure that defines a simple multi-point shape made up of the lines that connect latitude/longitude points. Without extrusion, a `Polygon` would draw a simple shape. With extrusion and altitude you solidify the polygon. The basic structure for a polygon is as follows:

```
<Polygon id="packagingstructure">
  <extrude>1</extrude>
  <tessellate>1</tessellate>
  <altitudeMode>relativeToGround</altitudeMode>
  <outerBoundaryIs>
    <LinearRing id="packaging">
      <coordinates>
          -97.59277582168579, 35.282008632343754,100
          -97.59277582168579, 35.278137436300966,100
          -97.59017944335938, 35.278137436300966,100
          -97.59017944335938, 35.282008632343754,100
          -97.59277582168579, 35.282008632343754,100
        </coordinates>
    </LinearRing>
  </outerBoundaryIs>
</Polygon>
```

The outerBoundary element defines the outer line of the polygon. Everything inside is considered part of the solid shape. The coordinates are specified, one per line, but really you need only separate each coordinate by a space. Remember, just as with bounding boxes in Google Maps, you must specify at least one more point for each side of the shape because you are drawing lines from point to point to point. In this case, four sides require five points, each of the four corners and the first corner again to complete the polygon.

You can also generate shapes based on multiple polygons by using the MultiGeometry option, including each Polygon definition within the MultiGeometry element.

Using these techniques, the simple flat image overlay demonstrated earlier could be redeveloped into a 3D model of the office building using the following KML:

```
<?xml version="1.0" encoding="UTF-8"?>
<kml xmlns="http://earth.google.com/kml/2.0">
  <Document>
    <Style id="myDefaultStyles">
      <LineStyle id="defaultLineStyle">
        <color>ff000000</color>
        <width>1</width>
      </LineStyle>
      <PolyStyle id="defaultPolyStyle">
        <color>77777777</color>
      </PolyStyle>
    </Style>
    <Placemark>
      <name>Sales Building</name>
      <description>The new sales building, showing a readical structure to ⤶
provide a view for
        clients.</description>
      <styleUrl>#myDefaultStyles</styleUrl>
      <MultiGeometry>
        <Polygon id="lowerfloors">
          <extrude>1</extrude>
          <tessellate>1</tessellate>
          <altitudeMode>relativeToGround</altitudeMode>
          <outerBoundaryIs>
            <LinearRing id="lowerfloor">
              <coordinates> -97.58590936660767, 35.27654336061367, ⤶
50 -97.58590936660767,
                35.28360260045482, 50 -97.58260488510132, ⤶
35.28360260045482, 50 -97.58260488510132,
                35.27654336061367, 50 -97.58590936660767, ⤶
35.27654336061367, 50 </coordinates>
            </LinearRing>
          </outerBoundaryIs>
        </Polygon>
        <Polygon id="middlefloors">
          <extrude>1</extrude>
          <tessellate>1</tessellate>
          <altitudeMode>relativeToGround</altitudeMode>
```

```
            <outerBoundaryIs>
              <LinearRing id="middlefloor">
                <coordinates> -97.58590936660767, 35.279, ⊃
100 -97.58590936660767, 35.28360260045482,
                100 -97.58260488510132, 35.28360260045482, ⊃
100 -97.58260488510132, 35.279, 100
                  -97.58590936660767, 35.279, 100 </coordinates>
              </LinearRing>
            </outerBoundaryIs>
          </Polygon>
          <Polygon id="upperfloors">
            <extrude>1</extrude>
            <tessellate>1</tessellate>
            <altitudeMode>relativeToGround</altitudeMode>
            <outerBoundaryIs>
              <LinearRing id="upperfloor">
                <coordinates> -97.58590936660767, 35.28, ⊃
250 -97.58590936660767, 35.28360260045482,
                250 -97.58260488510132, 35.28360260045482, ⊃
250 -97.58590936660767, 35.28, 250
                </coordinates>
              </LinearRing>
            </outerBoundaryIs>
          </Polygon>
        </MultiGeometry>
      </Placemark>

      <Placemark>
        <name>Administration building</name>
        <description>A straightforward office structure</description>
        <styleUrl>#myDefaultStyles</styleUrl>
        <Polygon id="adminstructure">
          <extrude>1</extrude>
          <tessellate>1</tessellate>
          <altitudeMode>relativeToGround</altitudeMode>
          <outerBoundaryIs>
            <LinearRing id="adminoffice">
              <coordinates> -97.58904218673706, ⊃
35.282008632343754,150 -97.58904218673706,
              35.278137436300966,150 -97.58638143539429, ⊃
35.278137436300966,150 -97.58638143539429,
              35.282008632343754,150 -97.58904218673706, ⊃
35.282008632343754,150 </coordinates>
            </LinearRing>
          </outerBoundaryIs>
        </Polygon>
      </Placemark>

      <Placemark>
        <name>Packaging/delivery warehouse</name>
        <description>A lower structure, open plan internally.</description>
```

```
<styleUrl>#myDefaultStyles</styleUrl>
<Polygon id="packagingstructure">
  <extrude>1</extrude>
  <tessellate>1</tessellate>
  <altitudeMode>relativeToGround</altitudeMode>
  <outerBoundaryIs>
    <LinearRing id="packaging">
      <coordinates> -97.59277582168579, ↵
35.282008632343754,100 -97.59277582168579,
        35.278137436300966,100 -97.59017944335938, ↵
35.278137436300966,100 -97.59017944335938,
        35.282008632343754,100 -97.59277582168579, ↵
35.282008632343754,100 </coordinates>
    </LinearRing>
  </outerBoundaryIs>
</Polygon>
</Placemark>
</Document>
</kml>
```

The resulting 3D office plan can be seen in Figure 17-12, and, because it is a proper 3D structure, Figure 17-13 shows an alternative view.

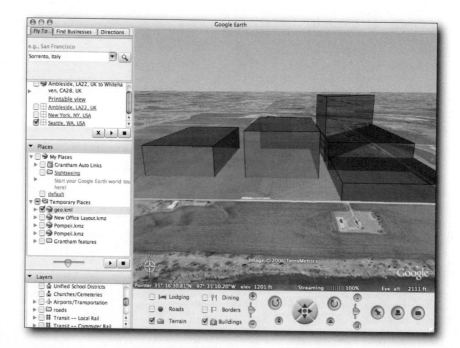

FIGURE 17-12: A 3D office demonstration.

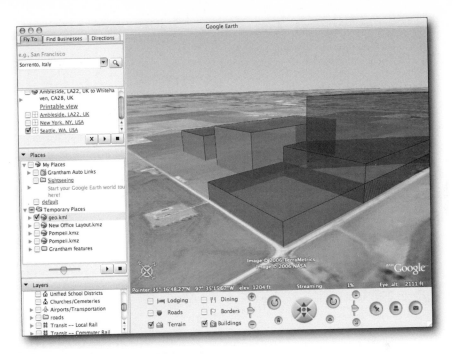

FIGURE 17-13: An alternative view.

Unfortunately, I am no 3D artist, but you can find numerous other examples of 3D structures defined within the Google Earth application when you add the Buildings overlay to your map.

Wrapping Up

The facilities in Google Earth can turn the basic principles learned in Google Maps into a much richer environment for showing information. Because the map can be rotated and manipulated, unlike the flat model used by Google Maps, you can develop much more interesting views of data and information, such as holiday photos. Because direction and orientation are implied in the display, the photos are given much more context than simple pushpoints on the map.

Using built-in 3D modeling, you can represent offices, buildings, and other elements in a way that provides a much easier-to-understand representation of a structure. With some manipulation of the camera, you could even give a representation of what a buyer could expect to see through the windows of stores in the buildings.

Resources

Google Maps has generated a significant following, and this has, in turn, led to a stunning array of web sites that provide information, examples, tutorials, and help for working with and developing Google Maps applications. I've distilled the basics of these links into this appendix.

Please note that the information in this appendix was correct at the time it was written. For a more complete and up-to-date resource page, please visit the MCslp Map Works web site (`http://maps.mcslp.com`).

Google Resources

As a web company, Google has done a lot to provide access to as much information as possible on as many different sites as possible. The primary considerations for this appendix, of course, are the main map sites that Google uses to provide the information.

You can view any part of the world through the Google Maps interface. Google also has specially allocated URLs that take you to specific countries so that you don't have to go to the generic U.S. site and search or scroll until you find the area you want. Of course, you can go wherever you like when developing your own Google Maps.

Table A-1 provides a list of the main sites, including Google Moon.

Table A-1:   Google Map Services

Map	URL
Google Maps USA	`http://maps.google.com`
Google Maps UK	`http://maps.google.co.uk`
Google Maps Japan	`http://maps.google.co.jp`
Google Maps China	`http://bendi.google.com`
Google Moon	`http://moon.google.com`
Google Earth	`http://earth.google.com`

The Google Moon site is unique in that it shows only the area (and the associated markers) used for the moon landings. The site was released on July 20, 2005, to mark the 36th anniversary of the *Apollo 11* moon landing.

Google Maps API

`www.google.com/apis/maps/`

You can find more information, read the documentation, and view help pages on the main Google Maps API site.

Google Maps API Documentation

`www.google.com/apis/maps/documentation/`

This is the main documentation page for the entire Google Maps service. The information provided on this page is the current version of the Google Maps API documentation. You should visit the site regularly to ensure that there have not been any important changes to the documentation and API.

Google Maps API Help

`www.google.com/apis/maps/faq.html`

Here you can find the FAQ for working and using the Google Maps API.

Google Web API

`www.google.com/apis/`

The Google Web APIs provide an interface to the Google system for searching the Google databases for information.

Google Maps Groups

There are two groups for Google Maps:

- The Google Maps group (`http://groups-beta.google.com/group/Google-Maps`) provides basic information and discussion on the Google Maps service.
- The Google Maps API group (`http://groups-beta.google.com/group/Google-Maps-API`) provides discussion of the Google Maps API and information on how to construct web sites based on the Google Maps system.

Information Sources

To get the most out of the Google Maps service, you will almost certainly need to make use of additional Google Maps resources and web sites. This section lists some of the key components, including sites that themselves provide more information on and links to the Google Maps service.

Google Maps Mania

`http://googlemapsmania.blogspot.com/`

This blog documents Google Maps services, changes to the documentation and service offerings, and general information on the web-mapping world. Overall, it provides one of the best ranges of resources, as well as links both to vital resources and to example Google Maps services.

Maplandia.com

The Maplandia site provides links to Google Maps pages that take you straight to a specific country, town, city, or other location through a series of geographical locations. Once you've found the location you want, you can further search for locations within the specific area.

Google Maps on Wikipedia

`http://en.wikipedia.org/wiki/Google_maps`

The Google Maps entry on Wikipedia provides a range of additional links and information on the Google Maps service and associated web sites.

Google Sightseeing

`www.googlesightseeing.com/`

This site shows images taken from Google Maps and Google Earth that show interesting structures or images.

Geocoders

Google does not provide a geocoding mechanism (that is, a way of mapping a given address or worldwide location into the latitude and longitude required to redirect Google Maps to a specific location). This section lists a number of solutions to this problem. You can use some of them directly within a Google Maps browser application; others can be used from within a server-side application to build a list of points for your main application.

MGeocoder

http://brainoff.com/gmaps/mgeocoder.html

MGeocoder provides a JavaScript overlay that enables you to search directly for a given location.

Geocode America

www.geocodeamerica.com/

This is a web service–based interface to a Geocode database for America. You can supply any U.S. address and obtain the Geocode information you require.

Geocoder

http://geocoder.us/

This is another web service–based interface for finding Geocodes from addresses. Primarily a U.S. service, Geocoder also provides a Canadian and Argentinean service.

Google Maps Tools

A number of tools have been produced to make it easier to produce Google Maps and to provide examples and extensions to the Google Maps functionality.

gMap it!

The gMap extension for Firefox allows you to find and search for information based on publicly listed phone numbers, which can then be used to display the location and directions within Google Maps.

Mobile GMaps

www.mgmaps.com/

Being able to use Google Maps on a mobile device is obviously a good combination, and Mobile GMaps enables you to use Google Maps on mobile devices (phones, PDAs) that support the J2ME (Java Mobile Environment) standard.

MapBuilder

www.mapbuilder.net/

MapBuilder provides a complete web environment for building Google Maps. You can specify locations, add HTML (to be displayed in map points and pop-ups), and choose your point icon. The result is a web page that you can download and use in your own applications once you use your own Google Maps API key.

MapKi

`http://mapki.com`

A Wiki that provides information and resources on using mapping APIs, including Google Maps.

Competitors and Alternatives

Although Google Maps and Google Earth are not the first search services available on the Internet, they were the first to make a publicly available API to enable programmers and other individuals to embed Google Map–based applications into their own web pages instead of redirecting users to another site.

MapQuest

`http://mapquest.com/`

The MapQuest site provides street maps only of the U.S.; Canada; and much of western, southern, and northern Europe. MapQuest is part of AOL.

Virtual Earth

Virtual Earth is part of the Microsoft Network (MSN) web site; it overlays satellite imagery and aerial photography of the earth over a 3D map. As well as providing map-search functions, Virtual Earth can also show maps according to specific addresses, towns, or cities, or via a business name or type search.

Yahoo! Maps

`http://maps.yahoo.com/`

Yahoo! Maps provides mapping information for the U.S. and Canada.

A9 Maps

Amazon's search engine, A9, has a mapping service that provides U.S. street maps and driving directions. In an interesting twist to the basic street-mapping service, A9 Maps also provides street-level photography that allows you to see what a street looks like in addition to viewing its location on the map.

Multimap.com

www.multimap.com/

Multimap.com is a U.K.-based provider of mapping information. It is a full road-mapping service (for the U.K., continental Europe, and the U.S.) combined with aerial photographs and local information. Multimap was one of the early Internet-based mapping companies, and U.K. companies often use the site to direct people to businesses.

Map24

http://map24.com

Map24 is an Internet mapping application that uses a Java-based interactive interface for building the maps and providing the interactive elements of the Map interface. The site currently supports the U.S., Europe, Brazil, and the Middle East.

Index

Index

Continued

Continued

Continued

Continued

Continued

How to take it to the Extreme.

If you enjoyed this book, there are many others like it for you. From *Podcasting* to *Hacking Firefox*, ExtremeTech books can fulfill your urge to hack, tweak, and modify, providing the tech tips and tricks readers need to get the most out of their hi-tech lives.